Also by the same author:

Church History in the Age of Science

A Century of Church History:
The Legacy of Philip Schaff   (*editor*)

CHURCH HISTORY IN AN AGE OF UNCERTAINTY

Historiographical Patterns in the United States, 1906–1990

Henry Warner Bowden

SOUTHERN ILLINOIS UNIVERSITY PRESS
Carbondale and Edwardsville

Library of Congress Cataloging-in-Publication Data

Bowden, Henry Warner.
    Church history in an age of uncertainty: historiographical
patterns in the United States, 1906–1990 / by Henry Warner Bowden.
        p.   cm.
    Includes bibliographical references.
    1. Church history—Historiography—History—20th century.
    2. Church historians—United States.   I. Title.
    BR138.B685   1991
270′.072073—dc20   90-34008
        ISBN 0-8093-1621-8   CIP

The paper used in this publication meets the minimum requirements of
American National Standard for Information Sciences—Permanence of
Paper for Printed Library Materials, ANSI Z39.48-1984. ⊚

To the memory of
EDITH HENDERSON BOWDEN
(1918–1986)

with thanks
not for what she had
but for what she was

Contents

Preface

Historiographical analysis is the study of historians, and this book focuses on twentieth-century American scholars who wrote about various aspects of the Christian church. Another kind of historiographical study looks at histories of particular topics, tracing changes in the way historians have interpreted Puritanism, religious freedom, or pietism, to name a few. But here I propose to analyze historians themselves, noting what theories they expounded regarding method and interpretation. Prima facie material is only the beginning, though, because it is much more important to investigate what historians actually did. In their body of writings, historians disclose what they really think about their subject matter, what they accepted as satisfactory evidence, and how they constructed interpretive patterns. After studying representative historians in several successive generations, one can also notice shifts in emphasis and procedure that illustrate how the historical profession has moved collectively to its present state.

Many observers have noted that each age rewrites history in light of its own experience. This does not mean that history is "bunk" or consists of tricks we play on the dead. It means rather that every generation adds its insights to accumulated information about the past. Whenever someone writes history, he or she brings to the task all the "virtues and deficiencies, the enlightenment and prejudice, and the liberating and restricting experiences of his own life and his own time." Finished products reflect the age in which they were written, indicating the intellectual currents that helped bring studies to fruition. Those like myself who treat written histories as primary sources do so in order to identify and assess those intellectual currents. As one such analyst put it, "What historians have to say about the nature, method, and substance of their craft . . . should have more than parochial interest; it should aid in understanding the quality and texture of the era of which they are a part."[1] By concentrating on church historians in the twentieth century, I hope thereby to illumine one facet in the overall field of modern American intellectual history.

Identifying a historian's central ideas and values is not always as straightforward as it may seem. For the most part, historians are likely to be vague about their theoretical and practical ideas. Historical enterprises are often fluid and unsystematic, without the writer moving from clear conception to practical application in planned projects. "Connections between theory and practice in historical work are usually circuitous and indistinct," another observer noted. Those of us who watch a historian at work should remember that, as he struggles to "discern the shape and order of a concrete situation, he may feel his way into it quite successfully without clearly formulating the preferences that guide him."[2] So I acknowledge at the outset that the following interpretation of church historians gives my own set of inferences. There are variables and nuances extant in the field which others would interpret differently. The same is true regarding the way I have classified people into schools of thought or categories exhibiting distinctive emphases, purposes, and intentions. What follows is simply one historian's honest reading of past and present colleagues. If these chapters help some readers think about how and why different historians have written the way they did, my effort shall have succeeded. If they provoke others to produce their own studies of these historians in disagreement, it shall have succeeded even further.

Perhaps not least controversial is my view of the modern era, as expressed in the book's title. If there is a thesis at all in the following study, it is that historiographical ideas based on a scientific model collapsed by the 1930s, and no ideas of corresponding magnitude replaced them. During the prior sixty years, most historians looked to science as their ideal for studying evidence objectively and for interpreting it without preconceptions. When the old paradigm faded, historians began to acknowledge that subjective interests affected their study of evidence and that presuppositions influenced their view of the past. After professional scholars admitted to subjectivism, it was impossible for them to agree upon another single standard for their craft. The end of scientific ideals in history gave rise to several alternative viewpoints, but no single view won all historians to its support. Many practitioners doubted whether one should, ever again. This air of uncertainty pervades the modern period, and church historians share this characteristic attitude with scholars in other subfields. The variety of definitions, approaches, and interpretations of religious topics in the twentieth century shows that church historians are quite diverse among themselves. This multiplicity echoes the richness found in modern historiography as a whole, and it shows church historians to be as divided as other colleagues over what standards best apply to their studies.

The uncertainty that characterizes modern historians is best understood in contrast to the earlier, now lost, uniformity. Modern historians do not despair that all knowledge of the past, necessarily derived from subjective angles of vision, is worthless. They are simply more realistic about the limited value of their findings. As one specialist put it, "The proposals we have on hand, ranging all the way from Turner's frontier hypothesis to the consensus theories propounded . . . by Louis Hartz and Daniel Boorstin, now sell at a heavy discount. Consequently we have today no unifying theme which assigns a direction to American history and commands any wide acceptance among those who write it."[3] And a perceptive church historian expressed the modern attitude when he noted that "we must keep in mind that there are no matters forever settled and beyond question in historical knowledge. There is no finality about any of the assertions."[4] Each historian may reach conclusions that seem final to his personal satisfaction, but all such findings are open to challenge and revision by others. That is the attitude about history that remains in force today.

In the late nineteenth century, few church historians cooperated with the scientific ideal. During early decades of this century, increasing numbers of them adopted scientific ideology, but their paradigm eventually collapsed under stringent criticism. In the aftermath, church historians developed several new approaches to their material, resembling their secular counterparts who applied the same ideas and procedures to other topics. Some adopted a viewpoint that emphasized the importance of environmental conditions in historical explanation. Chapter 1 mentions early exponents of that perspective. Others defined churches as social institutions and as we shall see in chapter 2, traced their impact on different cultures. A few church historians such as those mentioned in chapter 3 argued that, since subjective insights did not

rule out metaphysics, church history could once again build its
edifice on theological foundations. Still others aligned themselves
with consensus history, and chapter 4 discloses how they applied
that perspective to religious subject matter. Chapter 5 traces the
way some church historians focused on ideas as causal agents
while others thought ideas were worth studying in and of themselves. Chapters 6 and 7 point out other emphases and accomplishments, but these major categories are enough to show that church
history in the twentieth century has been marked by lack of a
dominant interpretive scheme. Uncertain as to uniformity and
finality, most of them would agree with a secular counterpart who
reflected this way on the nature of the craft:

> We are the people who have to look for the truth with the eyes that never saw;
> the people who must comb through the chaos of trash and falsehood, the
> disjointed reports and the uncertain traditions and tales, and try to make
> something meaningful out of it all. Complete certainty is forever out of our
> reach. If our work has any final value, that value must depend very largely on
> our ability to see the essential truth beyond the darkness and the error, and to
> create a faithful picture out of something that never makes itself explicit.[5]

I would be the first to admit that the categories in the following
chapters are my own construction, as are the judgments about
which church historians belong in them. I also acknowledge that
my choice of scholars has omitted many worthy of consideration.
Selecting representative writers resembles choosing stones to
build a dry wall. Many different stones could do the job, but some
seem to fit better than others in the overall pattern. The combination of twenty-five major church historians in this book strikes me
as fitting and useful to form a serviceable structure. These chapters follow a general chronological sequence, but my view of
twentieth-century historiography is that it does not have a beginning, middle, and end. There is no clean, connective sequence
where one idea or point of view neatly succeeds another. There are
instead differing phases that overlap, shift around, and mix together. Loose periodization allows for some sense of early and late,
but some of the options that were alive in 1900 still exist today. And
no normative criterion can show that anything is hopelessly outmoded.

So, after admitting that my own limits and choices have shaped
this study, one might conclude that its selectivity, arrangement,

and personal judgments mark it as a product of twentieth-century historical scholarship. Its larger value will be that readers might find the work useful in their own thinking, and it is offered with such a hope in mind.

(2) options
  1) environmental factors
  2) social institutions
  3) oical factors
  4) consensus
  5) ideas

CHURCH HISTORY IN AN AGE OF UNCERTAINTY

♪1
A Fresh Start:
Continuity with Innovations

In 1888 those who considered church history to be a distinctive field organized a society to further their interests. Various factors, particularly financial embarrassment, brought about the organization's demise in 1896, but convictions persisted among supporters that their topic had special qualities. Those convictions reasserted themselves in 1906 when the American Society of Church History emerged again as the forum for scholars who studied the rather inclusive subject of churches. The reconstituted ASCH did not signify a new era in writing church history, and it settled nothing on questions of procedure, subject matter, and interpretation. But it served as a meeting ground and clearing-house where church historians could discuss various options within their discipline. Those who valued traditional concepts met there with historians proffering contemporary methods to produce different approaches to history, and each perspective had its advocates.

SCIENTIFIC, REVISIONIST, AND TRADITIONAL VIEWS

Presiding over the renovated professional society was Williston Walker, a stalwart from the previous era who stood for depicting religious activity in a scientific manner. His German university training and many publications sustained an approach to church topics that defined them as human institutions, studied them with materialistic assumptions about causation, and interpreted them within a naturalistic context.[1] His version of the craft had strong affinities with views held in the American Historical Association, church history's secular counterpart and recent superintending

1

agency. Fellow exponents of scientific church history such as Ephraim Emerton also felt at home among historians who studied other subjects, and they made no special pleas for evidence or interpretation of past events beyond commonly shared norms for accuracy.[2] Another perspective in the original ASCH that survived to the new century was represented by Arthur C. McGiffert. As a supporter of liberal reforms, McGiffert used history to show how changing contexts eventually made various doctrines and ethical standards obsolete. His perspective stressed the transient qualities inherent in all systems, thus by implication calling for adaptation to modern trends. For McGiffert, liberal theological preferences and standard historical procedures worked hand in hand to enhance both secular knowledge and religious improvement.[3]

A third and probably the largest segment of historians in the resuscitated ASCH studied religious traditions for doctrinal and ethical guidance. Those scholars usually held pastorates or taught in theological seminaries, and they looked to history for proper teachings and behavioral examples. Church history frequently served as a defense of Protestantism and focused more narrowly on justifying some denomination's practice regarding baptism, ordination, or worship. They often chose a single confession or polity for study, that choice usually corresponding to personal religious allegiance. Working selectively within ecclesiastical parameters, these traditionalist scholars did not make overweening claims about what their researches yielded. Few referred to divine influence in causal explanations, and they did not interpret their topics in ways that applied exclusively to religious phenomena. They did not insist, as had Philip Schaff, their nineteenth-century progenitor, that faith preceded understanding or that references to providential guidance were necessary in narratives about divinely led institutions.[4] This conservative majority employed no procedures alien to other historical studies, but it still focused on subject matter that was religiously useful. And though church history comprised part of general knowledge about the past, many thought its edifying content justified treating it as a special field of inquiry.

These scientific, revisionist, and traditionalist views about the uses of history produced tensions within professional circles. Some were unhappy with the way many church historians regarded their subject as a repository of wisdom for present-day instruction. In 1904 a fact-finding committee sharply criticized those who used history to bolster orthodoxy, and it faulted them for keeping their field separate from general studies. It noted, moreover, that church historians failed to publish as much as political historians or even those engaged in biblical studies. The reason for such meager output, the committee charged, was "a lack of that spirit and method which defines the problems of church history as problems of historical science." These critics blamed this parochial shortsightedness on the fact that "the instructor, being chiefly confined to theological schools, is shaped too much by dogmatic and ecclesiastical interests." They urged seminaries to "realize the highest university ideal" and thus foster better research and writing. In broader terms the report concluded that "desired results could not be obtained until the study should be released from the monopoly of theological interest and offered . . . as a matter of general culture to a wider audience than the clergy."[5]

At the turn of this century, there were many who thought church history shared the "spirit and method" of historical science, and they regretted antagonism between "dogmatic interests" and "the university ideal." One who held this view was George P. Fisher, church historian at Yale, president of the ASCH in 1896, and elected to the AHA presidency two years later. In his 1898 address, he defended studying religions as a means of making moral judgments in history. This could be done properly only when such evaluations rose above "the influence of personal or party prejudice." Fisher appealed to "the better tone of history" to which all scholars should aspire in order to avoid narrow perspectives and thus treat "the requisite materials of judgment . . . with . . . greater impartiality."[6] In 1903 Henry C. Lea, another president of the AHA interested in church history, disagreed with moralizing about the past because he thought it led to "unfortunate conclusions as to the objects and purposes of history." He seconded Fisher's call for studying religion impartially, but Lea argued that such detachment precluded imposing moral standards on prior epochs. "History is not to be written," he maintained, "as a Sunday-school tale for children of larger growth." For him human motivations were bound by their times, and it was improper to judge previous acts by later standards. Lea's respect for the integrity of causal relationships limited historians to a single purpose, viz., to make "a serious attempt to ascertain the severest truth as to the past and to set it forth without fear or favor."[7]

Several secular historians also suggested ways in which churches fit in the larger purview of historical topics. In 1906 Simeon E. Baldwin declared religion to be an important factor in explaining human behavior. Far from discounting ecclesiastical influences, he valued religious principles as a key factor in understanding the dynamics of group action. Alluding to Napoleon's maxim, Baldwin held that historians should appreciate churches for the mystery of social order rather than for the mystery of the incarnation.[8] The following year J. Franklin Jameson continued that line of thinking. As one of the most respected and influential historians of his generation, Jameson sanctioned research in ecclesiastical documents, while limiting the value of its results. He considered religious statements useful because they unwittingly disclosed forces at work in human culture. Quite apart from their explicit rationale, such materials instructed historians about the society in which they originated. Religious authorities wanted to influence people through either "edification or conversion," but Jameson urged secular-minded students to shrug off those original intentions and to read documents from a different perspective. Making allowances for the "general prepossession of the preacher," religious materials could afford trustworthy reflections of the social milieu in which they were set. To those discerning enough to appreciate it, church records provided evidence for social history. Despite their doctrinal or ethical focus, church archives gave general historians the means to "enumerate all the little ways in which the lives of the American saints may enlarge our knowledge of the social background, the substantial warp of our American fabric."[9]

Though many historians distrusted studying ecclesiastical record for purposes of edification, they accepted work that was congruent with a wider, more intellectually respectable frame of reference. Ephraim Emerton, resident gadfly in the ASCH, repeatedly charged that when theological considerations were applied to historical data, "the resulting picture has been a hopelessly distorted image of what really happened." This "mistaken zeal," as he called it, placed the good name of church history under a cloud, creating "a loss of confidence, a suspicious distrust of conclusions on the part of those whose good opinion was of the highest value." It was unfortunately too often true, according to Emerton, that "the work of Church writers has been discredited because they were believed to be untrustworthy in their methods of work." Emerton, therefore, urged that scholars remedy the situation by studying churches not from a religious perspective but from what he termed "purely historical considerations."[10]

The real difficulty in analyzing historiographical patterns at the turn of this century lies in the fact that most church historians agreed with Emerton's remarks and did not think themselves guilty of the flaws he derided. On the whole, they honored ideals of accuracy and impartiality that pertained within general historical studies. Few claimed special treatment for their topic, and they did not think their findings distorted what had really happened. Standards within the profession were broad enough to admit several conceptions of proper procedure, and church historians worked alongside others in the conviction that they shared general views about method and interpretation.

One such church historian was Samuel M. Jackson, who utilized rigorous guidelines for historical excellence in his chosen field. Much of his activity consisted in collating the latest research findings as prelude to additional inquiries. He also provided biographical studies and textual expositions of Christian authors who lived between the sixth and twelfth centuries, a period that always fascinated him. In another medium he compiled a large bibliography of nineteenth-century source materials for the American Church History series. Interests in bibliography and editing made him a collaborator in the most comprehensive study of Huldreich Zwingli produced to that time. His talents and preferences culminated in coordinating a revised edition of the *Schaff-Herzog Encyclopedia*, a massive compendium of data on religious subjects.[11] Church history as Jackson practiced it had a rather modest profile. His matter-of-fact collections and translations indicated that he tried to rise above personal or party prejudice. His circumspect interpretations were clearly intended to surpass what H. C. Lea had characterized as Sunday-school tales for adults. In addition to providing improved research tools, Jackson offered restrained narratives that encouraged better scholarship in future efforts.

Another scholar who placed church history within the general field of historical science was Edward T. Corwin. Though affiliated vocationally with a seminary most of his life, he did not consider his topic chiefly confined to theological schools or unduly influenced by ecclesiastical interests. Corwin moved easily between parochial circles and general historians. He did not tailor methods to suit one audience and then change to suit another. His publications bridged the supposed gap between cultural history and information palatable to clergy. As if to demonstrate how churches were pertinent to both religious and cultural interests, Corwin produced a manual of discipline for the Dutch Reformed Church in America, and he wrote his denomination's history in the American Church History series. He searched through archives in Holland and printed the valuable results in several different places. It is indicative of Corwin's acceptance in the larger historical guild that his materials were used in the *Ecclesiastical Records, State of New York*. His translated documents also appeared in the *Narratives of New Netherland*, edited by no less a discriminating historian than J. Franklin Jameson.[12] Corwin's work showed how some church historians could study religious topics for both their intrinsic worth and the light they shed on developments in larger social settings.

Joseph C. Ayer, Jr., was similarly determined to honor the standard of historical objectivity in the subfield that interested him. He taught seminary courses on early and medieval church life, and his published essays made some notable contributions to those classic areas of study. Most of the essays centered on Roman juridicial authority in canon law and in the development of conciliar activities. His most durable service was to assemble a source book on early church history, one that went through six editions in his lifetime. Ayer knew that secularists criticized church scholars for using faulty historical methods, and he addressed the problem candidly. In the most general terms, every serious writer wanted, he said, to avoid distortions, "to treat the matter objectively and to render his book useful to all." But theory never led to perfect practice, and Ayer contended that no student could flatter himself by thinking he had fully eliminated "the personal equation." Some writers, he believed, let their personal interests dominate so much that their studies served unconsciously to "illustrate or support [a] particular phase of Christian belief or ecclesiastical polity." But Ayer insisted that the problem of trying to reach complete impartiality cropped up in church history "no more than in any other branch of history." Students everywhere had to admit their biases, whenever pointed out, and to curb them in search of greater detachment. He urged that scholars abandon church history "as a branch of polemical theology or as an apologetic for any particular phase of Christian belief or practice." Investigators could achieve greater disinterestedness, and their increasingly objective approach would place their work on a par with that done "in colleges and universities in conjunction with other historical courses."[13]

Perhaps the historian who best represented majority opinion in the renewed ASCH was Robert H. Nichols. He was convinced that approaches to church history materials presented no more of a problem to understanding events impartially than did studies in any other historical field. He also embodied the widespread interest among church scholars who wanted to use information derived from sound methods for religious purposes. Nichols pursued his work in a seminary context, and as an aid to ministerial education, he produced a survey of church history from its beginnings to modern times. With specifically religious expectations, he cooperated with the national Presbyterian committee on religious education. He also supplied the same information for wider use in writing course outlines and syllabi on Christian development for the home study service of Columbia University.[14] In these various capacities, Nichols felt he related historical information drawn from sound investigative procedures which all serious students held in common. Histories differed not in the way people searched for facts but in subsequent ways the information was put to use.

Nichols had ministerial education uppermost in his mind when he discussed the ways history could be put to use. He reminded members of the ASCH that, were there no training for clergy, "there would be little teaching of the subject to which our Society is devoted." In that context he thought lessons from past ecclesiastical experience could sharpen minds and temper the character of those who performed pastoral duties. Church history aided ministerial candidates by demonstrating the impact of beliefs on thought and action, of "the impression [faith] has made on society." Parochial details were secondary in such lessons, and Nichols urged historians not to get sidetracked into championing denominational polity, ritual, or doctrine. From a broader perspective, he said history could help church scholars "grasp the essential truth" in various expressions of their religion. History indicated "what Christianity can do in the world to-day" by detailing "its achievements in other days." Studying past records could also train minds to weigh evidence and to calculate motives underlying events. It could nurture moral growth by expanding experience to touch other times and cultures. Nichols held, moreover, that a historical perspective helped clarify contemporary situations and equipped students for the duties of citizenship. All these benefits would caution ministers against treating evidence impressionistically and making hasty conclusions about influences or results. Properly oriented church history was a discipline geared "to make Christian preachers more careful and reliable thinkers."[15]

This identification of church history with ministerial activity goes to the heart of ambivalent attitudes about the subject, and it shows why different historiographical conceptions have persisted throughout the twentieth century. On one side secular historians used religious materials only if they contributed to cultural developments, while on the other side, many religious students investigated their topic to enhance contemporary Christian effectiveness. Between those polarities, historians with various perspectives have found ecclesiastical data pertinent to the mosaic of human impulses that affected historical movements in complex ways. Students in the middle of the spectrum invoked common procedures and purposes as endemic to all investigations, but advocates at each extreme have found the opposing viewpoint to be inadequate. Irenic church historians tried to legitimize their work by grafting it onto general historical scholarship. They found ecclesiastical events no more specialized than those pertaining to political or economic history. Methods used in their subfield were not, they maintained, radically distinct from techniques employed in other arbitrarily isolated topics. But extremists emphasized particularities that divided history more sharply. Secularists accused religious historians of not operating wholeheartedly along common intellectual lines. Religionists replied that they employed universal norms for accuracy but used the knowledge thus gained for purposes defined by church life. The result has been confusion over what constitutes valid historical study, its content and purpose. It has also generated distrust over whose criteria defined acceptable scholarship. These multiple voices have perpetuated considerable uncertainty in modern times regarding what church history is, how it can proceed, and which results ought to command respect among peers in the historical profession.

THE ROMAN CATHOLIC PERSPECTIVE

Roman Catholic scholars participated minimally in historio-graphical debates at the turn of this century, and they were little affected by conflicting ideas. Part of their uniformity was due to intellectual isolation. Unlike their Protestant counterparts, Catholic historians had no national organization for discussing the techniques or results of investigative procedures. Both the American Catholic Historical Society in Philadelphia and the United States Catholic Historical Society in New York had existed since 1884, but each association catered to only a small clientele. Peter Guilday, a new instructor at Catholic University of America, attended the AHA convention in 1914 and was dismayed to find that his scholarly interests received no notice there. The following year Guilday founded the *Catholic Historical Review,* in part to compensate for that oversight. Additional promotion among historians who shared his topical interests culminated in 1919 when Guilday organized the American Catholic Historical Association. J. Franklin Jameson attended the organizational meeting, and his presence conveyed approval from AHA officials for such specialized studies. In cordial greetings he urged charter members to use in their chosen field the same standards already exemplified in general history. Such remarks had the effect, he recalled, of breaking "over the bows of the new craft when it was launched a bottle of mildly effervescent discourse."[16] By 1921 the once-independent *Review* was formally joined to the ACHA, and its pages moved beyond an American focus to cover the Catholic past in all periods and places.

A few historians in the early ACHA addressed the question of how their work related to regnant ideas about proper investigation and interpretation. They subscribed to generally accepted techniques and rejected any implication that Catholic truth differed from historical accuracy. One spokesman denied that Catholic writers were "more solicitous to glorify their faith than to tell the facts, as they really happened, without fear or favor." Catholic historians, he insisted, honored the integrity of what had actually occurred and did not "sacrifice historical truth in the supposed interests of Catholic doctrine."[17] Another ACHA member thought that American separation of church and state had created a false way of thinking about the two spheres. Modern culture had segregated church life from worldly affairs, and this situation encouraged some to ignore religion as an important historical factor. Secular historians who disparaged church history were, he charged, as guilty of bias as were those who ignored political or social elements in religious events. "The pity," he thought, "is that there should be sides." So to counteract this mistake, Catholic historians would align their work with "that of any other science — to determine the truth with regard to the phenomena which it investigates."[18] And they collectively rejected any work "if it shows signs of having been put together to make out a given case." It is clear, then, that by the 1920s several Catholic scholars embraced "the method of scientific history." Forty years after advocates had inaugurated scientific history in the AHA, and twenty years after a large segment of the ASCH affirmed that ideal, Catholic historians joined in the search for "facts solely with concern for their authenticity whatever their bearing happens to be." Historians sacred and secular avowed that "the primary aim now in dealing with events is to get a correct understanding of them."[19]

Peter Guilday stood at the forefront of American Catholic historical scholarship, filling a void left by John G. Shea who had pioneered the field in the previous century. Initially, Guilday specialized in British history, but once on the staff at Catholic University, he adjusted to its need for focusing on American experience. During his thirty-three years of teaching, he helped the same number of students publish their dissertations in his Studies in American Church History series. Guilday also drafted guidelines for graduate work, gathered original documents for university archives, and offered counsel to those writing parish histories. He edited the *Review* for almost three decades and through his own research program made secular historians more aware of Catholic contributions to national life. His presence at ACHA meetings was "the very life breath" of those annual gatherings. As dynamic promoter of a cause, exemplar of its standards, and tutor to those seeking academic excellence, Guilday is justly regarded as "the second founder of a distinct field of history."[20]

At first glance it seemed there would be no problem with incorporating Catholic history into the larger scientific field. When founding the ACHA, Guilday quoted Pope Leo XIII whose view of the historical enterprise could alienate no professional: "the first law of history is, not to dare to utter falsehood; the second, not to fear to speak the truth; and, moreover, no room must be left for suspicion of partiality or prejudice." Guilday endorsed the pontiff's words, saying they constituted "the fundamental principle which should guide the Catholic method in historical study."[21] This regard for detached observation and impartial judgment corresponded to ideals esteemed by historians in all fields. Another ACHA member underscored compatibility by saying that "all sincere scholars can cooperate in historical research conducted on such principles," and he added that no parochial idiosyncrasies would bar association with fellow historians in the AHA. He foresaw students applying the same methods of inquiry to different subjects, with such collaboration assuring "a systematic communication of intelligence which in its practical consequences amounts to a division of labor in the general movement of historical scholarship."[22]

But Catholic historians had additional ideas about their subject and the purpose of scholarship that other historians did not share. Many wanted to use "modern . . . works that keep abreast of the better historical methods and interpretations" in order to demonstrate "how thoroughly the American Church fulfills the teaching of our Founder and Redeemer."[23] Guilday supported this blend of apologetics and historical science, saying that the fundamental objective of the ACHA was "to promote among those who rejoice in the name of Catholic a more intimate knowledge of the history of the Kingdom of God on earth."[24] Others stated this ulterior motive more openly, asserting that the only way to make sense out of human history was to postulate divine origins and guidance:

History is the realization of a great divine plan, a vast supernatural process, more God's than man's. . . . For us, Christ and the Church cannot be considered merely as a department of sociology. . . . The history of man without Providence is inexplicable except by the suppression and mutilation of facts and sound logic. . . . For us, all history is related to this Redeemer, Jesus Christ. Christ is history, and history is Christ and the Church He founded to continue His work. All history has its roots in the Incarnation.[25]

Most Catholic historians could not see any discrepancy between such a theological definition of their topic and the scientific manner of studying it. They were convinced that, as natural law undergirded revealed truth, so historical facts displayed the efficacy of church experience. To their mind the secular findings of empirical investigation buttressed the higher realities of divine institution. For secular observers in the larger field, however, this juxtaposition raised grave questions about Catholic partiality and prejudice.

Guilday's publications did little to resolve the tension between an espoused investigative method and the way topics were actually treated. While a student at the University of Louvain, he acquired great respect for working with primary sources. He also learned the value of analyzing their content without distortion in order to "avoid all that could give offense." The ideal history, based on such work, was one that took no sides but represented every point of view "adequately and impartially." With that perspective, modern scholars could replace partial truths with wider knowledge. Guilday always handled evidence judiciously in his work, and yet he also conveyed such a defensive attitude about Catholic phenomena, erudition became linked to special pleading. He based his histories on impeccable documentation so he would have the means of correcting faulty opinions about his church "which today are the common property of a prejudiced reading public."[26]

In his first book, Guilday was anxious to defend English Catholics who had fled their homeland rather than abandon their faith. He extolled the "energetic resolution" to preserve proper life and doctrine that had sent them into exile. Their sufferings elicited "a strong sentiment of fellow feeling" from coreligionists and would, he hoped, command "profound respect" from even their enemies. Narrative and documentation undergirded an attempt to preserve the memory of a heroic people who struggled gallantly "against intrigue and calumny."[27] Guilday's admiration for fortitude among the faithful increased because he saw that it endured in the face of many injustices. He was convinced that the unadorned record alone proved Elizabeth I to have been a vicious and bigoted usurper. "She was a tyrant of the worst type, without pity; the willing tool of those who hated the Church for gain's sake." Protestants who seized power in 1558 had violated their country's laws "in direct defiance of the wishes of the majority of her subjects." This crime against God and lawful government succeeded in another travesty as well. It perpetuated "the Lutheran Reformation which had been grafted on the country during the reign of Edward VI."[28] In light of these comments, it is clear that Guilday's first book contained strongly partisan interpretations that favored the church he admired and excoriated those who opposed it.

In subsequent works Guilday continued to blend sound workmanship with high praise for model Catholics. His detailed biography of John Carroll remained close to the available sources without making extravagant claims about its principal. But it also accentuated the solid piety and noble efforts, the pure life and apostolic zeal in a churchman who labored as a "valiant soldier of the Cross." The prelate's sterling character stood in bright contrast to the dark "internal treachery" and "deception" that vexed America's senior ordinary. Still, those momentous trials "never seem to have chilled the natural tenderness of the man's heart."[29] Similarly, in treating the life of John England, Guilday repeated themes that made his church history distinctive. He endorsed strong central government in both church and state, arguing that developments which aided national growth would foster Catholic progress as well. His study of Charleston's first bishop displayed those twin convictions, especially where "the evil of disunion" under rebellious trustees threatened to divide "the seamless robe of the Catholic Church in the United States."[30] England's swift response to such license embodied the best hierarchical and republican leadership. His statesmanlike qualities exhibited "untrammelled Americanism" and a "thorough grasp of American idealism." England deserved admiration because he represented "justly and accurately to his own epoch the harmony between Catholic principles and the constitutional bases of the American government."[31]

A final historical survey furnished the same combination of painstaking analysis and parochial commendation. There Guilday recounted the experience of eleven conciliar assemblies and their canonical legislation. In such juridical history, he found guidelines for establishing the discipline essential to both a flourishing clergy and further ecclesiastical progress. His narrative soberly described events as borne out by original sources, and again it stressed the theme that Catholicism was integral to healthy American culture. Guilday saw no difficulty in blending scientific procedures with confessionalism because he thought historical study vindicated religious truth. Externally, history fastened on institutions, offices, and structured patterns. That kind of focus displayed tangible activity in missions, relations with governments, influence on social relationships, and contributions to art and science. A detached account of such topics vindicated the faith and drew on that which "is innate in the Catholic heart which must ever desire to see perpetuated through these volumes . . . the outward signs of that inward vitality which is the basic reason for our exceptional progress in this country." Internally, history touched questions related to hierarchical order and jurisdiction, doctrinal development, liturgy, moral customs, and devotional life. It was safe to investigate either aspect of church life with modern tools because such methods substantiated prior theological affirmations. Guilday and other scholars in the ACHA claimed parity with general historians because of their impartial study of sources. At the same time, they held that such work yielded "the truest history of mankind, since it embraces the story of man's progress toward his eternal goal."[32]

So Guilday's example stimulated debate about detached observation and partisan interpretation instead of resolving it. Some historians in the early decades of this century presumed that different organizations and their respective activities drew on common procedures and interests. But despite remarks about compatible methods in separate professional societies, there were many who doubted that either Protestant or Catholic church historians were pursuing essentially the same goals as their secular counterparts. Attestations of common method narrowed the gap, but special treatment of topics in both the ASCH and the ACHA aroused suspicion and held potential colleagues at arm's length.

THE NEW HISTORY: CHANGES IN TOPIC AND PERSPECTIVE

Early in this century, several historians turned away from the dominant fashion in their profession and chose a wider set of materials for innovative study. These scholars were not part of an ideological splinter group, but their ideas about new topics contrasted with traditional preferences enough to constitute a significant departure in historiography. By 1912 James Harvey Robinson had emerged as spokesman for this fresh viewpoint, and his collected essays entitled *The New History* gave the trend a name. Robinson was impatient with the old adage, "history is past politics and politics is present history." He rejected narrow emphases on governments and their wars, observing that in the past, the individual had been "more than a warrior, a subject, or a princely ruler; the State is by no means his sole interest." People had founded cities, erected universities, built churches, expanded commerce, created art, and improved technology. Historical materials in these vast fields made it possible to understand a fascinating spectrum of human activities. The knowledge thus gained was more informative than data confined to politics and legislative enactments.[33] Robinson was not the first to call for cultural history or "a history of the people," but unlike earlier pleas, his manifesto signified a developing momentum that eventually transformed the topical agenda of American historical scholarship.[34]

Several other scholars added their voices to this general trend of exploring new historical subjects. Among them was Frederick Jackson Turner who pointed out as early as 1893 that life on America's moving frontier was an important factor in explaining national development. His subsequent work with education, trade, and voting patterns in the Midwest led Turner to publish a volume in the American Nation series in 1906. His concentration on frontier experience influenced his generation and the next one quite heavily.[35] Charles A. Beard spearheaded another dimension of this widespread push for topical diversity. While many of his titles suggest outward conformity to conventional studies, he analyzed government from an energetic new viewpoint and revolutionized the interpretation of legal statutes. Economic interests provided the key to historical explanation for Beard, and he pursued questions about property interests in such areas as the drafting of the American Constitution and the growth of Jeffersonian democracy.[36] Beard's substantial contribution to economic interpretations in history and Turner's emphasis on developments in frontier settings opened many opportunities for students to explore under the protean aegis of "New History."

There was more behind choosing topics other than politics besides a simple wish to study something different. Social historians also harbored a serious determination to revise the overall understanding of what was important in American life and how past experience had created present circumstances. New Historians considered their methods to be scientific, but they asked new questions that went beyond the old range of subjects and institutional frameworks. Such a shift meant focusing on contexts rather than forms, on environmental conditions rather than structures. Historians with this new viewpoint wanted to understand changes by means of the social forces that caused them. Their emphasis on everyday life tried to make history more democratic by breaking down the artificial compartmentalization that earlier writing had created. As scientists they relied on empirical verification and were comfortable with the basic premises of evolutionary change. But instead of focusing on genetic development or hereditary traits, they attached more importance to environmental conditions as the matrix of emerging trends. Many New Historians embodied a progressive outlook that moved beyond questions of European origins and instead looked for beneficial changes later. They took Old World materials as a given and asked how the American context had improved matters since then. Progress occurred where previous circumstances had been modified; lack of change pointed to stagnation which needed more concentrated efforts at reform. This was the emotional significance of Turner's emphasis on the frontier as the testing ground for national development. This was the agenda behind Beard's emphasis on economic factors as the key to social progress.[37]

New Historians investigated topics with a view toward encouraging change in their own day. Knowledge of the past was essential to social progress because it lent perspective to further reform. In their kind of history, social conditions were not viewed deductively as fixed entities but rather as fluid circumstances. And progress occurred through struggle in the flow of events; beneficial change resulted from conflict. Furthermore, institutions did not unfold unerringly from an inner logic. New Historians saw them as responding to clashes of vested interest and conflicts between different ideals. Progress had to be won at every step over entrenched opposition, and this new sort of history sought to explain the realities of conflict so human agencies could better direct their efforts. Turner, Robinson, and Beard were not the first to discover conflict in history, but their scholarly emphasis resonated with reformist agitation in the American culture of their day. That larger impetus made progressive history a significant professional option for the next fifty years. While conservative historians wanted to restrict power to a few, stressing the role of privileged minorities in the past, progressivists emphasized forces at work whose momentum encouraged greater democratization and wider participation in social reform.[38]

Historical study of this sort encouraged contemporary-minded students to select topics where improvements had already occurred and more progress might be expected. By depicting struggles over ideas and customs that resulted in beneficial change, investigators could apprise readers of other victories that possibly lay ahead. Robinson highlighted this element of society's effort to better itself. Active pursuit of reform depended, he argued, on an understanding of the processes that had produced existing conditions. "We must develop historical-mindedness upon a far more generous scale than hitherto, for this . . . will promote rational progress as nothing else can do." Knowing what had happened led to ideas about what more should be done. With that in mind, Robinson coined a slogan for progressivist history: "The present has hitherto been the willing victim of the past; the time has now come when it should turn on the past and exploit it in the interests of advance."[39] So precedent was not binding, and inherited absolutes could be overturned. New combinations of thought and behavior were possible for those willing to fight for popular acceptance in the cultural marketplace.

This new sort of historical scholarship tried to uncover the techniques of progress by showing where outworn beliefs and institutions had been overthrown. Such a focus utilized the past for present concerns and emphasized previous experience that related directly to contemporary needs. It kept citizens abreast of changes in their environment and, by foreshortening their perception of cumulative development, freed them from thinking that any particular result was inevitable. This freedom from the past implied relative, impermanent values. It derived criteria about historical progress from whatever standards that happened to be widely accepted at a given time. New Historians were nevertheless confident that they could incorporate their limited grasp of cultural priorities into the scientific uniformities of historical change. During this century's early decades, they thought the democratizing tendencies in human conflicts could be empirically verified as the most important general laws of historical science.[40]

During the 1920s a few church historians began to apply the concepts of New History in their work. Encouraged by general historians who made religion part of social history, these more innovative church historians studied churches to understand the dynamics of religion and more importantly to appreciate the cultural influences that affected them. They discussed materials with a heightened regard for environmental conditioning, and they embodied a progressivist attitude about the meaning of change. With such perspectives, several scholars opened new paths in church history and explored fresh ways of interpreting their topics. Compared to secular historians, they were somewhat late and derivative, but in contrast to those who still looked at churches for edifying teachings or moral guidelines, they approached their craft with a noticeably distinct set of principles.[41]

Peter G. Mode was one of these scholars whose brand of church history closely followed trends in environmentalism and social adaptation. At the University of Chicago, he was primarily responsible for developing curricula in American religious life, an area pioneered and virtually monopolized by that institution through the 1920s. In 1921 he published the first collection of primary sources related to this new field. It was intended to complement extant sourcebooks on American political, social, and economic history, and Mode brought together a remarkably broad range of documents on American religious groups. Instead of restricting attention to Protestant churches, as most earlier historians preferred, he underscored American diversity by including Catholics, Jews, Indians, and blacks as well. By viewing religious groups as social institutions, Mode announced that he regarded no church "as the custodian of some divinely-revealed deposit of truth, nor as supernaturally detached from an environment that is ever affecting her inner life and organization." Instead of any concern for separate denominations, he looked rather for what contributed to the development of American Christianity as a whole. His new way of synthesizing materials was to choose "only such documents as most significantly set forth the contribution that the church has made to the progress of American society." Those reciprocal sets of influences would help illustrate "the manner in which from time to time [Christianity] has adjusted herself to her new and changing environment."[42]

Compiling documents did not allow much room for interpretation, but Mode's next book fulfilled most of the promises incipient in his groundbreaking anthology. There he made pointed reference to Frederick Jackson Turner's emphasis on the frontier as a dominant factor in American cultural development, adding that by following Turner, he hoped to keep church history abreast of contemporary historiographical patterns.[43] Mode also reiterated a humanistic definition of ecclesiastical bodies that fit secular standards for social history. Instead of viewing Christianity as a core of timeless truths, he proposed to study it "as a product and expression of life [that] has manifested a keen sensitiveness to its environment." Religion adjusted to its surroundings, and the historian's task was to note those variations which produced distinctive characteristics in differing times and places. Such adaptations were natural in all social institutions, Mode affirmed, and religion was part of general culture. The essence of church life lay not "in some static quantity of experience, doctrine, conduct or ritual derived from certain privileged periods of the past." Religious vitality lay rather "in the power by which persons worked out their religious problems in immediate contact with their several worlds of reality, the process being renewed in the experience of each new generation."[44]

In discussing the effect of environmental conditions on human institutions, Mode formulated as cogent a theory of causation as Turner ever did. He was not one-sided in arguing that environment determined action or that human effort transformed conditions. For him the most important thing was the context. There, inherited values faced new situations, interactions occurred, and new phenomena emerged. In this country Mode thought that the moving frontier provided a fecund context for such change:

In removing to new scenes of residence, people are unlikely to completely retain the habits and mental attitude of their former place of abode. A change in environment is usually productive of a changed outlook upon life. Fresh impulses are awakened, new interests are quickened, and prejudices are dissipated when men are placed in altered surroundings. This is no less true of groups than of individuals nor of religion than of culture and politics.[45]

For Mode, the West was where American Christians had ceased reproducing European religious patterns and acquired fresh, more fitting characteristics. The challenge of keeping up with westering populations had caused religious leaders to adjust their forms and methods to meet new demands. Reciprocal influences of spiritual responsibility and pragmatic necessity produced novel religious expressions. "All this was part of the gigantic enterprise to which American Christianity set its hand when it undertook to Christianize its frontier."[46] Mode's appreciation of context allowed him to keep a balance between overemphasizing materialistic causation and discounting it altogether in preference for ideals. Both types of influence counted in his view, and historians who clung to a single type of cause were as doctrinaire as those who used history to serve a predetermined theological position. A candid reading of records showed, he insisted, that authority and privilege had flourished in some Western churches alongside democracy in others. Tendencies for voluntary cooperation were manifold, but so were rivalries that isolated denominations. The American West produced no uniform set of effects in religion, but that setting was still the place to look for signs of a uniquely American way of life.[47]

Of all the features peculiar to American Protestantism, Mode considered revivalism to be the most outstanding. He found that it had "supplied the landmarks in our religious history" for over two hundred years and that awakenings in frontier settlements had marked "the beginning of an aggressive American Christianity." Other Turnerians emphasized the conditions that led people on the frontier to embrace political democracy, social cooperation, and economic individualism. In a similar manner, Mode pointed to the cultural circumstances that fostered the emergence of revivals. He noted that pioneers faced isolation and anxieties about safety and success; they lacked education and social constraints; they faced a life of drudgery with few emotional outlets. Picturing frontier conditions that way and probing for factors behind evangelical activity, Mode explained revivalism in terms that set a precedent for following generations of historians. He wrote that "the routine of a life consumed in chopping trees, breaking land, and doing chores, made the settler an easy mark for whatever new interest crossed the threshold of his thinking. And on the camp ground, no matter by what motive he had been drawn, the listener was brought face to face with a compelling interest—that of personal religion."[48]

Mode wrote church history with a New History preference for social topics, and he gave high priority to environmental conditions when discussing causation. But he showed little interest in adaptations as signs of improvement, and his depiction of American religion is not a story of gradual progress. Perhaps a more lengthened perspective, stretching over two millennia of ecclesiastical events, kept him from viewing recent changes as triumphs of progress. He knew that conditions required adjustment, but in the long view, those changes always atrophied when conditions eventually altered. "Nothing is more axiomatic with the church historian," he observed, "than that the successful use of an instrument in one set of circumstances is no protection against its obsolescence under different conditions." Linking revivalism with the frontier as he did, Mode saw little future for it in urban surroundings. He considered twentieth-century revivals to be "a tenacious carry-over from a phase of social development now almost past."[49] This did not mean, however, that religion was incapable of adapting to cosmopolitan settings as well. In his final assessment of spiritual awakenings, Mode penned one of his most graphic characterizations of religion and its power to endure. Spiritual quickenings, he said,

> were rather spontaneous developments of evangelical Christianity. . . . an Awakening is the weapon that evangelicism always retains for dealing with critical, abnormal moral and social conditions that threaten its existence. . . . There is, therefore, the ever-present possibility of spontaneous seasons of refreshing long after civilization, having sloughed off its frontier primitivity, has relegated to limbo its dependence upon conventional revivalism and the professional evangelist.[50]

Another church historian who exemplified new departures in his profession was Henry K. Rowe, professor at Andover Seminary from 1906 to 1941. As denominational chronicler he wrote *The Baptist Witness*, a popular treatise that saw many revised editions. He contributed lessons and a teachers' manual to the Bible Study Union plus an inspirational volume entitled *Modern Pathfinders in Christianity.* But those works did not display the methods and definitions that distinguished Rowe's scholarship from commonplace church history. A more innovative perspective surfaced in a textbook, *Society: Its Origin and Development,* and in his seminary duties that covered both history and sociology. Modern concepts in social history gave Rowe a vantage point from which he produced significant surveys of Christian history, particularly in America.[51]

Rowe blazed new trails in church history by applying sociological concepts to the past. His emphasis on social forces made much of impersonal processes in causation, and he abandoned any mention of providence as an agent in the events he described. Like other researchers in social history, he thought mundane themes were sufficient for interpreting what really mattered in human experience. This shift from divine to mundane topics and causes went virtually unnoticed in his day because Rowe stressed a more immediate issue. Religion was a vital part of social experience to him, and it warranted study as a component of cultural patterns. So he defined religion as part of human life and sought the meaning of religious expressions within that sphere alone:

The Christian religion was always a part of the life and thought of the people, of men and women who lived in the midst of a social environment which compelled attention to business interests, to social relations, to customs and laws which determined much of their conduct, yet who were bound together by a common faith and hope and were affiliated with a church organization through which religion was expressed.[52]

Rowe quietly adopted secular priorities in church history and, by abandoning theological concerns, conformed to what conventional wisdom called the most up-to-date historical perspective.

As far as detachment and impartiality were concerned, Rowe made it clear that church history had no special status because of its method or content. "The history of the Christian people must," he maintained, "be written with the same regard for accuracy and impartial treatment as the writing of any history. The scientific method of research, the sifting of evidence by the canons of historical criticism, the reaching of conclusions and the interpretation of facts by an unbiased judgment, are all necessary." This was standard operating procedure in general historiographical circles, and Rowe insisted they pertained to ecclesiastical data as well. He self-consciously embraced New History categories and rejected notions that "the history of a Church . . . was unlike other social institutions in its sacred character." He hoped thereby to avoid studying churches from what he called "the clerical point of view." Such narratives were inadequate because they focused on doctrine, missions, sacramental systems, or sermons. Now it was time, he asserted, to regard religion "as an integral part of human life" where it was understood as a component of the social environment. With that perspective, historians could watch religion interact with other factors. When history took the cultural context into account, it was possible to interpret churches adequately as they adjusted to political and economic conditions.[53]

Rowe was more progressivist than Mode in his view of beneficial historical development. For example, he found American Christianity compatible with "the freer air" of social experimentation where "democracy prevailed." He did not insist that religion worked directly for freedom or that churches had struggled for liberty against conservative interests. But voluntaryism and toleration were direct consequences of historical evolution wherein church leaders had held fast "to that which seemed valuable in the past and refashion[ed] it for a new environment and a new age." In recounting previous interactions between religion and social forces, Rowe noted where traditions adapted to new conditions. And in the aggregate, he was convinced that American experience had contributed to the process of breaking away from outmoded thought and practice. As a result, churches enjoyed tangible progress in such areas as freedom from state intervention, movement away from liturgical formalism, and liberation from the dead hand of Calvinist theology.[54]

Rowe singled out religious freedom as the salient characteristic of American historical experience. Earlier scholars had emphasized this element, too, but in Rowe's interpretation, religious liberties were a consequence of democratic culture, not a contribution to it. In his scenario, Europeans had brought conservative ideas to the colonies and established them in effective institutions. Aristocratic government flourished alongside traditional ecclesiasticism in early times, and such a state of affairs would have continued indefinitely, had not leavening factors in American society been at work. Those factors appeared when common people secured rights of free speech and local initiative. In time, citizens expanded their prerogatives to include autonomy in religious matters, too. Rowe thought such a trend indicated progress, "as the pure democracy of the town meeting and the representative democracy of the colonial assembly fostered political liberty, . . . so the pure and representative democracies of the Protestant churches stimulated religious liberty and were a permanent consequence of that liberty."[55] Separation of church and state was part of a generally upward tendency in American life, a natural consequence of the humanitarian factors at work in an environment sensitive to opportunities for improvement.

After chronicling the emergence of revivals and a more optimistic theology consistent with democracy, Rowe assessed the state of religion in contemporary society. Not one to view progress as inevitable or inclusive, he noted that two conceptions of religion dominated the American scene. One tried to pacify an alien God by penitence and suffering. The other regarded faith "not a password to Heaven, but a potency that makes life rich and full in the present, a process of growth in grace and divine knowledge."[56] Rowe clearly sympathized with the latter opinion, but in his coverage of American pluralism, he acknowledged that both religious proclivities were there. It was a sign of healthy society for people to worship in different ways as they saw fit. Still, Rowe was convinced that the most vital elements were those congruent with national development:

The religion of America does not present unity of faith or organization in this land of diversity. It shares the independent spirit that is so characteristic of American business and politics and society. Religion has freed itself from state control, reorganized itself on a voluntary denominational basis, evangelized the multitudes of American citizens that were fashioning the nation East and West, discovered its relations to a needy social order, and to an expanding world of scientific ideas, and in the last generation has been drawing together its forces in a new consciousness of the unity of Christian faith and purpose.[57]

This sort of evolutionary adaptation could meet new situations as they arose and bring about further improvements when the internal dynamics of social forces produced additional change.

SHIRLEY JACKSON CASE: FOREMOST EXPONENT OF ENVIRONMENTALISM

The person who most effectively linked church history with social contexts and environmental conditioning was Shirley Jackson Case. Shortly after completing his doctorate in 1906, Case began a career of three decades at the University of Chicago where he strengthened historical studies at the Divinity School and made it one of the country's premier centers of learning. Beginning as an instructor in New Testament and theology, he shifted to historical studies and ended up as Professor of the History of Early Christianity. Case was a lucid exponent of new approaches and interpretive perspectives in his subject area. He not only spoke with great clarity about method but put those principles to work, producing what eventually became an impressive shelf of books. His efforts provided a distinguished example of how historical inquiry into cultural factors could illumine the development of Christian beliefs and institutions.

Beginning with a definition of his topic, Case viewed Christianity as the outgrowth of human spiritual experience, a source that had produced myriad religious expressions. The versions of Christianity found in every era were the result of "creative religious living," and Case regarded all of them as valid if they attempted "not to imitate but to transcend all past and present standards." He saw church history as the record of people in various time periods trying to work out their own understanding of God and human nature, sin and salvation, ethics and destiny. Those who were really sincere about their spiritual quest did not simply copy earlier theology and worship. Vital religion looked for new insights and affirmations that were conditioned by contemporary surroundings.[58]

It was this quest for "the attainment of experiential values in the life-process as a going concern" that gave meaning and purpose to human existence. People who constructed fresh affirmations used tradition to a limited extent, appropriating previous religious categories insofar as existential involvement confirmed them anew. But more importantly, people in later epochs pushed beyond inherited standards to find their own version of correct thought and practice. Living religion thus occupied an important place on the edge of continuing change. As a historian, Case used this progressivist conception to identify different versions of Christianity as they emerged over time. For believers, religion was genuine when it contributed positively to their lives. For historians, "the study of Christianity becomes the fascinating pursuit of the varied ways in which the people of the past have sought to realize their desires within that area of experience and attainment commonly termed religious."[59]

Case began historical studies with the inclusive hypothesis that "Christianity is primarily an affair of life, with varying characteristics according to the individuals and the circumstances which have determined its historical manifestation." He also noted that, as subsequent expressions changed, each one was shaped by environmental circumstances. Case did not regard every change as an incremental improvement, but he still approached his subject with "a vitally developmental conception of Christianity's character." Development to him was value-free and directionless, indicating only that change was inevitable and that all believers expressed their "fresh attainment of religious experience through personal religious living." Noting development in history was simply recognizing the fact that people in successive generations experienced different realities and created new constructs to confirm those religious experiences. Christian history did no more than recognize varying spiritual expressions that had "evolved under specific conditions in successive periods of history," their forms varying "naturally . . . with the changing circumstances of life."[60]

Scholars who emphasized continuity at the expense of change were guilty of slighting both religious vitality and historical awareness, Case believed. They threatened the creative process of understanding present and past affirmations by absolutizing a single norm and thus denying the flow of cultural metamorphosis. "This was a futile effort to give permanence to a phenomenon that by its very nature had to be subject to change." Living religion could not justify itself by relying on antiquity, according to Case, because "formulations of belief are only human devices" that try in concrete ways to communicate "honest convictions of religious people who in different ages and under distinctive situations phrase their thinking in the light of their particular type of intellectual, moral and spiritual outlook."[61] So historians should avoid the futile exercise of judging truth in Christian variations. That decision would free them to study a wide range of religious expressions and then explain their differences by means of the environmental conditions that shaped their content.

Case found it necessary throughout his career to remind readers about the fluid character of historical phenomena. That admonition probably stemmed in part from his own theological outlook which acknowledged religious diversity in the past and welcomed contemporary innovations. Historical knowledge proved it was not possible to think "that Christianity was a finished product in Jesus' day, or that it came into being full-fledged at some particular moment in history." Case never relented in arguing for movement and change as opposed to "a fixed point which one may isolate and call 'original Christianity.'" For him, "Christianity is not a static thing; it is a movement, to whose origin and development many factors contribute."[62] Scattered observations of this nature culminated in a succint declaration:

Christianity is, always has been and always will be, a way of religious living in a complex and changing world. It ever remains a quest rather than a finished attainment. Its only permanence is the permanence of changing life seeking to realize the highest moral and spiritual accomplishments which men are capable of envisaging in the concrete but multifarious situations of their living. Change is inherent in and indispensable to this religious process.

Christianity was not an abstract quantity, either of doctrine, ethics, or ritual. Of course various groups had produced dogma, defined rules of conduct, and established liturgical norms, "but these were secondary," Case thought, "to the vital activity of actual Christian persons." Candid historical assessment led him to observe that Christianity was "a hydra-headed movement within which unity has never prevailed for any considerable length of time."[63] Variety over time had been conspicuous through the course of historical development.

Change occurred when people added their own religious affirmations to extant categories. Differing cultural circumstances had shaped the priority and content of those additions. So Case described his historical task as one that looked for "the formative social experience of the early Christians in the various environments amid which the structure of their own society crystallized and their message took shape." This perspective which Case embodied was congruent with New History in that it stressed social themes over the genetic unfolding of any inherent ideal, over shopworn concerns about formal institutions. It also corresponded to the liberal theological position that would not defer to biblical documents as timeless norms for religious vitality. Instead of grounding his study on scriptural texts, Case pushed inquiry back "the the more remote Christian society within which the writings arose and were finally assembled into a collection to be used for purposes of propaganda and control." This allowed him to reiterate in yet another way that varieties of Christian expression were unique whenever they evinced a "personal religious reaction upon their several worlds of reality." And more important, it substantiated his conviction that every Christian position was historically conditioned, "interpreted under the impulsion of stimuli furnished by the actual world in which believers lived."[64]

Religion as mutable human phenomena, change as irreversible process, social environment as pivotal to explanation—all these infused Case's conception of historical study as "a sober science." Scientific history contrasted sharply with what he termed variously as an "Augustinian," "suprahistorical," or "dualistic" attitude about the past. That perspective declared providence to be the regulator of earthly happenings from the day of creation to present times. It allowed minimal human participation except to show where sinfulness had impeded divine purposes. In the last analysis, Augustinians regarded historical knowledge as a branch of theology because it provided supplementary data about God who controlled mundane affairs.[65] Case rejected such ideas and argued that historical science rested on humanistic methods antithetical to supernatural confessionalism. "Are the devotees of Christianity more loyal," he asked, "to tradition, to prejudice, to dogma, or to creed than they are to truth?" Such a dichotomy required an emphatic negative. Opposed to suprahistorical views, Case maintained that "history deals primarily with facts," and because of that orientation, "essentially it is a factual science." Rather than search for immutable truths, "the historical method seeks to set aside all blinding prejudices" because temporal events can be "ultimately and comprehensively conceived only in the developmental sense." Case announced that history as a sober science would remodel confessionalism and revise long-cherished opinions about the past. The science of New History did not seek knowledge of God but of "actual persons . . . in immediate contact with their several worlds of reality" where religion evinced fresh expressions in each new generation.[66]

Case applied his distinctive approach to the field of early church history. To the dismay of Augustinians, he declared that only his kind of investigative methods would yield a proper historical understanding of the period. Truly professional techniques avoided the pitfalls of confessionalism and moved away from the "Jesus of dogma and of legend in order to return to the human Christ of historical reality." Case relished the new approach because its more detached observations obviated "the confusion of modern varieties of interest in Jesus as sponsor for present ideals." It was admittedly no easy task to extricate oneself "from the mass of fanciful imagery now freely employed," but disinterestedness was good practice because, through it, historians learned not to absolutize any belief about the founder of Christianity. By threading one's way through successive strata of cultural developments and noting accumulated idealizations of Jesus, the historian could eventually penetrate to "that memorable day when the hopes of his expectant followers were temporarily shattered by the tragic event on Calvary."[67]

In his attempt to identify the characteristics of early Christianity, Case did not seek an "essence" or some standard that governed later developments. He thought Jesus' religious ideas and activity were important simply because later generations referred to them when they formulated their own views. Much of what happened later hinged on the fact that Jesus had emphasized fellowship with God instead of understanding the relationship philosophically. The outstanding feature of Jesus' religion stemmed from "the prophet's characteristic awareness of the presence of God." His teachings had force and vitality because "he felt the very emotions of the Deity throbbing through his own soul." This more intimate contact with the God of Israel led to a corollary emphasis on neighborly love and earthly justice. Case thought such emphases ultimately derived from "the maintenance of a clear conscience, the cultivation of a righteousness that welled up from within a pure heart" in each individual. And Jesus assumed that all his ideals were "capable of realization by every truly religious person in the fold of Judaism.[68] At the outset, neither he nor those who heard him considered any other option.

Jesus' death ended thoughts about him as a prophet who tried to reform Judaism. Matters did not stop there, however, and Case noticed that the apostles used their leader in reform programs of their own devising. The earthly Jesus had failed to inaugurate a new regime, but apostles decided that he could still function as the symbol for better days. References to the prophet Jesus shifted thereafter to Jesus as a messianic figure, soon to return from heaven and establish his ideals. Disciples adjusted to this new emphasis and prepared for the advent of Messiah by propagandizing this revised gospel. In Case's interpretation, Jesus' death shattered the disciples' political aspirations, but "it still left them their vivid recollections of his personality on the basis of which they reared a new messianic faith. They no longer looked for an earthly leader, but for a heaven-sent deliverer in the person of the crucified Jesus. Out of the 'Jesus of history' enthroned in their memory they proceeded to construct the 'Christ of faith' who became central in their hope."[69] So Christianity entered the evolutionary stream, and its early advocates gradually embraced a religion about Jesus instead of the religion of Jesus. Reminiscences of the historical figure always gave later Christian expressions a concrete reference point, but all later formulations also met new needs and perceptions, giving them the malleability necessary for survival.

Survival depended on providing creative answers to spiritual needs, and since they addressed questions shaped by time and culture, the answers varied with different circumstances. Case's ideas about Christian origins depended on a sense of process and the inevitability of change. He never tired of saying, "the movement was a growth; it did not spring into being full-fledged at a specific historical moment. From the very start, its nature was developmental."[70] Within scant decades Christianity acquired new emphases, adapting to conditions and interests dominant in non-Jewish settings. People in the larger Greco-Roman world made Christianity into a religion of redemption with a divine savior who provided salvation for immortal souls. They developed sacred rituals that appealed to the imagination and emotions. Their versions of Christianity also sounded a strong ethical note through a system of rewards and punishments. This transition divested Jesus of characteristics which early followers had prized and gave him attributes more appealing to those who sought answers unrelated to the founder's earthly ministry. "Thus it has come about," Case observed, "that a Palestinian Jewish artisan, who was rejected by his own countrymen and crucified by the Romans long ago, is today remembered, honored, and worshipped throughout a world-wide Christendom."[71]

Christianity experienced many transformations within the Gentile milieu. Fortuitous combinations of needs and perceptions made it "possible for Christianity as a new movement to secure a degree of success denied to it in a Jewish environment where social conditions were of a distinctly different character." In meeting several needs, the message created new images. Jesus came to be appreciated not just as a martyred prophet but as one who actually triumphed over death. Successive portraits included an apocalyptic Messiah with God-endowed authority, a divine hero subordinate to the Almighty, an object of worship who granted terrestrial success, a preexistent Logos, and finally a trinitarian figure who shared the metaphysical essence of full Godhead. The historical Jesus was gradually overshadowed in Mediterranean Christianity by popular enthusiasm for a heaven-exalted Christ and an eternal Son of God. Case depicted such changes and the conditions that fostered them for purposes of instruction, not for normative judgment. His narrative merely pointed out that the original moral and spiritual emphases had been "gradually overlaid with a veneer of otherworldly imagery that obscured the fundamental nature of the new religion." In his view it was natural for later exponents to imbue Christianity with new priorities. Any detached observer could recognize that the "decorative garment in which it was clothed to please the eye of a miracle-loving age [had taken] precedence over the essential body of religious ideals that inspired worthy Christian living."[72]

Christianity successfully permeated the ancient world by changing its features. It supplemented religious individualism in order to meet social expectations of divine help in economic, political, and cultural life. The Roman world embraced Christianity as a means of making people happier, healthier, and politically more powerful. And the religion responded in kind. Missionary efforts boomed whenever proponents adjusted "to sponsor those interests which gentile society had long regarded as essential to human welfare, and had thought capable of being preserved only by the protection of heaven."[73]

One of the last areas wherein evangelism triumphed was philosophy, and Case identified Cynic-Stoic thought as the crucial viewpoint in that mediation. He saw Christianity as reinforcing the same concern for virtue and duty as held in the other intellectual system. So religious and philosophical notions of universal fellowship, based on divine fatherhood, reinforced each other. Both perspectives cultivated forbearance to others and scrutiny of one's interior life. Christian thinkers found these and other ideas among philosophers, and they took pains to emphasize their mutual compatibility. Historical development thus made Christianity all things to all people. And for the most part, it satisfied popular religious need by harnessing supernatural power. Individuals needed supernatural aid to be successful, and the state needed it for security. Christianity protected its converts from demons and healed diseases. It gave devotees a sense of union with a human-divine hero who had experienced their misfortunes "and through his own triumph, could insure to them a victory even over death, and a firm hope of bliss in a life to come."[74]

Varieties of Christian experience attracted supporters in increasing numbers throughout the civilized world. By the fourth century, Christianity had developed from an illegal sect to a respectable alternative among tolerated religions. Case thought one significant factor behind this transition was that churches, once indifferent to worldly goods, began actively to accumulate material resources. Altruistic ideals of fellowship and charity were gradually elided with an ethic that created institutions with economic prestige and social respectability. At length the previously obscure and other-worldly organization became guardian and guarantor of its host society. Churches accepted responsibility for social stability, monitoring public behavior to foster the general welfare. Christianity evolved to a level where its leaders felt obliged to address the needs of society as a whole. For centuries thereafter ecclesiastical policy pursued the sum of all good things, both material and moral, which people sought in this life and in the one to come. This goal for temporal and eternal achievement was expressed theologically as a search for "the community of men under the mandate of God."[75]

Comprehensive programs of this sort made the ancient Catholic church one of the "most formidable institutions produced by Roman society," the other being its system of political administration. Case noted that both church and state were regarded as sacred entities. Patriotism required loyalty to the state's divine protector, and fidelity to the church necessitated support of political officials. The church triumphant had changed considerably from "a religion so utterly lacking in social prestige at the outset" to one that ultimately became "the only respectable faith for men of culture and high position in the Roman Empire." Some time after Constantine, the day finally arrived when church membership was essential to social status. For many centuries thereafter, political power survived in the eastern part of the empire, and princes shared authority with bishops. In the western portion, however, secular power collapsed, and bishops assumed guardianship over every facet of human life. In that part of the world, ecclesiastical dominance in society was complete.[76]

Case restricted his professional attention to the early Church, starting with Christian origins and tracing their maturation through half a millennium. He was also interested in showing how historical knowledge might help modern Christians keep their expressions fresh and vital. In contemporary times his major contribution was to provide object lessons for one principle, viz., that copying the past is futile. One could not meet modern spiritual needs by imitating ancient patterns. History in its variety demonstrated that no doctrinal system or behavior standard applied to all situations. Case warned that any reduction of Christianity to a single creed, polity, or ethic "would be to fall into the error of making the whole equal to only one of its parts." He berated those who looked for permanence in history and clung to features that were "only external concretions of the movement's continued existence." A proper historical perspective acknowledged that vital religious energy came from living experience. Such energy led people to adopt intellectual frameworks and institutional patterns congruent with their "functional efficiency for nourishing the religious life." So in modern times those engaged in religious quests could explore new expressions because they knew that "organized Christianity is ever subject to the processes of change that underlie the course of human living."[77]

Historical awareness stimulated creative experience. Case thought that, after seeing the zeal with which earlier Christians had worked out their own salvation, one could "scarcely fail to become a more zealous and effective servant of his own generation." More important, recovery of the past produced liberation from it. Once people knew that previous religious expressions had been conditioned by cultural factors, they were free to try formulations more in keeping with modern contexts. Case argued that all religious ideas are limited, each the product of social conditions. So "historical events . . . are significant for the present chiefly as a means of enlarging our sphere of reality, thus supplying a domain for the enrichment of thought and experience." Understanding the dynamics of religious experience encouraged people to search for their own affirmations. Knowing the origins and limitations of earlier expressions released people from obedience to external authority. History taught one the importance of remaining on the growing edge of Christian development. Truly religious contemporaries remained alert to new impulses of divine energy, and "upon their shoulders has been placed the responsibility of learning and pursuing God's designs for bringing his kingdom to realization on earth."[78]

Case repeated ideas such as these in historical publications that appeared through the early 1940s. But by that time, several church historians had begun pursuing different approaches. His prestige could not keep the liberal approach perennially viable, and Case is better remembered as the epitome of historical perspectives that prevailed in the first quarter of this century. He agreed with Walker and Emerton that the proper focus for religious studies is mundane phenomena, tangible products of human thought and values. He shared a theological outlook with McGiffert that welcomed religious innovation. Case also seconded Jackson, Nichols, and Guilday in supplying knowledge about the past for present-day use. Each one differed over which lessons history actually taught, but all of them wrote so their version of the past would show contemporaries how to appreciate religion more fully.

Case's ideas about church history were compatible, too, with the views put forth by Fisher, Lea, and Ayer. Those scholars represented shades of differences in their chosen subfields, but varying topics did not entail different approaches. All of them shared a common conviction that their work belonged squarely within the general field of historical science. Case agreed that church history required the same objective detachment and accurate reporting as did other inquiries into the human past. Alongside Mode and Rowe, he subscribed to the social emphases found in New History. Their stress on religion as part of human culture met Robinson's call for themes that illuminated new areas of the past. And Case also corresponded to historians like Turner who relied on environmental conditioning as the chief factor in causal explanations.

Case resembled most of his colleagues by accepting the idea that history was a science. Generalists and specialists might argue over the importance of churches, liberals and conservatives could disagree about whether religious traditions had value, but they assumed their information came from scientific knowledge of the past. On the whole, historians felt comfortable with shared assumptions about procedure, and they were confident that their basic operating principles would continue indefinitely. But the foundations of scientific history were in jeopardy. While most historians debated topical priorities and interpretive issues, a few in this quarter century had begun to undermine the foundations on which information was presumed to rest. Critics reassessed procedural principles and found them to be unscientific. By the late 1920s, attacks against history as a science created a revolution within the professional guild. This devastating critique made it impossible for historians ever again to function with the confidence which Case exhibited to such a remarkable degree.

2

The End of Scientific Objectivity, the Emergence of New Apologetics

The ideal of scientific history dominated professional historiography for more than half a century. After Johns Hopkins University began its graduate history program in 1876 which copied German research techniques, several other graduate schools followed suit. American professors trained in Germany patterned themselves rather loosely after Leopold von Ranke by advocating a conception of history that stressed objective phenomena, detached observation, and a recounting of events as they actually happened. In the twentieth century, this scientific ideal continued without serious challenge for at least another generation. Professional historians assumed that data about the past existed in a natural state which they could observe without distortion after eliminating all biases and preconceived judgments about such material.

The major critic of this comfortable attitude was Carl L. Becker, who questioned the fundamental assumptions that supported history as a science. Becker had labored almost single-handedly for two decades to show his associates that their actual practices differed from the professed scientific ideal. By the 1930s Charles A. Beard added his own critique to Becker's arguments, and their cumulative weight brought an end to naive ideas about objective facts, detached observation, and disinterested reporting in history.

Becker made critical comments about the received historical method as early as 1910 when he noted that progressivist colleagues scanned past epochs for lessons on social improvement.

35

This initial observation led him to conclude that every historian viewed earlier times from some perspective shaped by present interests. Whenever researchers focused on a historical topic, their choice already contained tacit assumptions about what they would find and why it was important. A candid assessment of investigative procedure showed that every historian operated with preconceptions shaped by contemporary culture. Students of the past changed their viewpoint when differing conditions altered their values and interests. In light of such fluctuation, Becker held that historical inquiry obviously yielded variable rather than absolute results. History for one generation could not be precisely the same as history for the next, nor was it even possible for observers in a single era to agree on what was really important in the past. Instead of history being uniformly objective and factual, Becker declared it to be "rather an imaginative creation, a personal possession which each of us . . . fashions out of his individual experience, adapts to his practical or emotional needs, and adorns as may be to suit his aesthetic tastes."[1]

Just as it was impossible for historians to choose a subject without preconceptions, neither could they observe events with completely neutral eyes. There were no patterns inherent in events, and historical significance could not be recognized simply by observing it in a detached manner. A historian did not "stick to the facts," in Becker's view, but rather "the facts stick to him, if he has any ideas to attract them." Actual historical procedures contradicted popular axioms about scientific detachment, and Becker wanted to be more realistic in describing how his colleagues pursued their work. In contrast to the old shibboleth, he held that "complete detachment would produce few histories, and none worth while; for the really detached mind is a dead mind."[2] Disinterestedness was an unobtainable goal because historians carried their own set of interests back into earlier times instead of accepting a bygone era on its own terms.

Experience belied another of the most widely supported assumptions about history as a science, viz., that events contained their own explanation. Becker found no fixed meaning in events, and "to suppose that the facts, once established in all their fullness will 'speak for themselves' is an illusion." In ridiculing this jaded creed, he displayed his renowned rapier wit. He said that to claim objectivity by screening out current interests simply created a situation where "the scientific historian deliberately renounced philosophy only to submit to it without being aware." Becker scoffed at the attitude of "hoping to find something without looking for it, expecting to obtain final answers to life's riddles by resolutely refusing to ask questions—it was surely the most ro- mantic species of realism yet invented, the oddest attempt ever made to get something for nothing."[3]

Turning to another aspect of the outmoded canon, Becker delved into the nature of documents and the events they represented. Historians spoke of events, but Becker insisted that they could not witness previous occurrences because those events had them- selves disappeared. The only reality with which historians could deal were statements about events, mere affirmations that certan incidents had taken place. So in treating documents related to past developments, historians had to sift through various attestations to the truth. For Becker, this was "a distinction of capital impor- tance to be made: the distinction between the ephemeral event which disappears, and the affirmation about the event which persists." And it was important to notice that "for all practical purposes it is this affirmation about the event that constitutes for us the historical fact."[4] There were two kinds of events in history: those that had actually occurred and those affirmed by data. The first kind of historical event was absolute; it had also vanished and was irrecoverable. The second kind survived in documents, "traces of vanished events," that lived in the minds of contemporary historians. Documentary sources were the only tangible connec- tion to the past, and narratives of events based on such traces provided a tenuous sort of factual report. Becker rejected a favorite scientific maxim in saying that the historian's reconstruction of facts was not absolute but relative, "always changing in response to the increase or refinement of our knowledge." Far from being a compilation of facts that spoke for themselves, he said, "for all practical purposes history is, for us and for the time being, what we know it to be."[5]

Detached observation was impossible; predetermined interests were inevitable. Events in selective memory disclosed no inherent meaning; documentary references attested to events insofar as historians affirmed their relative merit through culturally condi- tioned judgments. It was clear to Becker that "the past, regarded as objective reality, is an abstraction" because "facts, simply restored to their original position, convey no intelligible meaning." There was no substance to the old assurances that facts existed outside the historian's mind or that investigators could observe and describe past reality without distortion. Contemporary historians had to acknowledge that "the historical fact is in someone's mind or it is nowhere." Becker thought students could pursue their work more effectively by admitting that "if the historical fact is present, imaginatively, in someone's mind, then it is now, a part of the present."[6]

Charles A. Beard also challenged scientific history in the early 1930s, using analysis Becker had been exploring for two decades. Beard had stimulated American scholarship with economic interpretations of national experience, and he cultivated the field of popular narrative as well. Then late in his career, he began to reassess basic procedural principles. As Becker before him, he came to see the futility of thinking that historians simply observed past events from a neutral standpoint. His professional experience proved that assumptions about historical objectivity were false. Historians did not regard documents with indifferent minds, nor did evidence mirror events as they had actually occurred. No matter how historians tried to filter out biased presuppositions, everyone remained creatures of time, place, sex, and circumstance. Beard denied the possibility of remaining disinterested because "into the selection of topics, the choice and arrangement of materials, the specific historian's 'me' will enter." Though some still clung to presumed objectivity, Beard insisted that "the historian's powers are limited. He may search for, but he cannot find, the 'objective truth' of history, or write it, 'as it actually was.'"[7]

In a more explicit and thorough analysis than Becker ever provided, Beard explicated the assumptions behind the idea that it was possible to find absolute truth in history. First, to think one could observe events as they actually happened assumed that the past existed independently, constituting a series of objects outside human minds. Scientific historians also assumed they could know and describe this series of events (Beard preferred the German term *Gegenüber* to label presumably objective events) in its objective existence. Thirdly, historians of this persuasion were convinced they could divest themselves of all religious, political, social, economic, and moral interests, "and view this *Gegenüber* with strict impartiality, somewhat as a mirror reflects any object to which it is held up." A fourth assumption was that historical events possessed an inherent structural organization which impartial historians could discern and accurately portray. Finally, this ideal perspective held that historians perceived causal sequences and their significance by means of purely rational effort. This confidence derived from a naturalistic conviction that nothing transcendent permeated or sustained historical phenomena. Beard enumerated all these assumptions as a prelude to dismissing them. But he looked wistfully at the scientific historian's frame of mind and called it "that noble dream."[8]

Beard maintained that there were three kinds of historical reality. History as past actuality comprised everything that had occurred, "all that has been done, said, felt, and thought by human beings on this planet since humanity began its long career." History as record was the second type, and it comprised all the evidence about past occurrences, "the monuments, documents, and symbols which provide such knowledge as we have or can find respecting past actuality." But history in its third and most general sense related only indirectly to actuality and record. Beard called this category "history as thought" because it derived from contemporay ideas about past actuality. In practical terms it was instructed and delimited by history as record which always needed critical evaluation. This third category, the product of a historian's conscious effort, was "the final, positive, inescapable definition" of history in modern life. Every written history denoted a selection and arrangement of facts. The recorded fragments of past actuality did not automatically arrange themselves into fixed schemes. Historians selected and arranged them according to ideas absorbed from contemporary culture. In Beard's view those who think and write about the past base their work on "an act of faith." The historian believed that something true could be known about history, "and his conviction is a subjective decision, not a purely objective discovery."[9]

Colleagues responded to criticisms such as these in different ways. Some argued that implications of the Becker-Beard critique required historians to accept radical subjectivism and relativism. Most historians avoided those extremes. Another group linked their investigative procedures to the latest standards for knowledge in the social sciences, humanities, and physical sciences. In this aspect of ongoing debate, historians continued to respect science as a paradigm for their work, but they redefined science with a new understanding of the limits built into human learning. No one in the 1930s or thereafter chose to defend the old assumptions about objective truth, absolute reality, or universally valid criteria for disinterested history. Some scholars at midcentury still invoked scientific ideals, but their idea of science differed significantly from earlier categories that had perpetuated a naive reliance on detached observation of an objective past.

The barrage mounted by Becker and Beard wrecked easygoing attitudes, and as the outdated categories fell, fresh ones took their place. Becker ended pretensions to scientific objectivity by showing that bondage to present interests prevented any detached view of the past. Beard tried to restore the primacy of humanistic values in the intellectual process, replacing naturalistic determinism with hopes for social progress. But strangely enough, Beard yearned to grasp reality objectively, even while he denied the possibility of doing so. He stressed the unscientific character of history and yet accepted science as the only authoritative mode of inquiry. The result was that, "in spite of his desire to enhance history's status as an intellectual discipline, his argument had the effect . . . of discrediting it." Both Becker and Beard contributed to the dialectic of historical discussion and did much to increase philosophical self-consciousness among their colleagues. Each was provocative enough to open "an overdue debate on the nature and terms of historical understanding, a debate which was to unseat the established complacency of the American historical profession about its assumptions."[10]

In the aftermath some scholars moved from complacency all the way to anxiety. Since objective truth about absolute reality was impossible, they argued, history was unknowable, and every account of the past was a mere patchwork of subjective inferences. More thoughtful historians refused to accept such an extreme conclusion. They pointed out that, even though observers had an imperfect view of events and could see only traces of past actuality, such knowledge was still worth serious consideration. History came alive in the minds of historians at the point where they glimpsed a vanishing past through affirmations that survived as evidence. New pieces of evidence enhanced and refined historical awareness, confirming some ideas with additional affirmations and revising others by showing where they were inadequate. As one respondent put it, "The greater the knowledge from freshly discovered evidence, the higher the degree of probability in the inference that we make of what the past actually was."[11] Becker's criticism of naive objectivity did not mean that the past was totally inaccessible. His perspective led historians to see that ideas about the past were reliable as long as they were based on the full range of affirmations found in the evidence.

Beard complicated the debate by seeming to espouse radical conclusions himself. He correctly pointed out that historical knowledge is not final. No written history ever conveyed the full truth of a single event or accounted for all pertinent factors in a sequence of events. But in light of such a flawed epistemology, he implied that all historical integrity was undermined. More balanced practitioners found they could accept Beard's basic epistemological point without moving to thoroughly skeptical conclusions. Salvaging respectability from impending bankruptcy, some commentators made the crucial observation that lack of finality is endemic to all human inquiries. If Beard's skepticism held, "not only would every historical account ever written be condemned as a necessarily mutilated and distorted version of what has happened, but a similar valuation would have to be placed on all science, and indeed on all analytical discourse."[12]

Beard had accurately depicted the imperfect basis of human knowledge, but colleagues thought his pessimism was unwarranted because it was obsessed with absolutism and ignored the virtue of limited success. One participant in the debate argued that, while historians began with hypotheses derived from the present, evidence about the past took precedence over preconceptions and often revised them. Factual relations indicated by the record could also suggest new hypotheses. Critical historians had come to the point of rejecting the idea of absolute fact, but they continued to assume that affirmations of past events are not completely independent of the facts that generated them. They regarded history as an interaction between contemporary ideas and those contained in the evidence. Most historians refused to despair over relativism and subjectivism because they still found value in the knowledge that evolved in their own minds.[13]

RELATIVITY, INDETERMINISM, AND DISCONTINUITY

The end of scientific ideals meant abandoning simple reliance on a Baconian conception of knowledge, but that did not make principles of selection completely arbitrary. By the late 1930s, historians admitted that contemporary values influenced scholarly investigation, and yet this did not produce unqualified historical relativism. A few advanced thinkers noticed how their more complex conceptions of history tallied with current standards for human learning in other fields. As if in echo of the earlier paradigm, they suggested that modern science contained useful guidelines for other types of inquiry. They did not use natural science as a perfect analogy, but some historians nevertheless drew on physics for a new way of looking at things. Biology had served as the idiom for nineteenth-century inquiries, and physics served that purpose in the twentieth. That new perspective highlighted three elements of modern existence: relativity, indeterminism, and discontinuity. Historians profited from philosophical self-understanding drawn from those elements. Their scholarly endeavors benefited from an epistemology that found no meaning in isolated facts apart from values supplied by contemporary observers.[14]

Relativity meant, for historians as well as for physicists, that things were not absolute; the world took on significance only when related to some frame of reference. Indeterminism followed from acknowledging that events are not inherently linked in sequence. Rather they occurred haphazardly, and chance variations were always a possibility. Discontinuity recognized that natural and human processes were often fortuitous and apparently unconnected, not a chain forged by obvious causal relationships. These fundamental principles, supported by the most forthright scrutiny of physical reality in the twentieth century, were of immense importance for reassessing the nature of historical understanding. A world view based on relativity allowed modern thinkers to accept what the old historiographical model had deplored: "Historical facts . . . gain their meaning when by order, selection, and interpretation they are related to a frame of reference. . . . Without relation to some theory the fact is an isolated entity of dubious validity and little meaning."[15]

Instead of lamenting the loss of history based on absolute facts, scholars in a relativized world dismissed the old ideal as unrealistic. Historical facts parallelled physical data in that their significance needed correlation according to some frame of reference. Historians had to supply their own judgments about pertinence, and that subjective contribution was deemed valid in the modern concept of knowledge. An indeterminate world encouraged historians to see that their perception of causal connections was also part of a subjective-thought process. Events seemed to be more the product of chance than the outcome of inherent principles. Causes in written history stemmed from a human determination to bring some order to events. Discontinuity further confirmed historians in their new way of looking at the present, and thus the past. As discrete events formed no developmental pattern by themselves, modern historians admitted that any pattern found in the past came from someone who perceived it through a frame of reference.

In these ways, then, modern physics offered valuable intellectual guidelines. With this kind of help, modern historians acquired a more critical understanding of physical evidence and the internal components of human knowledge. Earlier history had been tested by comparing it with absolute reality. After those assumptions were abandoned, contemporary historians found they could judge their work "by pragmatic criteria as to whether they served their purpose of giving . . . significance, connection, and continuity" to known data. If modern researches met such pragmatic criteria, its products were acceptable because they "tended to make history intelligible and valuable and . . . conformed to similar theories in other fields of knowledge."[16]

Secular historians have usually been the first to create new standards in the profession, and church historians have lagged behind, contributing little to developments in the craft. This has been a common pattern in American intellectual history, and it held true during the first two decades of this century. If one cites the work of R. H. Nichols or S. J. Case as examples, the pattern continued much longer. But a few exceptions occurred shortly after World War I. Some church historians criticized the ideal of scientific objectivity, voicing their own version of insights commonly ascribed to Becker and Beard. For once, ecclesiastical scholars were as up-to-date in their thinking about historical procedure as were their secular counterparts. This critique of scientific ideals in church history did not, however, generate wide discussion. Church historians seemed to take for granted that there had always been a problem between preconceived ideas and the goal of disinterested observation.[17] This difficulty did not cause them, as it did secular theorists, to rethink questions of method in order to form better conceptions of empirical investigation.[18] By the 1930s church historiography slipped back into secondary status again. For at least another decade thereafter, it featured histories that were apologetical in content. And this failure to stay abreast of the professional consensus kept alive the old question of whether religious topics were a legitimate part of general historical studies.

INFLUENCE OF HORR AND ROCKWELL

During the unusual interim, however, it is important to see that two church historians helped terminate scientific ideals in their profession. George E. Horr was one of those analysts who argued the same way Becker did. He may have noticed the problem earlier, but World War I forced him to rethink the way contemporary interests belied the ideal of disinterested information. The collapse of world peace and its tragic aftermath made Horr recognize as never before that modern circumstances strongly influenced the way historians selected topics and framed inquiries into previous epochs. History was not simply an antiquarian exercise, he concluded, because "the present situation does much to interpret the past." Contemporary priorities defined what was important in history and sparked curiosity about how affairs had developed to their present state. So Horr began his discussion with colleagues on the church history side of things by observing that "we only know the past in the light of the present."[19]

Turning to a question that no longer interested secular historians, Horr asked how spiritual causes fit alongside natural ones in history. He did not exclude spiritual influences as entirely irrelevant, but he clearly thought mundane factors were more pertinent to historical explanation. Studies in church history had "suffered greatly from the fact that too little regard has commonly been paid to the forces that are simply human," he declared, and the results were inadequate or unrealistic narratives. Social, economic, and political factors had affected religious ideals in every time period, and church histories that ignored such elements produced one-sided interpretations in which authors could only "generalize from insufficient data." Horr urged his ASCH colleagues to acknowledge the role of natural causes in religious history. Mundane explanations were particularly needed "in the present complex issue" where wartime conditions made people wonder how the country that began the Reformation could have become an aggressor nation.[20]

Military clashes around the globe had stretched European provincialism to a broader consciousness, and Horr suggested it was time for church historians to expand their horizons, too. Modern contacts with Turkey, Egypt, and Persia offered new occasions for developing studies of Nestorian, Armenian, and Coptic Christianity. Horr thought it was shortsighted to dismiss eastern churches as exotic or ineffectual groups, and he chided historians for undue fascination with European and American subjects. "It may be," he mused, "that closer knowledge of these faiths will reveal important human reactions to the Christian religion we have not appreciated." New factors were at work in modern life where more participants formed greater complexities, and Horr anticipated richer content in church history as a result. He looked forward especially to a better reporting of history of Eastern Orthodoxy, a more adequate treatment of that venerable tradition "that will at least bear some faint comparison with what has been done for the more obscure divisions" of Christianity in western countries.[21] Horr's challenge to provincialism still has merit seventy years later because American scholars have yet to develop much expertise in Orthodox history.

Postwar developments also created opportunities for studying old topics more comprehensively. Horr was particularly intrigued with the nature of democratic states and their relation to individual freedoms, churches, and more autocratic regimes. Recent events were a reminder that churches had always been involved in these vital questions, and Horr wanted this awareness to foster new investigations into the ways religion influenced secular developments. He bemoaned the fact that church history too often confined itself to doctrinal evolution, ecclesiastical factions, and denominational trivialities. If historians would avoid such ephemera and "consider the history of the Church from a novel angle," he was sure their work could shed light on questions of contemporary import. Church scholars also had much to contribute to fresh investigations into common law, the new League of Nations, individual rights in different political systems, and relations between religious groups and civil power. Moreover, Horr believed that the upheavals of modern experience should make church historians want to search the past "for a more intelligent and sympathetic insight into every phase of Christian development." As with other progressivists of his era, Horr thought historians had their "own important contributions to make to a more adequate utilization in our modern world of all the resources of our common faith."[22]

William W. Rockwell was the other notable analyst in church history, and his critical essay, "Rival Presuppositions in the Writing of Church History," considered how bias posed a problem to the ideal of objectivity. Drawing on an impressive range of ideas about investigative procedures, he pointed out that Herbert Spencer had punctured assumptions underlying scientific history as early as 1873. Spencer had said that very little historical narration stemmed from immediate observation because most of it "comes through channels which color, and obscure, and distort; while everywhere party feeling, religious bigotry, and the sentiment of patriotism, cause exaggerations and suppressions."[23] In 1901 Theodore Mommsen reiterated the old ideal about writing church history without any presuppositions. Rockwell reported the fierce European controversy that had ensued, and when most professionals rejected detachment as a viable goal, he embraced the conclusion as his own.[24] Continental theorists tangled again over flaws in the scientific ideal in 1910, and following those arguments, Rockwell based his ideas about procedure on the conviction that a strictly presuppositionless learning was impossible.[25]

Intellectual bias was inevitable, an aspect of human perception noticed by theological as well as secular observers early in this century. Emotional bias was an attendant pitfall, and the Great War convinced Rockwell that feelings exerted an overwhelming influence on one's perspective. During the way, propagandists had distorted facts behind a facade of patriotic fervor. If historians prior to international hostilities believed they could describe facts with neutral eyes, accusations and recriminations since 1914 had exploded that myth beyond repair. National loyalties blurred everyone's vision in situations where "the beating of drums, the rhythm of marching feet . . . may sometimes be misused to silence critical judgment on matters of fact." Intellectual honesty became a casualty of the war, and Rockwell wryly remarked that, while under the influence of emotions, "we are all drafted into the Light Brigade." In describing how passion could distort perception, his prose glowed with eloquence:

Emotion, spontaneous in the individual, contagious in the crowd, or calculated by the cunning masters of the show, blunts the edge of discrimination, and makes men . . . avid of atrocity stories which cry to be avenged. . . . Feeling crashes heavenward in hymns of hate, earthward in shrapnel and poison gas. The balances of historic justice are weighted down by mud-slinging.[26]

Experience on both sides of the trenches proved that observers were never free from bias. And the simple presence of emotions in historians prevented their work from being objective, too.

In Rockwell's estimation church history was doubly plagued by presuppositions because there, theological convictions came into play. Beliefs associated with religious institutions led to controversies over the relative merits of different polities, liturgies, and ethical guidelines. And beneath those conflicting loyalties church historians faced the more basic problem of claims about supernatural influence in human experience. Confronted with purportedly sacred events in a secular context, church historians had to recognize, Rockwell insisted, that the ideal of detached observation and disinterested narrative was impossible to achieve. Once dogma declared that a certain event had occurred, historians in that church felt constrained to affirm it. Rockwell despaired over such cases because "it is no use for a critic to point to the silence of other sources, conflicting traditions, or antecedent improbabilities; historicity has been guaranteed by revelation."[27] Beliefs, like emotions, precluded a clear view of things as they actually happened.

Once faith predisposed historians to think that God acted in earthly affairs, Rockwell complained, it could also exalt a church's historical importance. As representative and mediator of divine presence, human organizations could acquire characteristics originally attributed to God. Belief in special institutional qualities led to history based on miracles and providential intervention, and this placed religious history at odds with the rest of mundane experience. Ecclesiastical historians had followed that logic too often, in Rockwell's view, and expectations of infallibility or indefectibility blinded believers to the fact that "however perfect [a church] may be as an ideal to those that love her, too often her performance has been lamentable."[28] Conservatives in many denominations were offended by modern notions that history should confine itself to natural causes, "giving attention to phenomena only and leaving God and His interventions entirely out."[29] Rockwell's main point was that, whether church historians adopted a modernist or traditionalist position on the issue, their attitude was a subjective element in their studies of the past.

Bias was inevitable in church history, then, whether it derived from a mundane or a providentialist orientation. Rockwell found in his subfield the same deficiencies and naive epistemology that Becker and Beard discussed in greater detail. And speaking for church historians, he too said it was time to relinquish the dream of impartiality. "We all have presuppositions," he declared, "whether we recognize them or not. We all have some bias, due to imperfect knowledge of facts, to the defects of our experience and training, to our wishes and aspirations, and to our beliefs." The important thing was to acknowledge preconceived ideas and then confirm or revise them in light of tangible evidence. After working through the question of how beliefs played a role in historical inquiry, Rockwell reached two conclusions. As far as supernatural claims were concerned, he saw no merit in any more sacred narratives. History focused on people, and its content sought to explain the lives of "ignorant, forgetful, self-absorbed" human beings, not describe "the One who knows the end from the beginning."[30] But even when historians used mundane explanations, it was impossible for them to study churches objectively. The only hope for improvement, he suggested, was to regard presuppositions as fluid hypotheses open to investigation, not fixed convictions opposed to further inquiry.

Critiques of this sort were rare among church historians, and they elicited little response compared to the debate Becker and Beard stirred up in the general profession. There is no evidence to indicate that Horr and Rockwell stimulated anyone to think through the problems of limited empiricism. But their ideas were timely and pertinent, and after the 1930s, most American church historians did not pattern their work along scientific lines. Instead, their studies followed several different schools of thought. This diversity was a legacy of freedom in the modern period when a single standard for historical procedures ruled no longer.

The next types of ecclesiastical studies appeared at a time when historians were trying to come to terms with a world characterized by relativity, indeterminism, and discontinuity. As scholars realized that facts did not speak for themselves and that events had no meaning until assimilated to a frame of reference, the guild made room for varying perspectives and interpretations. If objective reality was an abstraction and observers did not mirror events without bias, it was now acceptable to admit the subjective aspects of historical understanding. Insight was not an obstacle to learning but part of a process that drew inferences from evidence and assessed knowledge on the basis of probability.

In this context of new possibilities, two American church historians dominated the next phase of writing. Each of them grounded their work in empirical research and utilized procedures common to the general field. But they also used factual data to demonstrate how vital religious forces had been in historical experience. These apologists emerged at a time when historians were probing relationships between frames of reference and research findings. Their work seemed all the more feasible since theorists had not yet reached a new standard for correlating presuppositions with the evidential record. It would be a mistake to think that critiques of scientific history created a vacuum which subjectivists rushed to fill. But for a time, after the demise of old guidelines, it was possible to write about the triumph of Christianity on America's frontier or its spread around the globe and to regard such work as congruent with contemporary rubrics. These two church historians flourished at a time when interpretive standards were broad enough for apologists to sustain their viewpoint within limits of the profession. Their massive use of factual information legitimized their efforts as history; their religious overview seemed at least plausible, given the way preconceptions were thought to influence every historian in their day.

NEW APOLOGETICS

Publications by two prolific authors featured a different angle of vision in the 1930s. Their work resembled apologetics because each series of writings stressed the prominence of Christianity in human affairs. Of course they were not the first historians to defend the importance of their faith. But instead of extolling doctrinal or moral excellence as had earlier works, these authors opened a "new" field by emphasizing Christianity's impact on social settings. The authors were also "new" in the sense that both used the latest critical thinking about method to substantiate their case. They utilized secular ideas about causation and relied on critical procedures to obtain accurate documentation. Each one acclaimed

Christianity as socially functional only after amassing enough empirical data to make their arguments seem irrefutable. Since most historians were admitting that subjective insights affected research, they thought it was legitimate to blend evidence and special pleading in their chosen areas.

The first of these was William W. Sweet who began his career in 1913 at DePauw University. In 1927 he moved to the University of Chicago where until 1946 he occupied the first chair of American Church History established in this country. Sweet used extensive archival research to make his topic more respectable. He faced a double challenge: one from secularists who slighted the whole subject of religious influence, and the other from church historians who gave little notice to events in America. In redressing that imbalance, he was careful not to claim too much. He did not insist "that the American churches be given a place of first importance" in national life. In a modest understatement, he simply pointed out "that the total life of the nation cannot adequately or truthfully be portrayed without giving them their due recognition." Sweet thought the only way to remedy the neglect, and possible contempt, for religious topics was to study church phenomena with the same care and rigor that other professional historians honored. His use of documentary evidence and quantifiable measurements served "to point out clearly and conclusively the significance of American church history."[31] They also facilitated his wish to demonstrate that religious activity was based on ideals and lasting values worth knowing about.

Sweet used critical empirical techniques to vindicate American church history as a respectable branch of inquiry. If earlier church history had been questionable because it did not observe rigorous secular standards, he vowed to surpass such work with the best of modern procedures. He would show from primary sources themselves that religion was influential in American life. Solid methods and reliable data would make his work superior to those that harbored partisan denominational biases. In contrast to self-serving treatises, he would survey materials as fairly as possible, with "no side to defend, no party to uphold." Despite the impossibility of operating with a completely objective viewpoint, Sweet still valued evidence over theory, the record of events over theologies about them. His task of finding and interpreting evidence was the means to serve an end, stated simply as telling "the whole truth without fear or favor" about religions in America. This truth, substantiated by the record, would allow him to assess the role Christianity played in this country's cultural development.[32] Sweet's lectures at Chicago and a dozen other institutions, his research seminars and supervision of more than thirty dissertations, plus his tireless efforts to collect documents for ongoing investigation helped achieve this goal.[33]

Sweet had been trained in secular historical methods which led him to see common ground between himself and all other professionals in the guild. He considered religion to be an aspect of human culture worth studying, and his subject matter alone distinguished him from other historians. He also conformed to secular patterns by emphasizing the importance of frontier themes, developing an orientation already familiar in church history. Sweet did not merely copy the ideas of Frederick J. Turner or those of Peter G. Mode, his predecessor at Chicago, but much of his emphasis on distinctive qualities of life in the American West has a Turnerian flavor. Focusing on characteristics that emerged in the trans-Allegheny heartland, he stressed the role religion had played in forming values of lasting significance to the nation. Sweet regarded life in Western regions as an experimental seed plot "where new forms of life, whether of institutions or types of thought, are germinated."[34] The most notable features of American religion, he believed, had also grown from the seedlings that sprouted during frontier experimentation.

In Sweet's estimation almost every valuable aspect of American Christianity had stemmed from frontier experience. The vast territory drained by the Mississippi River and its tributaries, protected from European corruption, was the land of emergent national character.[35] As Turner before him, Sweet held that "the American spirit—the traits that have come to be recognized as the most characteristic—was developed in the new commonwealths that sprang into life beyond the seaboard."[36] This perspective emphasized frontier conditions and consequent human adaptation, excluding almost every other historical consideration. Sweet admitted that some innovations had occurred in eighteenth-century colonial churches, but "it was not until population began to move away from the Atlantic seaboard and . . . turn its back more and more upon European influence that a distinctively American religious scene begins to appear."[37]

In the new environment, away from European influence, people worked out pragmatic approaches to the problems and opportunities they faced. Responses to frontier challenges produced experimental innovations that became the touchstones of a new way of life. Success confirmed habits that eventually became character traits such as individualism, hard work, recklessness, violence, upward social mobility, and democratic social cooperation.[38] Frontier circumstances were the key to cultural development in this hemisphere: "The greatest accomplishment of America has been the conquest of the continent, Sweet maintained. "It is not exaggeration to say that the most significant factor in the history of the United States has been the Western movement of population."[39]

Following this dictum, Sweet made his own contribution to thinking about the place of the frontier in American church history. Not surprisingly for one interested in statistics and mundane evidence, he held that the churches most capable of adapting to New World conditions had become the most important agents in American religious life:

The greatest task which the American churches faced during the latter years of the eighteenth and the early years of the nineteenth centuries, was that of following this restless and moving population with the softening influence of the Christian Gospel. And those churches which succeeded in devising the most adequate means of following population . . . were the religious bodies destined to become the largest, and to that extent, the most influential forces in extending religion and morality throughout the new nation.[40]

Successful adaptation nurtured growth, and from Sweet's perspective numerical strength indicated qualitative superiority. Evidence drawn from naturalistic, empirical investigation enabled him to highlight what he considered the most effective characteristics of American Christianity. But in a significant departure from Turner, Sweet argued that Protestant denominations played a crucial role in *making* the region typically American. The natural environment did not impose characteristics on the people who lived there; their religion created new human values as they struggled to cope with new conditions. Frontier churches made life more humane and effective because of the influence they brought to bear. Protestant Christianity, especially its Methodist component, served as a defender of democracy, a guarantor of social stability, a safeguard of moral standards, a template of education and civilized manners. Instead of environmental conditions affecting the content of religion, Sweet argued that Christianity had been a vital factor in shaping the development of American culture.[41]

Of all the priorities that motivated people on the frontier, Sweet thought their determination to improve social conditions had been the most important. Religion lay at the core of those concerns, and it was in turn affected by them, so that "the great American evangelical churches [became] the most socially minded of all the churches in Christendom."[42] This effective and long-lasting emphasis on the social aspects of Christianity grew from practical difficulties which religious leaders faced in borderland settings. As ministers kept pace with the advancing frontier, their work met the task of "attempting to bring the softening influences to bear upon the life of the raw, rough, and often blasphemous communities of the great new West."[43] Morality on the frontier was haphazard; individual freedom permitted unchecked license, and western communities found it difficult to preserve order or to uphold decent standards. The pressing issue of the day for religion was to enforce, through persuasion and discipline, some adherence to fundamental principles of moral conduct.

Sweet maintained that the major evangelical churches had enhanced their stature through moderating frontier behavior. The strongest and best churches supported social reform—morality in families and business, temperance, abolition of slavery, and subsequently the Social Gospel program in cities. Denominations worth historical notice were "those which came to power and influence as a consequence of their successful coping with the frontier."[44] Saving the West from barbarism set the stamp of practicality on American religion. As long as churches grew by advocating moral activity, they gave little concern to doctrinal matters. This indifference to theological questions was another result of frontier experience. Evangelical Protestantism reformed pioneers by insisting on vigorous morality, and this concern for social behavior stamped American religion with a lasting commitment to practical issues, discounting ideology and placing a low premium on intellectual comprehension.[45]

The frontier challenged religious agencies to keep pace wtih westering peoples. Sweet thought that challenge was "largely responsible" for stimulating the modern missionary impulse, "one of the chief influences in the life of the American churches."[46] Another beneficial result of interaction between Christianity and the new American West was the appearance of many denominational colleges.[47] Missionary outreach and efforts to provide educational personnel were substrata for a third major feature of American Protestantism: revivalism. This unique mode of evangelization emerged on the frontier as religious leaders contended with the conditions they found there. According to Sweet, "American society through much of its history may be characterized as a society in motion. . . . such a society is always strongly individualistic. Revivalism arose in such a society as a way of bringing Christianity to individuals; and revivalism flourished in frontier society because it was religion applied to individual needs."[48] Sweet thought people on the frontier inclined naturally to personal religious experience, not to doctrinal niceties or questions of institutional propriety. Since the great majority of them were isolated from organized religion, they developed a sense of independence from catechetical precision and liturgical uniformity. Revival techniques reached those people in ways congruent with their social and political experimentation. They met popular needs by experimenting with a new religious idiom. In Sweet's estimation, revivals were perhaps the only medium through which Christianity could have influenced such a scattered population.[49] And as frontier experience confirmed its utility, revivalism became one of the most distinctive characteristics of American Christianity.

Religious freedom was another basic feature that American churches derived from practical experience in the West. Arguments for religious freedom had some precedents in left-wing groups of earlier centuries, but Sweet insisted that the frontier was where those ideas flourished best. Protestants facing immense spiritual challenges realized the value of letting every denomination freely exert itself. Toleration of differing viewpoints culminated in the American heartland where a workable religious freedom proved to be "the greatest contribution America has made" to the cumulative expressions of Christian witness. By civilizing and Christianizing the frontier, evangelical agents had promoted "all the great concepts for which American democracy stands today, individual rights, freedom of conscience, freedom of speech, self-government, and complete religious liberty."[50] Freedom did not dilute religion's social influence, and competition among churches did not make them hostile to each other. In fact,

although there were sharp differences in theology and church polity among the most successful frontier churches, yet their differences were often less in evidence than their likenesses. The religious diversity of the frontier was underlaid with a certain uniformity which made possible a large degree of unity of action. The frontier churches placed theology as distinctly secondary to the practical work which the needs of the frontier demanded, and they found it possible to work together in spite of their divergent views and polities.[51]

Frontier churches also nurtured the seeds of democratic cooperation. Their concern to meet pressing needs among the people led them to a higher regard for mutual toleration, and it laid the groundwork for broader ecumenical efforts to achieve common religious and cultural objectives.

Why did Sweet emphasize frontier experience and assert that its distinctive features included revivalism, social reform, and religious freedom? These themes were nothing new in American church history. Writers since Robert Baird in the 1840s had repeatedly mentioned them as central to religion on this continent. The work of Frederick J. Turner had been an intellectual force among secular historians after 1890, and this may account for Sweet's early fascination with the frontier. But granting Turner's influence at the time of Sweet's graduate training, the "frontier thesis" had lost impetus after World War I. Why did it survive as a dated concept in Sweet's narratives long after it faded elsewhere? Frontier topics dominated his perspective through decades of research, perpetuating well into the 1950s a rather one-sided focus that excluded urban problems, ethnic pluralism, and confessional complexity. His overemphasis on Western priorities cannot be sustained even by some of his own statistical tabulations.[52] Sweet amassed empirical evidence, but he used it selectively to fit a preconceived interpretive pattern. What remains is to suggest why he employed it so persistently and for so long.

As a protagonist of accepted historical method, Sweet confined himself in church history to practices laid down by secular theorists. At the same time, he admired the values and standards contained in American Christianity, so the spadework of conventional research became a basis for extolling mainstream churches as having social significance. His reliance on frontier themes suggests that he wanted to use tested historiographical canons for apologetic purposes. Sweet may have felt that utilizing an accepted perspective, even one past its prime, made his work more respectable. Thus grounded in an approach and focus already sanctioned by general historians, he was free to champion Christianity as essential to the development of national culture.

Looking at his apologetics in another vein, there may have been a second reason for Sweet's distinctive church history. He could have emphasized the functional importance of spiritual influences because he lived in a time of social turmoil himself. Possibly, he sought reassurance from examples of how religion solved problems in the past in order to counteract the despair that gnawed at his own cultural setting. Sweet's mature years were beset with race riots, lynchings, labor unrest, a resurgent Ku Klux Klan, anti-Semitism, economic depressions, hot wars, cold wars, and nuclear weapons. Reacting to a time of national insecurity, he may have felt a sense of ineffectiveness compared to previous eras of tangible achievement. Studying periods when religion had exerted wholesome effects on American culture might provide guidelines for its doing so again.

Sweet focused on successful interaction between religious and social forces in American life. His emphasis on durable American qualities always fit within an interpretive framework where religion stabilized social uncertainty and rooted national characteristics in collective experience. Highlighting a spiritual heritage that could also meet contemporary challenges, Sweet observed that

it is the past which unites us. We differ about present leadership and policies; we unite about the great ideals, the noble achievements . . . coming out of the past; and it is . . . these achievements, these ideals which keep us a united people. This is true of the nation and it is equally true of the church. . . . We need the knowledge of the past . . . to counteract the many divisive influences of our time.[53]

From this perspective, American experience on the frontier offered valuable information about how Christianity and the commonwealth could deal with current problems. Sweet thought history could tell people about the ideals that had sustained their ancestors, helping them to identify with the country and its churches by embracing a shared past.[54] Most often he discussed events of the early national period, and whenever alluding to modern difficulties he urged readers to rely on ideals that had triumphed over earlier problems. He saw urban conditions as just another setting in which religious leaders could follow a mobile population and apply again the social teachings of Christianity. Cities for him were the new frontier, an environment ripe for another wave of revivals.[55]

Sweet hoped Americans would retain their historically acquired character. He used lessons from the past to encourage the faint-hearted and to indicate possible courses of future action. On the other hand, he warned that past achievements did not ensure continued success. Vigilant social activism based on religious ideals was always necessary because "the great freedoms cannot be taken for granted, even in the land of the free." While proud of America's record, Sweet said the watchword of history was "no great and good cause is ever finally and completely won."[56] History did not disclose providential deliverance but rather struggles where-in people with religious principles had raised their society to higher levels. When cherished ideals were being attacked, histori-cal wisdom called for courage to act from spiritual promptings for the public good. Sweet thought church history might help identify the best religious ideals and thus facilitate continued action for cultural advance. With these goals in mind, he used empiricism and mundane criteria to depict Christianity as a vital force in historical contexts, a reservoir of spiritual energy to be used whenever situations called for reform.

Kenneth S. Latourette was the other historian who employed secular standards in order to demonstrate the importance of Chris-tianity. Trained when scientific history was at its zenith, his prodi-gious labors made him one of the most prominent scholars in the first half of the twentieth century. Beginning in 1921 he taught at Yale for thirty-two years, occupying various chairs associated with Oriental history and the study of Christian missions. One key to his importance lies in the fact that secular colleagues accepted Latourette as an expert in the Far East. He produced more than a dozen books on the development of Japan, the history and culture of China, and Sino-American relations. These works secured his reputation as a careful historian who provided reliable information based on the best investigative methods. They also earned him the presidency of the American Historical Association for 1948. Other aspects of his work show how much he correlated spiritual inter-ests with research and writing. Latourette stayed within common-place guidelines of his craft and used the data he gathered to

buttress a Christian interpretation of events. His search for interpretive patterns led to apologetics, and he used secular standards
of historical exactitude to support that ulterior purpose.

Latourette followed the debate that modified scientific ideals in
his profession. As absolutist standards crumbled, he noted there
was room for historians to pursue their task with different approaches and goals in mind. But naturalistic explanations still
dominated the minds of most historians everywhere. Latourette
mentioned this mundane orientation in order to define his own
position in reference to it:

> The author has been trained in the school of modern history which looks
> askance at the supernatural and sees in the flow of events simply mechanical
> and human factors. . . . Most members of this school decline to affirm any
> cosmic significance in human history. If in the story of the human race they
> discern any determining causes . . . they find them in some factor or combi-
> nation of factors which by themselves cannot be labelled as "supernatural."[57]

Even if one wished to ascribe some higher significance to history,
one could not go back to the old confessionalism that claimed to
see the hand of God at work. So Latourette avoided talk of miracles
and providential intervention. But he was convinced that it was
possible to trace events with strict historical accuracy and then
interpret the whole scheme of things from a Christian perspective.
He sought to "narrate the facts" as objectively as possible, and
while not using an overtly supernaturalist viewpoint, he dealt
selectively with evidence that demonstrated the importance of
religion in human affairs.[58]

Developments in science and philosophy had refined ideas
about how historians treated materials. In Latourette's increasingly
sophisticated appreciation of historical procedure, every investigator brought subjective insights to observed data. He knew that

> no one can hope to write history without presuppositions. The professional
> historian of the nineteenth and twentieth centuries has aspired to be "objec-
> tive" and to tell "what actually happened." Yet every attempt to view the
> human story, whether in some small segment or as a whole, involves a
> selection of events from the stream which constitutes the crude stuff of
> history. Back of the selection is a conviction of what is important. Governing
> this "value judgment" is, consciously or unconsciously, a philosophy.[59]

Historians of all subjects had to acknowledge biases in themselves.
Their narratives included personal values as well as selected factual

information about the past. Instead of despairing over this epistemological state of affairs, Latourette developed operating principles within the revised limits of modern research techniques.

Secular historical theory recognized that value judgments affected research and interpretation. Perceived facts, rational interpretations, and personal convictions formed complex substrata in every investigation. In light of this, Latourette considered it legitimate to maintain that "the history of Christianity is the history of what God has done for man through Christ and of man's response."[60] Every history was relative to the author's frame of reference, and in this case, it was plausible for carefully gathered evidence to support the view that "much seems strangely to fit into what Christians have believed about the universe, mankind, God, and the fashion in which God works."[61] Since historians had many options after scientific standards gave way, Latourette thought his particular interpretation of data could hold its own with other scholarly efforts in the profession. Many of his works rested on the belief that God created physical reality and, because of both origin and continuing dependence, the world of historical events had some intelligible relationship to divine purpose. This emphasis on empirical spadework coupled with spiritual insight has remained a paradigm for many church historians in later generations.

Latourette described his conceptual overview by relating faith and factual affirmations as precisely as he could. Since evidence substantiated apologetics, it was crucial to the believer's historical synthesis. The historian used reason to search for and to authenticate factual evidence. "But truth is not attained by reason alone," Latourette insisted. "The insight that is born of faith can bring illumination." Of course faith was not naive credulity that ignored rational analysis and natural causes. But history suffered from relying on reason alone. Defending a more balanced perspective, Latourette argued that "confidence in reason as the sole or final criterion is a blind act of credulity" in itself, an act which denied rich possibilities to historical interpretation.[62] Truths perceived through personal insight interacted with those discovered by means of research. The historian blended ideas about past events and their meaning in an interpretation that accorded with all points of reference, ideological as well as empirical. In one of his most lucid characterizations of this viewpoint, he maintained,

We must take account of facts. But as every historian who is honest and informed knows, even in the selection of facts the judgment of which are important cannot be avoided and depends largely on the observer's convictions. For the Christian this means that his faith is involved. It is his faith which enters into his appraisal of what is pertinent. Yet if that appraisal is to approximate the truth the Christian must be aware of observable facts and dodge none of them, including those which challenge his conclusions. He must be willing to modify or even reject his appraisal if it is not in accord with the facts.[63]

History could not be history without critically researched data, but it would have no significance without ideas, beliefs, and values.

Various combinations of fact and ideology were not equally plausible, and historians could not arbitrarily impose on the record a meaning they wanted to find there. Latourette urged investigators to keep an open mind regarding cumulative factual knowledge and to revise their interpretations accordingly. If faith assumptions conflicted with historical evidence, then beliefs should be modified to accommodate known data. Faith should supplement, not dominate, a critical treatment of historical materials. There was a discernible tension in Latourette's ideas on this point. He sensed perpetual difficulty in dovetailing religious convictions with mundane details. "From the Christian standpoint," he said, "the usual historian has an entirely distorted view of history and misses the most important features . . . of . . . ecclesiastical as well as political, economic, or intellectual history."[64]

Despite this tension, beliefs could help synthesize isolated facts unearthed by research. And if the historical record substantiated one's confessional viewpoint, their compatibility gave an added dimension to understanding the past. Such an endeavor was worth pursuing, and "limited though they are, the historian must employ such tools as he possesses." Latourette was convinced that "when he does so, much comes to light which tends to support the Christian understanding of history. The historian as historian can neither refute nor demonstrate the Christian thesis, but he can detect evidence which suggests a strong possibility for the truth of the Christian understanding."[65] History alone could never persuade unbelievers that God moved temporal events to good purpose. But for those like Latourette who already believed in providential guidance, history could give empirical support for that conviction.[66]

Latourette was a historian of Christianity, not a historian of churches. He preferred going beyond a focus on institutions to observe the broader influences Christianity had exerted in various cultures. "A complete history of Christianity must include every phase of the impact of that faith upon mankind," he said. It should cover institutional developments, too, with attention to forms of organization, leaders, and controversies. It must account for changing ideas about doctrine and worship as well as appreciate different ways in which faith had transformed the inner lives and conduct of individuals. A well-rounded study would also note the effect of cultural environments on the faith and in reciprocal fashion, point out what impact Christianity had made on different local settings. In this last category, Latourette was ambitious. He wanted nothing less than a survey of how his religious tradition had affected all phases of human civilization: its arts, music, literature, education and philosophy, plus social, economic, and political institutions. Expectations for this larger canvas lay behind his assertion that historians "need a fairly thorough reorientation in our study of the history of Christianity." Church history in its normally modest versions produced "a distorted view of the course of Christianity, and of its place in the human race."[67]

To rectify such distortion, Latourette recommended three changes, beginning with studying the faith wherever it was expressed instead of only in Christian churches. Then he urged focusing on human experience around the globe, moving beyond Europe and occidental priorities to appreciate all representations of Christian life. Finally, he called for more attention to recent rather than ancient times. If church historians adopted a more comprehensive vantage point, he was convinced their studies would yield gratifying results. "Seen against the background of the world as a whole, it will become apparent" to those adequately apprised of the facts, "that Christianity has been a growing, rather than a waning, force in human history."[68]

All of Latourette's publications on the history of Christianity followed a definite thematic structure and used a cogent set of interpretive criteria. He explicated standards for determining periods of religious vitality, and by applying those tests, he found patterns that both chronicled past accomplishments and anticipated future effectiveness. Among the criteria he used were geographical expansion, the emergence of new movements from within the living tradition, and basic improvements in human welfare. Regarding improvements, Latourette sometimes chose to emphasize Christian influence on individual religious experience, and at other times, he stressed the effect of faith on various aspects of human culture.[69] This gave him remarkable flexibility in highlighting first one area as proof of Christian triumph, then another. It let him switch from themes that did not, at some given point, bear out the importance of Christian presence, to others that put the faith in a better light.

Fortified with such evaluative formulae, Latourette related the history of Christianity as a series of vigorous advances and partial recessions. He discerned a period of early success from the time of Jesus to A.D. 500 when the initial impulse spread through the Roman Empire. Between 500 and 950, the faith sustained threats to its existence when cultural disorientation attended the collapsing Empire. From 950 to 1350, there was encouraging renewal as missionaries converted new barbarian peoples to Christian principles. The years between 1350 and 1500 marked a slight decline because Moslem advance and inroads by other non-Christians entailed loss of territory and influence. Christianity expanded again from 1500 to 1750 alongside aggressive European outreach, particularly through Portuguese and Spanish efforts, and it receded between 1750 and 1815 when those national powers faded. In Latourette's estimation, Christian history reached unprecedented heights in "the great century" of 1815–1914 due to global expansion and cultural effectiveness. The years since 1914 had been filled with uncertainty, but he still perceived hopeful advances through troubling storms.[70] These periods disclosed "successive pulsations" of religious influence which historians could assess in order to "take the full and accurate measure of Christianity" in every epoch. While taking that measure against the background of human experience around the world, facts enabled him to show how "Christianity has been a growing force in the life of the race."[71]

Through Latourette's many writings, the assertion rings out repeatedly that Christianity has been a truly vital and beneficial force in human endeavors. This conviction recurs most forcibly in his treatment of the period since 1815. Perhaps Latourette was concerned to maintain such a positive interpretation of modern times because this was the era in which Christian eminence had been most widely assailed. He was aware of attacks on Christianity's contemporary relevance, and he responded with corresponding vigor. To him the faith had been more influential over the course of the last 150 years than at any previous time. Many historians fostered the impression that Christianity had declined since the Renaissance as religious concerns increasingly gave place to secular interests. Latourette noted that many Christians subscribed to this unfortunate interpretation, accepting secondary status and defining their day as a "post-Christian era."[72] But he argued that historical evidence in its widest scope would not support such a myopic interpretation. Judging from a world perspective, not from one tied to western European experience, it was more accurate to conclude that "never has Jesus had so wide and so profound an effect on humanity as in the past three or four generations."[73] Millions of individual lives had been transformed; cultures had been improved by reforming political systems, upgrading health standards, and nourishing minds with beauty and learning. In a time of social and economic instability, international hatred, and war, Latourette did not counsel despair. He thought a firm grasp of historical facts supported an optimistic future for Christianity.

As the twentieth century advances, and in spite of many adversaries and severe losses, it has become more deeply rooted among more peoples than it or any other faith has ever before been. It is also more widely influential in the affairs of men than any other religious system which mankind has known. The weight of evidence appears to be on the side of those who maintain that Christianity is still only in the first flush of its history and that it is to have a growing place in the life of mankind. In this Christianity is in striking contrast with other religions. Here are much of its uniqueness and a possible clue to its significance.[74]

Such an assessment did not allow wishful thinking to override sober realities. Latourette thought his optimism justifiable because it used tangible factors as the basis for historical evaluation. Since every historian began with presuppositions and then modified them with the widest possible grasp of pertinent data, a church history that stressed Christianity's cultural importance corresponded to the latest reflections on method. Judging from geographical diffusion and cultural penetration, Christianity seemed clearly to be a potent force in human affairs. Moreover, its relevance as catalyst for beneficial change proved to be continually on the increase. As to any higher significance, Latourette drew from confessional insights to address that issue because "the answer cannot be given on the basis of facts ascertained by observation and appraised by human reason." There, he said, "It can come only as an act of faith." But even there, a Christian understanding of history could not "contradict observation and reason." It needed grounding in accepted evidence. Using measurable phenomena, it was still possible, though, to speak of "a conclusion of faith supported by what is deemed to be fact interpreted by reason." Viewing history through the eyes of faith also provided "intelligibility . . . to what otherwise seems confusing and contradictory."[75]

This intelligibility stemmed from viewing Christian activity in its widest scope, not restricting it to any single creed, institution, or behavioral norm. Amid events that led some observers to bemoan a loss of Christian effectiveness, Latourette thought world history confirmed a view of divine superintendence that bent adversity to higher purpose. "Indeed, it is conceivable that [God] never allows the abuse of free will to get completely out of hand, but has placed such resources at the disposal of those who, also of their free will, respond to the promptings of His Spirit that they bring good out of evil."[76] All his studies of Christianity rested on this modest yet unshakable optimism. In a final declaration toward the end of his career, Latourette drew on the metaphor of wheat and tares to recommend patient scrutiny of all temporal events. Though it seemed "the chronic ills and evils of mankind are increasing," he spoke as both historian and believer in pointing out that "the forces issuing from the love of God in Christ are also mounting." Latourette's faith and dogged realism preserved the conviction that a student of mundane events could see "much in history which puzzles him but nothing that clearly makes this hope illusory."[77] Faith and scholarship were compatible, and experiences in neither the past nor present precluded hope.

$\mathcal{S}3$
Higher Ecclesiology as a Basis for History

When historians stopped believing that facts existed by themselves, disclosed causes, or conveyed their own significance, they inaugurated the modern era of American historiography which we still occupy. An underlying premise of all modern work is that "individual subjectivism always has and always will dominate historical research and writing as the controlling factor in the formulation of projects and selection and interpretation of data." The whole past cannot be reconstructed; accounts can never be definitive; new viewpoints from successive generations or differing cultures will rewrite history according to changing priorities. The truth of historical narratives is always relative to their authors' frames of reference, values, and preferences regarding what really mattered in bygone events.[1]

Every written history is bound by some frame of reference, but subjective elements do not preclude a concern for accuracy regarding historical evidence. Modern practitioners agree that researchers can cope with their biases if they recognize preconceptions for what they are and notify readers about them. Historians who shape information through their own experience are better off if they say so. The best results stem not from claims about detached reporting but from a candid viewpoint "which spurns the bitterness of partisanship while yet embracing the passion of involvement."[2] Historians no longer contrast "factual" accounts with "theoretical" ones but recognize combinations of the two in every narrative. If assumptions remain unrecognized, they are detrimental to the best use of documentary materials. "Evaluative generalizations, solemnly exorcised at the front door," warned one analyst, "will inevitably creep in at the side entrance, and the historian will be their victim less often if he fixes them with a steady eye than if he insists they are not there."[3]

Practical discussions about historical method in the 1930s and thereafter accepted the idea that preconceptions were inevitable in all human inquiries. Secular historians led the way in reformulating theories of objective research that also made room for subjective insights. Church historians either accepted the new formulations without self-conscious scrutiny, or they pursued their own conceptions of what the discipline allowed. Scholars like Sweet and Latourette relied on revised methodology and emphasized the roles Christianity performed in various societies to prove its cultural worth. Another group refused to define churches as social institutions or to confine their studies to cultural effectiveness because such a perspective lacked theological dignity. These other church historians stressed the spiritual nature of the Church, and they investigated past occurrences to determine events of religious significance. And although the otherworldly hypotheses of "high-church" historians seemed to be recidivist, their renewed defense of the Church as a metaphysical entity fit, albeit uneasily, within broad principles developed in the profession at large.

The more open attitudes about various perspectives made it easier for church historians to postulate the spiritual nature of Christian communities. There were other factors behind the rise of fresh theological impulses, but general historiographical theory accommodated religious definitions of churches when they appeared. Some observers suggest that high-church history resulted from modern ecumenical consciousness with its questions concerning faith and order among denominations.[4] Others surmise that theology was rejuvenated by the trend known as "neoorthodoxy." It is impossible to ascertain what really stimulated this new emphasis on religious values in special institutions, but it came at a time when church leaders were "conscious of a fresh sense of vocation after the aimlessness or self-apology" found in socially oriented history. Church history with a theological rationale "recovered both the self-esteem and the outward respect" it had enjoyed before science banished transcendence from causal explanation.[5] Now that revised epistemology made room for metaphysics again, these ecumenical, neoorthodox historians had secular as well as religious justification for emphasizing distinctive qualities in their subject.

Roman Catholic historians had asserted the importance of their church since the days of Peter Guilday and earlier. Catholic historiography changed little during this century's first four decades and needed no stimulus from neoorthodoxy or ecumenism to maintain that focus. While secularists touted critical method and encouraged mundane explanations, Catholic scholarship kept its distance from popular norms. Since it had not conformed to those trends, it was in a better position to capitalize on revised theory once the latest thinking again allowed for different perceptions. Representative statements over the decades illustrate how Catholic history persisted in orienting research around a distinctive ecclesiology. One classic articulation agreed with revised theory by acknowledging that there was no discrepancy between Catholic truth and "the fierce light of history." The logic of such a conclusion depended on suitable definitions, and in this case, history was seen as "a patient . . . study of all the available evidence, in the light of the Catholic doctrine on Divine Providence and the distribution of grace."[6] Locating providential grace and consequent salvation in an institution that spanned the centuries made it possible to recount spiritual history through empirical evidence.

A generation later many Catholic historians were less interested in writing for the conscious purpose of edifying the faithful. More candid attitudes about painting warts and all prevailed, but even there it is apparent that organizational and temperamental preferences set their church history apart from secular efforts.[7] Even more recent thinkers have continued to defend the unique placement of historical scholarship within preconceptions about Catholic eminence and certitude. Latter-day apologists note that a complete separation between observer and the observed is neither possible nor desirable. They reason that, since historical knowledge is participant knowledge, acceptance of Catholic affirmations is essential to producing acceptable historical understanding. "Is it merely the subject that determines Catholic history alone?" asked one parochialist, implying that it is not. A proper history of Catholic development necessarily involves the observer's confessional viewpoint. Apologists of this sort continue to defend the position that adequate scholarship includes active participation in church life. This vital relationship will affect students' attitudes about their tradition as the pivotal institution of Christian nurture, and it will guide their method of studying its importance throughout the ages.[8]

THREE PROTESTANT EXPONENTS

Cyril C. Richardson

Protestant historians who worked within a theological framework were rare and thus more noticeable than their Catholic counterparts. A strong voice among these advocates was Cyril C. Richardson whose career at Union Theological Seminary enhanced that institution's educational program at midcentury. His expertise in early church materials was such that the ASCH chose him as its president early in 1948. But a serious tubercular condition marred future prospects for Richardson and he resigned the presidency in April. Thoughts about the society's customary presidential address must have been on his mind, though, and in 1949 he published an article that would probably have served that purpose. In it Richardson summarized his ideas about the Church's true nature, reasons for studying its history, and the proper manner in which to pursue investigations.

Richardson defended studying church history, saying "one enters into the communion of saints" through acquaintance with the past. Knowing what others had accomplished in broader fields of action freed one from parochialism and pointed the way to more courageous action. Church history also yielded vital religious benefits. Heroic examples from previous eras did more than broaden one's horizons: "They steady us in loyalty to the one faith. We catch from them a spirit more fervent than our own, and through their trials we stumble on our own victories." Proper church history for Richardson pertained to more than human collectivities because the Church was also "the Holy Community entrusted with the means of salvation." He thought inquiry into the spiritual core of ecclesiastical bodies involved the scholar in "a prophetic role, disclosing God and His ways with men." Of course this required something more than looking at institutions that happened to call themselves churches. In rebuttal to socially oriented perspectives, he maintained, "On the contrary, Church History is the tale of redemption; and while in a sense it embraces world history, its central thread is the story of the Holy Community (known under various guises and found in manifold and surprising places), which is the bearer of revelation and through which God acts in human history."[9] So from the beginning, Richardson apprised his readers of how history would contribute to a more adequate theological understanding of past and present reality.

Richardson urged students of the Church to write history in its fullest, sacred sense, not confining themselves to simple narratives of events. A historian who wished to enrich theology had to penetrate beneath surface phenomena: "He has to tell the story against the background of ultimate meanings. He has to recognize that he stands on the boundary between symbol and fact, between myth and history, because the events with which he deals are transfigured by the Holy."

Richardson did not allow his convictions about ultimate meaning distort the evidence. He dealt with facts of record as responsibly as historians of other topics. But when he discussed meaning as distinguished from facts, there his distinctive emphasis came into play. It was his conviction that historians who interpret the importance of church life "have to clothe a concrete, historical event in a vesture woven by the religious imagination." Combining the two aspects of method into a single process, "We have to speak of events in their historical settings, to investigate just what did happen, and its relation to what occurred before and after. But we have, too, to recognize how these incidents themselves reveal something to us of God, and in consequence are more than events, because they are the medium of revelation."[10] The solemn task of church history was to recount previous ecclesiastical experience with scrupulous accuracy in order to facilitate seeing the hand of God at work there.

So much for prolegomenon. When Richardson employed these views in practical historical studies, his publications did not exhibit the triumphalism which readers might have expected. He rarely alluded to divine action while describing human activities, and any understanding of ultimate meaning in history was only implied, never stated. Most of his researches centered on ecumenical concerns that commanded attention on the seminary campuses of his day. But knowledge of the past did not, for him, furnish easy lessons which churches could use to blend their present creeds, ministries, or rituals. Richardson depicted past ecclesiastical differences in graphic prose that showed how difficult it would be to achieve a satisfactory reunion of all Christianity. He thought this kind of church history was an aid to ecumenism because it discouraged shortsighted optimism. History served churches best when it described failures that still needed to be overcome, not when it highlighted bygone patterns for current imitation. In this way it served a higher purpose by stimulating serious theological reflection on all the problems that ecumenism had to face.

One of these imponderables concerned doctrines of the Church itself, and Richardson elucidated various definitions to show how irreconcilable they were. He hoped historical information would further the cause of unity, but this could happen only if it exhibited the limitations found in both Catholicism and Protestantism. Richardson singled out such topics as ordination, the Eucharist, and apostolic succession to underscore difficulties with the basic concept of grace. Many believed grace was limited to the ordinary means of sacraments administered by priests, but history also disclosed multitudes who experienced divine presence in unregulated ways. For those who took the past seriously, this meant that there were "not merely diverse forms of one Christianity, but different Christian religions."[11] In a similar analysis of trinitarian theology, Richardson concluded that all existing creedal statements were incapable of comprehending the God who revealed himself in Jesus Christ. Doctrinal formulae were artificial constructs, arbitrary impositions that engendered more bewilderment than belief in individuals, more hostility than fellowship among groups.[12]

The historical record displayed antithetical conceptions of revelation, and that posed another problem to modern ecumenism. Church history challenged religious leaders to grapple with such serious diversities because, Richardson said, "a type of Church unity which evades the fundamental fact that there is not one Christianity with different forms, but actually different Christian religions, would be little more than formal and have small chance of survival." Historical awareness might suggest that hopes for Christian unity were futile, but Richardson truly believed that new institutions and ideas could advance the cause. Despite his sober recognition of long-standing problems, he was sanguine of future possibilities because he saw every church as having a role in God's plan. His inclusive concept of the New Israel acknowledged that it had in historical fact "split into warring tribes." Each tribe was involved in the sin of schism and hindered the full operation of grace by not living up to the ideal of the true Church. Dialogue among traditional factions was worth pursuing because, as he doggedly maintained, "all do in some measure participate in the Church Transcendent."[13]

In another survey Richardson stated somewhat more clearly how he combined metaphysical ideals and mundane realities. Still focussing on basic concepts of the Church, he analyzed ancient and medieval Christianity to trace reliance on ecclesiastical offices as the source of grace. Then he pointed out that many believers in the sixteenth century and thereafter preferred scriptural to institutional authority, a religion of faith to one of works. Sacramental theories also abounded in later times, and these multiple religious options created in modern times an atmosphere of tolerance. This more lenient attitude stemmed at least in part from competing ecclesiologies, and their historical differentiation proved one thing to candid observers: all religious institutions were human, not divine, constructions. If history offered no sure guide to the future, what did it encourage modern church leaders to do? Or as Richardson put it, "What can and ought the Church to mean for our generation?" It was not enough to know what Christianity had meant previously because earlier conceptions of the Church only hinted at what it could mean in contemporary life. The important question was not how tradition was grounded in the past but how it related to the present. Modern churches were free to seek new understanding, to apply "the eternal element in Christianity to that which is unique in the life and thought of our generation." As a historian, Richardson was convinced that knowledge of other Christian expressions would aid this theological quest. "It is only as Christians become conscious of themselves as a world-wide community, sharing a divine life and a common faith," he held, "that they will be able to withstand the movements that threaten the very foundations of the Gospel of Christ."[14]

Temporal institutions and the transcendent ideal were complementary, not exclusive, realities. Richardson valued human religious constructions because they drew inspiration from the Church as their ultimate reason for being. He maintained that "churches are not merely local expressions of cultural life or even aggregations of believers. They are historical manifestations of the people of God." Religious life at various times and places gave the historian examples of how different groups had approximated God's

Kingdom. Each effort had meaning, but their success was always partial. Historians found them useful not as absolutes to copy but as concrete expressions that taught something more about God's full purpose. The Church as "the transcendent unity of The Faith" existed in perfection outside mundane expressions, and yet it could be discerned only through imperfect human efforts to reflect it. For Richardson, the eternal had "historical meaning and existence, when it is embodied in the churches and denominations which share its life and witness to its divine origin and gospel."[15] In this manner high-church historians could combine a close scrutiny of historical documentation with belief in an overarching verity that gave importance to the whole Christian past.

Richardson usually confined his scholarship to describing earlier versions of Christian life as they evolved into a variety of ideas on salvation and worship. Beyond that, he occasionally speculated on an eclectic view of the Church, and that conception can serve to round off his thoughts about religious progress. Not surprisingly, he suggested that the best concept of the Church would draw on examples from every major historical period. Early churches contributed a vision of the Church as the fellowship of salvation, of people living in a new age governed by the rule of Christ. Catholic development provided ideas of the Church as a divine institution dedicated to fulfilling its appointed mission. Protestants retained the crucial reminder that human institutions could never be absolute and that only God's Kingdom was eternal. Modern denominations made the important point that moral vigor and spiritual freedom were essential qualities in the true Church. Contemporary ecumenism emphasized unity in the Church's life. That yearning for reunion led Richardson to blend all previous historical elements into a summarizing affirmation. History did not reveal the Church in its fullness, but it provided glimpses of "the divine creation, the body of those whom God has called through His Son and send into the world to do His will." Facts and beliefs were reciprocal. Mundane institutions were imperfect reflections of the eternal, and "in the Church [each temporal expression of] Christianity is made alive." Richardson sought to understand the Church by studying some of its previous expressions. His fundamental presupposition was that Christian truth "is embodied in a living community, which preserves, reinterprets, and hands it down to successive generations."[16] Since the Church made Christian traditions vital, a careful depiction of historical varieties enlivened the past and enriched the present.

James H. Nichols

Another scholar who wanted to rejuvenate church history by aligning it more closely with theology was James H. Nichols, professor at Chicago Divinity School and later at Princeton Theological Seminary. In his view Western society had derived its only genuine understanding of historical processes from a Christian perspective. Before the advent of the Church, ancient chronicles had recounted wars and erratic political fortunes to no lasting purpose. Christianity gave meaning to human experience, but modern historians had largely abandoned that orientation by rejecting teleology and replacing it with a naturalism that left basic questions unanswered. And worse, many church historians had capitulated to such myopic views, failing to appreciate the exalted nature of their subject. Those who explained history through environmental factors were, in Nichols's opinion, spiritually impoverished. Those who emphasized the social function of religion "put second things first" and were guilty of ignoring the religious quality of what they studied.[17]

To remedy this decay, Nichols advocated a return to sound definitions of the Church and a reassertion of theological conceptual guidelines. His reaffirmation was timely because it appeared when modern epistemologists agreed that all interpretations included elements of faith. Since events had meaning only when related to a transempirical perspective, he felt justified in positing that "interpretations must have a verifiable factual basis, but it is the eye of faith alone which discerns in concrete facts their transcendent significance." Eschewing the vagaries of shortsighted interpretations, he declared that church history had a "particular vocation." And he urged students of his day to expand their task "beyond ecclesiological and doctrinal considerations to include the whole moral and spiritual life of those called to Christian loyalties."[18]

Nichols wanted to rescue his profession from the inadequate historical perspective that hampered most studies. His general target was what he termed "positivistic history," the outdated reliance on absolutes in scientific detachment. This view had seemed infallible to practitioners in earlier generations, but Nichols found it, as did most modern analysts, no longer convincing or important. There was a hollow ring to claims that the dignity and perquisites of scholarship depended on writing history without particular convictions. He said such a view rested on a poor understanding of how historians actually functioned, and it suffered from an overdose of "naturalistic philosophies . . . which mark a late degeneration of the unique Judeo-Christian conception that mankind has a history worth recording." Positivistic history embraced secular values that ignored religious activity as either inconsequential or not amenable to scientific observation. Challenging those assumptions, Nichols argued that history would be more realistic and relevant if it adopted a religious perspective and focused on "the ultimate loyalties and values of human societies." Scholars would contribute more pertinent studies if they abandoned naturalistic reductionism and used instead the insights available in religious history.[19]

Few historians seemed interested in theological relevance, and Nichols used his 1950 ASCH presidential address to win some of them over. He began by charging that their kind of church history contributed nothing to religious thought because it was too secularized. As a result, it had lost its distinctiveness and became just a subcategory of the general field. The history that needed reforming was any study of "those institutions called churches which could be pursued as one might study legal history or the history of art." Such students of the Church's past had sold their spiritual birthright in order to win recognition from other professional historians, Nichols believed. They had been too quick to accept the "misconceived scientific method" as a means of gaining intellectual respectability, and now they feared losing status if they gave it up. Nichols was irritated by this reluctance because it stemmed from the wrong priorities. Historians who saw churches as social institutions were tied to "such a positivist reconception of the meaning of history" that their efforts "effectually eliminated the Church." They were timid about returning to the only conviction that could distinguish their work. As a remedy he called on them to recognize "that in fact the life of the church was the focus of the meaning of history in general."[20]

Nichols's hectoring comments to church historians illustrated his standards for scholarly value. He considered the work of Philip Schaff, completed a full century earlier, to be the latest and best full-length survey written in English. The fact that Schaff's effort had not been improved upon suggested to him that later historians had been "unable to sustain the faith of his vision of the Church."[21] One of those epigonic successors was Shirley Jackson Case whom Nichols rated as "one of the most conspicuous American writers on early Christianity." But Nichols faulted Case's work because it was based on "a kind of evolutionary humanism" that had become dated and irrelevant in light of recent theological changes.[22] As far as William W. Sweet was concerned, Nichols thought his oeuvre ranked alongside that of Samuel E. Morison and Arthur M. Schlesinger, Sr., but not "with the church historians proper." He considered Sweet to be a social historian "who specialized in religious institutions and movements as a major aspect of the American social pattern." Sweet was not acceptable as a church historian because by method and orientation, he avoided theology, "describing religious aspects of national culture, rather than the American expression of the church catholic."[23] As one might expect, he spoke approvingly of Cyril C. Richardson and quoted his viewpoints as his own. Drawing on yet another scholar of similar persuasion, Nichols held that sociological analysis "is not the history of the church . . . but that of various Christian movements." Any "purely empirical manner of observation" was inadequate because it failed to see the invisible Church inside visible institutions. Church history patterned along secular lines failed because it could only deal "with institutional churches irrespective of the life of the real Church in them."[24]

Several factors helped create the intellectual climate that fostered church history of this sort. In an era when subjective insights were once again admissible, Nichols mentioned two impulses that shaped his own priorities. One was a resurgent interest in historical theology. He defined this as a concern for doctrinal development, not a direct result of Barthian or neoorthodox fascination with systematics. This new theological sensitivity focused on classic soteriological categories such as sin, grace, and atonement. These made for more relevant historical insights, and Nichols left no doubt about his conviction that "new openness to traditional Christian tenets . . . qualified historians better for the task of interpreting the past." Perspectives nurtured by Christian redemption were infinitely superior to anything based on evolutionary humanism.[25]

The second component that helped reinvigorate church history was what Nichols called "a heightened perception of the character and significance of its subject matter." He did not say the ecumenical movement stimulated him thinking along this line but referred only to "the events of the 1930s" as prompters for a high ecclesiology. Whatever the causes, Christians had been "made newly conscious that they belonged, not just to this or that national community, but to a universal society transcending cultural barriers." And as historians acquired fresh insights into the universal Church, they recovered a "specifically Christian understanding of human fulfillment as in part distinguishable from social progress."[26] This beginning point and subsequent studies inevitably meant that church history would differ from social or cultural history. Nichols welcomed the distinction because it accentuated the special quality of church history and enhanced its potential for contributing to religious vitality in contemporary church life.

A theological conception of the Church was fundamental to both religious renewal and improved historical studies. Generalities and specifics reinforced each other, and Nichols was convinced that "one cannot discern direction and meaning in history in general without a concrete perception of particular redemption and new life in the Church." He argued that students could attain "the Christian vision of history" if they looked for the Church in every tangible example of the faith they investigated.[27] This was the basic orientation church historians should adopt. If they retained a proper appreciation of the Church as a transcendent reality, its overarching presence would help them understand the common heritage that gave separate traditions a single destiny.

A proper theoretical orientation led to correct perception of events. Nichols thought such an orientation allowed historians to focus on "the manifestations of redemption and the release of new life in the concrete historical community of the church."[28] But it was not enough to accept external definitions and investigate the fortunes of purportedly Christian institutions. The higher purpose that distinguished church history from other studies was a concern to know "how much of this belongs to the story of God's redemption of mankind." Even though he confined himself to mundane evidence, Nichols still felt that "after our own earthbound fashion we must agonize over the question 'Where and what is the Church?'" Those who inquired into previous church experiences had a duty to use verifiable data to show how particular doctrines, rituals, and institutions had served as vehicles of Christian deliverance. In short, the task was "to trace the actualization of the Gospel in human history, to discern and describe the signs of the Kingdom, to reveal the subtle indications of the presence of the Risen Christ to his adopted brethren."[29]

Guided by this larger conception of their subject, church historians were thus enabled to perform three important functions. First they were free to scrutinize ecclesiastical phenomena and compare historical incidents with transcendent ideals. As a practicing historian, Nichols held that "all revelatory facts, . . . can be analyzed in objective, secular fashion, and need to be." This scrutiny taught humility because critical history eventually found limitations in every human religious expression. Using transcendence to judge the mundane inevitably proved "the fallibility of all books, all churches, all reason, all the sacramental agencies of life to which we are constantly tempted to trust our security."[30] Second, church history could also show members of various churches what they held in common with others in the Christian tradition. For instance, the communion of saints touched all generations and enlivened simple religious patterns as well as sophisticated ones. Historians could engender respect for earlier churches by spreading accurate information about those who had fought the good fight.

Nichols thought church history could do more than enlarge parochial horizons and highlight the inclusive scope of Christian fellowship. Its third function could "actually lead to the knowledge of God, to faith." Since Christian faith stemmed from the dramatic intrusion of a personal God in Christ, the historical record of that communication was crucial to its validity. Mundane records pointed to higher meaning; if properly constructed, the "history of Christ and his Church is a medium of the self-revelation of the living God." Church historians could seek out other examples of God's revelation in Christian experience to show that "the normative element of the tradition is not any given philosophy of religion but a living personal communion undergoing reinterpretation generation by generation." Nichols linked the phenomenal and the noumenal aspects of his vocation in this manner: "In contrast to all humanist religions, or all otherworldly mysticisms, the God who was in Christ, the God of Abraham, Isaac and Jacob, summons a personal response from each individual at his particular post inextricably involved in the irreversible cumulative network of historical relations and traditions."[31] All Christian expressions derived from ways in which people responded to Christ. Those who wanted to know more about divine-human encounters in general needed the specific data of historical examples.

Putting this theory into practice, Nichols hoped to advance theological understanding by studying a number of different religious expressions. In those sustained investigations, he viewed concrete phenomena as elements of a continuous, dynamic process. Each Christian expression was valuable as it sought to understand and respond in its own way to divine impulses. "Every individual believer is both expositor and learner of the message of salvation," Nichols thought, and since none of them was infallible, none should be dismissed as irrelevant. So he looked at specific traditions with great care because each one made its own contribution to discerning "the unbroken life of the evangelical fellowship from the days of the apostles to our own." Of course he did not expect to find a perfect embodiment of evangelical faith. Critical history stemmed from the conviction that mundane forms contained only partial religious truth. But critical history with a high-church perspective could still serve contemporary religious thought by recounting "the unending dialogue of the evangelical community with the God who makes himself known there."[32]

In an early publication on Protestant principles, Nichols demonstrated how investigative procedures and theological insight could work in tandem. His treatment of ecclesiastical records was a model of comprehensive coverage and accurate analysis. Protestant and Catholic institutional forms provided glimpses of "the will of the living God speaking through the mutual ministry of believers." Those previous witnesses were limited by context, however, and they never evinced full knowledge of God. What history really taught was that earlier religious expressions were inadequate and that it was disastrous to copy them indiscriminately in present circumstances. Church history aided theological awareness by showing how previous religious forms had been misused as "substitutes for the personal trust in the living God and the acceptance of his free grace taught by the evangel." In Nichols's estimation, Romanism had erred more than Protestantism by equating human patterns with divine presence. But both types of Christianity were at fault in trying "to set up false securities, to seek salvation in institutional loyalties, moralism, creedal orthodoxies, or Biblical literalism."[33]

Nichols did not neglect social and economic factors in various episodes of Christian history. Cultural determinants were important, but he concentrated more directly on Christian experience because it had "its own energies and purposes." He was interested in appreciating "the religious heart of the movement" more than measuring ways other conditions affected it.[34] History repeatedly demonstrated that the faith which transcended earthen vessels should not be confused with polities, liturgies, and systems of thought. Rather than champion some stale orthodoxy over others, Nichols preferred to regard all ecclesiastical traditions as "part of the Christian society, . . . as if the church were to be found in significant measure within them."[35] This perspective allowed him to respect various churches as bearers of Christian experience while remaining skeptical about any claims regarding perennial value. Churches could fail in their witness and need correction, even from heretics or sectarians. Awareness of the central thread in historical experience made studying all the traditions relevant: "It was the Christian *life*, or the insight of the heart, which gave them stability through the intellectual problems, thus illustrating that faith was more fundamental than doctrine and confessions. It was the living sense of the Presence that was basic, prior to conduct and virtue as well as to teaching."[36] A sense of historical evolution could help scholars break down provincialism and aid the process of ecumenical understanding among Americans and Europeans, Protestants and Catholics alike.

Of particular interest to Nichols was the question of how Protestantism and modern Catholicism had contributed to the rise of liberal democratic culture. He viewed Protestants as rooted in fundamental affirmations that persisted from the apostolic age, through Latin medieval times and Reformation revivals. Protestantism stood in the mainstream of Western Christian history, he held, but modern Romanism was mired in a reactionary creed, government, and worship.[37] Protestantism, especially its English-speaking Puritan forms, had exerted a positive influence on the rise of democratic practices. This contribution came not through doctrine or social ethics but through "folkways of the religious community itself." Protestant communities used their faith and discipline to form larger behavioral standards, and these gradually transferred to the civil state. Social and economic factors played their part, too, over the course of three centuries, but to Nichols, Puritan Protestantism was clearly "the Christian nurse of democracy."[38]

The Protestant values that had affected political practice included free discussion of public issues, voluntary consent in social contracts, and individual responsibility in monitoring their use. Nichols noted that concepts of sin and salvation became highly individualized, while political and economic ethics moved away from the sphere of biblical authority to secular criteria which no church could dominate. Crucial to this whole development was the idea that every ruler, political and ecclesiastical, was liable to sin. So liberal democracy made all citizens responsible for holding themselves and their representative executives to proper standards. Thoughtful, voluntary participants in church and state were bound by the dictates of conscience to curtail officials when they exceeded the bounds of propriety.[39]

Nichols argued that such principles did not operate in countries influenced by Roman Catholic, Eastern Orthodox, or classic Lutheran traditions. The few democratic impulses which emerged under those types of "illiberal ecclesiasticism" were not vital forms of collective participation. Such limited efforts at reform produced nothing better than what he called "egalitarian and illiberal democracy." And their fate in modern times could not stand the strain of extremist political tendencies. Religious resistance to evolutionary democracy eventually caused revolutions and the rejection of all religious influence: "Roman Catholic political absolutism contributed to the development of anticlerical and illiberal democracy, of Marxist Communism, of anarchism." Nichols said that events in modern Russia, Germany, and Catholic Europe were largely due to a fatal combination of extremist politics and autocratic churches.[40]

Several religious groups harbored repressive attitudes about church and political life, but Nichols singled out "new Romanism" for excessive vituperation. In new Romanism, church membership did not mean belonging to an organic community of Christ, he charged; it meant submission to an ecclesiastical sovereign. Catholics did not delegate power to their rulers, nor could they withdraw authorization. Executives in church and state did not solicit opinion or consent from the governed. People had to accept decisions and policies on the strength of external authority without inquiring into their intrinsic worth. "Dissent was treated as disobedience and sin in the penitential discipline of the Church, which inculcated habits of unquestioning submission," he maintained, and liberal activity based on "the democratic principle of discussion was diametrically opposed by the system of the Index and Inquisition." Nichols made several such comments on the basis of his historical overview. He was firmly convinced that Catholic societies were not knit together by mutual public concerns as were Protestant ones. Catholic influence produced "submission to . . . one central and superimposed autocratic rule."[41] According to one of his more graphic depictions,

the Catholic alliance with Fascist counterrevolution in this last generation pointed up again the purely external and opportunistic basis on which Roman Catholicism had come to terms here and there with democracy. Unlike Protestantism, the Roman Church had never fought for democracy when democracy was weak. The Roman Church had accommodated itself to democracy when democracy, supported by other systems of thought, had proved itself a power to be reckoned with. And then it had never given wholehearted support to liberal democracy, but only to those democratic liberties by which the Roman Church itself could profit. . . . And where a monarchist restoration or a military dictatorship became a possibility, the Roman Church generally turned with relief to such types of governments as more familiar to its tradition and better suited to its methods. . . . These traditions, as we have seen, are not merely undemocratic, but antidemocratic.[42]

This judgment was offered as an interpretation of evidence. But such observations make one wonder when language moves from description to diatribe, when a perspective distorts fairness into sour invective.

Another major theme that attracted Nichols's attention was secularization in modern culture. This broad topic allowed him to investigate relationships between Christian faith and society in ways similar to his study of democracy. Here, too, his distinctive viewpoint led to predictably black-and-white conclusions. This schematic overview posited two basic types of secularization that evolved between 1650 and 1950. One version occurred where Catholicism had been the predominant Christian influence. There "the medieval tradition of a priest-controlled society, state, and culture, on a static hierarchical pattern remained normative" for most of the time. As social, economic, and political concerns became more strident, clerics tried to face them down by reasserting the old hierarchical pattern. But medieval prototypes could not solve modern problems, and secular thinkers refused to accept them. Confronting confessional rigidity that insisted on obedience, humanist leaders rejected church influence because its priorities had lost touch with practical circumstances. The resultant secularization denied all Catholic influence because it could not adapt to anything new. Emancipation of this sort was sometimes gradual, sometimes abrupt. But either scenario involved rebellion against the church as an obstacle to progressive change.[43]

Protestant cooperation with modernizing tendencies, on the other hand, involved neither confessional ineptitude nor apostasy. In fact, Nichols held, Protestant countries were where leaders used religious impulses to deal creatively with secular issues. Laypersons and clergy in those places applied Christian principles indirectly to nurture political democracy and humanitarianism, scientific technology and capitalism. The result was a type of secularization in the sense that few thinkers accepted a biblical theocracy as their model any longer. But this sort of modern culture still operated on moral laws in society that were compatible with divine revelation. It embodied "a new synthesis of faith and culture not unworthy of comparison with the thirteenth century."[44]

Despite Protestantism's partial success, Nichols ended his study on a diffident note. He acknowledged that much of contemporary life eluded Christian guidance, pursuing what he called new tribal or utopian gods. There was, he noted, a widening "chasm between the tone of the industrial West and anything that might be called Christian." As a historian he did not prescribe how churches should adjust to the situation. Nevertheless, he offered a few speculations. Churches in secularized conditions might adopt a pre-Constantinian attitude, concentrate on their inner resources, and abandon any hope of transforming society. Or they might continue to search for ways to humanize the militarized, technological culture of their day in order to render it more responsive to Jesus Christ. Both options had historical precedent, though it was impossible to guess which direction the future might take. Nichols was encouraged to think, however, that later historians would still find church life relevant as they looked for intelligible patterns in cumulative experience.[45]

Leonard J. Trinterud

The third church historian who made concepts of the Church central to scholarly practice was Leonard J. Trinterud, professor at

McCormick Theological Seminary and later at San Francisco Theological Seminary. Together with Richardson and Nichols, he valued churches because they afforded glimpses of divine activity. But Trinterud recognized more clearly than the others that historical information was an inadequate means of exhibiting transcendental reality. After careful analysis he found it impossible to use tangible historical evidence and sustain a theological appreciation of religious institutions. His candid admission that a gap existed between worldly records and otherworldly ideals made Trinterud unique in this school of thought. His reflections on such difficulties pushed high-church historiography to its logical terminus, and that helps explain why the school had such a slight impact on the profession at large.

Trinterud specialized in American church history, and he felt it necessary to defend the legitimacy of his choice. The problem as he saw it was that historical study had been dominated for too long by European subjects and prototypes. Rich diversities found in Asia and the Americas had strained old categories, and a European understanding of history could not elucidate the new information. Histories of new phenomena could not be "patched on" to earlier models, nor could new experiences be interpreted according to the old patterns. As churches in America and other former missionary fields altered norms and structures, many worried about continuity with the old ways. They did not see how histories of fresh institutions could be relevant unless they conformed to traditions which Europeans considered important. Trinterud thought the way to comprehend all these variegations was to concentrate on "how much historical continuity . . . these younger churches have with these older churches if they are to be a part of the one, true, holy, catholic Church."[46]

Obviously, a proper beginning point helped achieve the desired result. Defining the discipline of American church history would be a simple matter after finding where the church existed in this country. Trinterud valued "the ecumenical movement . . . and the current theological debates" as aids to his task because those twin emphases were "bringing to the fore new and deeper understandings of the nature of the Body of Christ." He found this orientation helpful, and "as the conception of what the Church is becomes deepened, Church history will become more profound." From this theological perspective, Trinterud dismissed other historical approaches, including that of William W. Sweet, because none of them made "a frank attempt at a 'Church' history." Those interpretations which emphasized the functional importance of churches had in effect redefined the field to study "the sociological phenomenon of religion in American culture," not the Church itself. From a confessional point of view, that was clearly not the way to demonstrate the centrality of churches in human experience. The body of Christ was a living reality that historians should observe on its own terms, and "unless American Church history can come to grips with the problem of what it means to confess the Christian faith in a God who reveals himself mediately in history, it can never come into its own."[47]

In defending the legitimacy of American Christianity, Trinterud called for restructuring basic categories in all church history. Each historian, he pointed out, wrote about religious communities in specific contexts, and those studies captured expressions of a shared experience. That experience centered on redemption, and it undergirded all types of Christianity, though none of them embodied it fully. No church provided an adequate standard for understanding the others. Trinterud wrote, "From its very beginnings the Church has struggled with the problem of the tension between historical continuity in God's redeeming work, and the fact that it is God who is doing this redeeming work in history." Heightened sensitivity to providential action made the historian aware of what church life could disclose. "The present, on-going work of the Holy Spirit determines how man shall understand God's past work," Trinterud maintained. The difficulty was to mix worldly and otherworldly factors in proper proportion. "A very great part of the 'offence of the Gospel' is the freedom with which God moves man, even the people of God—his Church—out of the controlling center of the redemptive history in order that his life may not be hindered by the Church's claim . . . to dispense God's redeeming grace as it sees best."[48]

Trinterud looked to history for more than antiquarian lore. He expected it to divulge various types of redemptive experiences, all of which came through Jesus Christ. And for that reason students of "all the various corners and crannies of church history need to renew their awareness of the Church Catholic." Concentrating on particular churches could highlight the Church at work in local settings. So specializing in American church history was as informative as any other study bounded by time and culture. Choosing it as a topic pointed to the need for expanding procedural techniques that could investigate new expressions. The challenge to all studies in church history was to show how all variations pertained to the redeeming work of God through Christ. Trinterud knew that American religious history had to begin with criteria derived from local circumstances. The historian "can and he ought to check these criteria against those of his colleagues in other American fields, and against those of his colleagues in other parts of the Church Catholic." Beyond that, the right kind of church historian would make empirical research serve a theological purpose, remembering that "his function is to accept the responsibility of writing from within the American scene in order that there may arise from all parts of the Church Catholic a truly catholic history of the Church."[49]

Redemption was a noble theme, but how could mundane history shed light on it? After assessing the possibilities of empirical method, Trinterud admitted that there was considerable tension between assumptions prompted by faith and observations sustained by hard evidence. He respected practical investigative procedures too much to inflate limited findings beyond their capacity. All Christian groups referred to some type of redemption, but since historians were bound by earthly records instead of divine revelation, they could not say when or if such references were genuine. Using empirical methods to support religious insight, historians found that the only thing they could do was describe the various Christian groups who claimed to have experienced God's presence. A scholar could ask religious questions of the surviving record, but Trinterud insisted that one could not discriminate among the claims found there. One had to include "the whole group of those who have claimed to be redeemed by God through Christ" because the proper task was to function "as a historian, . . . not as a Prophet or an Apostle." Historians could describe what salvation had meant to different people in the past. They could not verify instances of divine action or presume to discriminate among diverse assertions. "However odd a group or denomination may be," he held, "the church historian must deal seriously with this people's faith that God through Jesus Christ did redeem them."[50] History lacked the capacity to determine what God did. The deficiencies of partial evidence and modern ways of understanding it kept historians from thinking that their work was another form of theological affirmation, Trinterud asserted.

Investigators might search for the redemptive experience, but all they could find was a variety of human references to it. They might try to identify the Church triumphant through the ages, but Trinterud found that historians were actually bound by institutional definitions. Transcendental ideals and higher meaning could inspire historical inquiry, but when students began looking into religious activity, they found organizations with creeds, governments, and liturgies. Historians could neither affirm nor deny the Church in such phenomena: "In varying degrees we admit that the Church as such is something more than and other than its institutional expression. But what is it?" This query laid bare the irreconcilable difference between theory and practice in the high-church scheme of things. Trinterud realized that historical method could not satisfy theological ends. He did not want to forsake the transcendent element in his calling, yet he would not prostitute the integrity of historical method. Incompatibility led to impasse, and Trinterud characterized it poignantly:

Wherever there is redemption through Christ in history, there is the Church his Body. . . . To be the Church, therefore, is always a confession of faith and not a matter of historical investigation and proof. How then can you write the history of the work of God, unless you are a Prophet or an Apostle? To be sure, some histories are written for groups who regard themselves alone as the objects of this redeeming work of God. Yet, church history as a discipline cannot so operate. The question remains, even so, how can you write the history of what God is doing? The answer, of course, is that you cannot.[51]

The narrow strictures of historical epistemology forced church historians to accept inclusive and nonjudgmental attitudes toward their subject matter. And the limitations of empirical observation prevented identifying the Church with people truly redeemed by God.

Historians could search for the Church only in settings where cultural influences had produced schisms, sects, and denominations. They had no way of determining which groups genuinely belonged to the Body of Christ and which did not. Trinterud knew that his professional apparatus could not bridge the gap between tangible materials and insights based on faith. Transcendental definitions of the Church stimulated historical research, but such ultimate conceptions could not be confirmed in the sphere where investigations took place. It was impossible to write American *church* history because mundane observations about religions in this country prevented it. So, Trinterud concluded, historians had to admit that "there is no 'church' in America of which a church history can be written." And instead of thinking this view was atypical, he ventured that "it seems indeed to be the destiny which awaits the whole of the Church Catholic in the future."[52]

Trinterud originally thought church history could utilize theological insights in the study of tangible materials. But he discovered that historians could not blend theological categories with the way they studied mundane evidence. The only viable alternative was what he called either "history of religion" or "history of Christianity." This type of study produced modest results because it was tied to institutional definitions and mundane phenomena. Trinterud wished his work could have been a history of the Church, but he admitted that it was only history of religion:

Here, then, is laid bare my bad conscience. I assume that I ought to present *church* history, but I end up with only the history of Christianity. What I do differs only by its lack of ability from the work of those in other historical disciplines who, in dealing with various aspects of the Christian Church in history, do so frankly disavowing my assumption about the Church. And from their works I have learned no small part of whatever I may know about the history of the Christian Church. What, then, shall I do?[53]

In theory Trinterud professed to high ideals; in practice he acknowledged that his studies were part of secular history. Richardson and Nichols turned this dilemma into a virtue, hoping that by process of elimination, their empirical analysis could underscore religious convictions about the Church. For Trinterud, such pretenses seemed untenable, and yet he had a bad conscience about abandoning the possibility of serving higher ends with his work.

One facet of the historiographical process offered his conscience some relief. Historians researched and wrote with assumptions that controlled their efforts, but in the same manner, readers also brought assumptions to bear when they assimilated historical information. However, historians need not despair of failing entirely to enhance theology because "some people will read *church* history where others see only the history of the Christian religion," Trinterud wrote. Empirical observation and transcendental conceptions could coexist, unrelated as far as procedure was concerned, yet potentially fruitful for readers who absorbed information into their own frame of reference. Confessional insight could transfigure concrete details in the consumption, not the production, of historical knowledge. It was even possible for a historian to "write with no real assumption that the Church is the redeeming work of God, and yet to a reader with different insights this historian's document may become *church* history." As a theological educator who took historical procedures seriously, Trinterud reached an impasse between theory and practice. He admitted to a professional dilemma and hoped others could resolve it where he could not. In the end he trusted that "the church historian may write even worse than he thinks, and the reader may read far better than he knows."[54]

Trinterud studied documentary materials with methods unaffected by theology. He based his interpretations largely on cultural conditions and human factors, commenting on the religious significance of his topic almost as an afterthought.[55] English Puritanism was his favorite subject, and he did most of his work within that complicated area, eventually broadening his view to include American Presbyterianism as well. His treatment of materials in this specialization is consistent with his theoretical reflections. He recognized, for instance, that one could approach Puritanism with "the belief that all definitive elements in the world were the acts of God." But he did not follow such an orientation and emphasized instead the social and political conditions that affected Puritan religion.[56] Similarly, his survey of American Presbyterians emphasized external developments from their roots in New England and Ulster to their first General Assembly after the Revolution. That meticulous work concentrated on controversies over creeds and revivals, schism and reunion, and attitudes about political and religious freedom. Only at the very end, on two pages entitled "Retrospect," did he suggest any larger significance which a reader might discern from that volume.[57] So Trinterud remained true to his perspective. He never wavered in appreciating the Church for its own sake, but he rarely used the tools of historical investigation to extol it.

Richardson, Nichols, and Trinterud form a distinctive school of thought, and it is clear that their interests produced a carefully articulated ideology. All three scholars agreed on the ultimate transcendent quality of their subject. Each one also used rigorous standards for accuracy when scrutinizing mundane evidence. None of them wrote triumphalist history or tried to exhibit a providential plan in events. They analyzed records, as Nichols characterized it, "in objective, secular fashion" in order to stimulate religious creativity with factual information. They did not try, as Trinterud pointedly said, to write as prophets or apostles. Taking their writings as a whole, it is clear that their distinctive conceptions did not create new methods or use familiar ones in ways different from other colleagues. Their goal of combining religious ideas and strict empirical standards was an option shared by few others, and it was ineffective in the profession at large.

In sum, the theory and practice of high-church history had limited utility. Faith tried to bridge the gap between ideal conception and historical research, but it did not affect method or uncover a new interpretive vein. Modern historians knew that all their efforts were relative to some frame of reference. When high-church references coincided with interest in ecumenism and neo-orthodoxy, its orientation seemed appropriate and contributive. As a type of scholarship dedicated to furthering a religious agenda, it flourished while that agenda commanded a great deal of attention. But since it was subservient to other interests and had no strong rationale of its own, it declined when cultural expectations regarding theology and church union gave way to other concerns. Meanwhile, other church historians had been using different models to make their work intelligible, and we now turn to those emphases which received greater professional attention.

ॐ4
Searches for Consensus and a Common Past

By the 1940s most historians had abandoned absolutes in procedure and interpretation. They accepted a certain amount of subjectivity as inevitable, but few went so far as saying that one viewpoint was as good as another. As a rule, students were reluctant to disengage completely from the goals and attitudes inherited from scientific history. Most scholars tried to mesh their subjective insights with accepted cultural assumptions and still respect the integrity of concrete data. They were no longer certain about recovering all of past reality, but careful attention to method could still salvage enough of what remained "to offer a decently objective and comprehensive historical picture," according to one historian. Facts existed in sufficient quantity for historians to continue ascertaining selected evidence and "get at the truth of things through a systematic accretion of knowledge."[1]

One of the areas where historians felt reasonably comfortable in choosing worthwhile topics had to do with traditional values that had developed within their culture. Instead of emphasizing change as the key to progress, scholars at midcentury doubted whether further innovation would always be good for society. A more cautious, less optimistic mood affected many thinkers after World War II, and rather than looking forward to a better future, they sought reassurance in lessons about historical continuity. Students of American life or the more extensive patterns of western Europe began to search for uniformities in society, stability in institutions, and persistence in values across the generations.[2] This concern for durable traits marked a new quest for consensus. It resembled some nineteenth-century attempts to highlight distinctive qualities in Western civilization, but the modern search for consensus was driven by a greater sense of urgency.

Many historians regarded fascism and communism as direct antitheses to Western cultural values. Strident, irreconcilable ideologies led them to search for liberal democratic principles embedded in the past and tested by time. Through wars and police-state pogroms, humanity was slaughtered on an unprecedented scale during the first half of the twentieth century. The reality of death camps and wartime atrocities demonstrated the fragility of concepts like human dignity and individual freedom. The cold war and the threat of nuclear annihilation convinced many historians to emphasize the best of their cultural heritage as an antidote to these contemporary barbarisms.[3] Scholars looked for principles that undergirded previous social development, ones that had survived to counterbalance the radical threats of modern life. In a context where basic ideals were being challenged, they responded by searching again for ideals that had already proved their worth. Consensus on such values and principles might rescue contemporary culture from disintegration.

While much of consensus history evinced a conservative attitude, it helped liberate students from misgivings about proper procedure. One analyst noticed that twenty years had made quite a difference: "The relativism of the Thirties, imprisoning the historian in his contemporary world, reflected a sense of the inferiority of history as a science. The relativity of the Fifties, emphasizing the possible opportunities of the historian's observational position, took the invidious sting out of the comparison."[4] One very important expression of this historiographical emphasis was the American Studies movement and its fascination with national character. In a context where scholars probed for what made western Europe distinctive from Soviet policy and Marxist ideology, it was an easy step to ask what separated America from all of Europe. National traits and differences attracted a great deal of attention in the 1950s. But whether students concentrated on the United States or some other cultural entity, consensus attitudes affirmed fundamental values that had survived past challenges to meet present ones. By emphasizing strong lines of continuity, this kind of history tried to illuminate previous developments as a means of enhancing contemporary social vitality.

CONSENSUS ON PEACE AND TOLERATION

Several students of Christian history fit within this general search for culturally beneficial values. One of the most prolific was Roland H. Bainton whose career at Yale University spanned four decades from 1920 to 1962. Bainton made a name for himself chiefly with sprightly writing on a wide range of topics. He produced gripping narratives and sharp character sketches with a portraitist's eye for color and detail. Much of his work centered on the sixteenth and seventeenth centuries, but his inclusive interests swept from early Christianity to modern times. In the best sense of the term, Bainton was a popularizer, making accurate historical information palatable through vigorous prose. His study of different subjects coalesced into a search for fundamental principles in past experience. Bainton was a consensus historian, aware of living at a time when traditional values were under siege. Knowing that "the last quarter of a century has seen retrogression," he listed major threats to social stability: "Fascism, first in Italy and then in Germany, was the earliest setback, and then the emergence of Communism has exhibited the major characteristics of a militant religion."[5] So he spent his long career trying to show how churches had embodied, and could still offer, ways of impeding further cultural decline.

Taking all of Christendom as his province, Bainton was confident that certain perennial values would have a beneficial effect on modern problems. He thought that especially the earliest Christian era and sixteenth-century Reformation experience could teach valuable lessons, or put more simply, "Survivals and advances through [those] crises suggest hope." Bainton did not underestimate the ideological threats of his day. He noted how

our rifts are deeper and our perils more ominous. Now we have Fascism and Communism, which drop God and yet carry over from the religious tradition a fervant [sic] dynamism, intolerance, and apocalypticism, with readiness to liquidate even millions of individuals in the present in order to realize a more equitable and enriching culture in the future. The West is basically conservative, but at the same time fluctuating, confused, bewildered. . . . The ancient values are questioned, scrutinized, rejected. With reason do we ask "What's next?"[6]

Bainton was convinced there could be no truce with secular paganism; the only hope for Western civilization lay in "the classical-Christian tradition of the unity of mankind." He proceeded to describe major aspects of that tradition through biographies, surveys, and thematic studies. The consensus he found in religious experience had proved strong over time. And he suggested that churches were especially qualified to alleviate modern ills because "no institution in these crumbling days has exhibited such constancy in resistance to tyranny, no institution has preserved its own international structure and mentality so faithfully, as has the Christian church."[7]

Three basic themes recur in Bainton's writings, each of them underscoring a particular type of freedom. The first concerned pacifism, freedom from the violence and cruelty of war. As a lifelong conscientious objector, Bainton researched many attitudes toward armed conflict, and he stressed nonparticipation as the best religious response to such madness. His second perennial ideal gave priority to open discussion, freedom to seek the truth and to criticize other positions while doing so. Attempts to clarify ideas were signs of healthy minds, and Bainton valued diversified debate over stultifying uniformity. The third principle was toleration or freedom of religious association. He was convinced that oppression in the name of orthodoxy had always been culturally harmful. Religious liberty contributed more to social harmony because it permitted different institutions to exchange ideas about worship and moral behavior in friendly coexistence.

Before he expounded Christian attitudes toward war, Bainton surveyed preceding ideas. He found that pre-Christian responses included pacifism (nonparticipation), just war (reluctant participation), and crusade (hearty participation). All three attitudes eventually appeared during some epoch of church history. But in one of his most notorious interpretive claims, Bainton held that all Christians in early times had been uniformly pacifist. They might have compromised with worldly attitudes regarding slavery and private property, but the ancient churches repudiated war, he insisted, as inimical to their true witness. Christians bore arms only after Constantine became emperor, justifying limited war as a defense of the faith and protection for the Christian state. "The just war of pagan origins," Bainton quipped, "was baptized by sprinkling." In later times he noted that the Christian Empire modified pacifism even further by fighting for just causes. And then when Christianity encountered barbarians and unbelievers, its original paci-

fism eroded to the vanishing point. The resulting crusades un-
leashed destructive violence beyond all constraint. When one
fought infidels, so the rationalization went, one need not honor the
constraints of just war theory. Bainton condemned this extreme,
finding not even a "residue of the Augustinian mournfulness in
combat. The mood was strangely compounded of barbarian lust for
combat and Christian zeal for the faith."[8]

Church history contained three positions on war, but Bainton
did not view them as equally valid. He asserted that the earliest one
constituted the normative standard. Later developments only demonstrated a sad decline from original purity; the primitive pattern
offered the best consensus for Christian thought. With chronology
as his dominant principle, Bainton argued that, since the first
church leaders had repudiated taking up arms, "then pacifism is
the Christian position." He expounded on Christian preaching
about love, a yielding spirit, and an aversion to killing, all based on
what he termed "the pacifism of the New Testament." There were
various emphases within such principles, but Bainton held that the
only approach to war contained in the gospels was nonviolence.
Pacifism could manifest itself in counsels of submission, or it could
stimulate peacemaking efforts when conflicts broke out. In Bainton's estimation of historical experience, it was clear that *the* Christian position on armed struggle forbade participation. Any positive sanction of war, reluctant or otherwise, repudiated the pristine
standard first held in the churches.[9]

After boxing the compass on attitudes about war and locating
the Christian position as true north, Bainton used it to plot a chart
for modern troubles. Pacifism was the original and only genuine
Christian response to violence; later compromises were mistakes.
Because modern technology could obliterate both the just and the
unjust, a return to the earliest Christian tradition seemed the only
sane choice. Reasoning on the basis of that presumed consensus,
Bainton pointed out why militant attitudes were unacceptable.
"The crusade suffers," he observed, "from the assurance, not to say
the arrogance, of all elitism." Using a host of medieval and recent
examples, he pointed out how crusades entailed "war of a theo-
cratically minded community which seeks to impose the pattern of
the Church upon the world. The saints are to rule. They are the
elite." But who could determine who the elite really are? Given rival
claims, carnage could not be avoided: "The enemy being beyond

the pale, the code of humanity collapses." At midcentury two military giants, the U.S. and the U.S.S.R., faced each other, "each possessed of the power to paralyze the other if not to liquidate the globe." Their crusading mentalities threatened coexistence and precluded magnanimity after defeat. Remembering perhaps Nuremburg or Tokyo, Bainton held that crusades always engendered self-righteousness where foes were tried for war crimes "by the victors under the fictitious trappings of impartial justice."[10]

If the crusading spirit produced exclusivist arrogance and heedless destruction, the just war theory was just as impracticable in present circumstances. Just wars needed proof that one side was in the right, and they had to limit violence to combatants only. But Bainton charged that modern warfare could not meet either criterion. It was impossible to decide which nation was an aggressor and which was justified in repelling attacks. There was never enough information to judge which side acted from just causes, and all pretensions to innocence were hollow. The capabilities of modern weapons presented further difficulties for a limited war: "The more war has improved at the point of technology, the more it has deteriorated at the point of moral discrimination. The code of the just war calls for the sparing of noncombatants. Today not even children are immune. . . . War obliterates all such distinctions. Modern war certainly cannot be squared with the code of the just war."[11]

So Bainton conflated the two arguments that supported warfare, and he condemned them both. There was little difference in his estimation between crusading elites and those who defended themselves from unjust attacks. Historical experience and the modern stalemate over superweapons made the first Christian attitude still the truest and most practicable solution.

The logic of Bainton's position placed his moral exhortation, not his historical accuracy, on solid footing. "If the crusade and the just war are rejected as Christian positions," he argued, "pacifism alone remains." Christian pacifism might achieve some practical good in world affairs, but it was especially notable for promoting spiritual health among coreligionists. Bainton recommended pacifism as a consensual value in Christian tradition because it afforded the best response to violent passions. And in many instances, this historic position had proved both personally edifying and socially productive. Critics called Bainton's position irresponsible and cowardly. He admitted that it did not always achieve peace or shield loved ones from suffering. But for the committed pacifist, "if he dissociates himself from the use of war to advance a cause however noble he is not for that reason irresponsible, and he may not be irrelevant."[12]

Modern times threatened the second freedom—experimentation with ideas and social programs—by demanding too much conformity. Bainton held that conflicting ideas and divergent practices were natural in human experience; efforts to suppress them were unwise. He thought it more beneficial to respect each person's thoughts and uphold the integrity of private convictions, the better to let everyone pursue truth as they perceived it. Like Erasmus whom he admired, Bainton wished to avoid acrimonious contention, even while admitting that thinking often benefited from the clash of divergent opinions. So he adopted the role of a "battered liberal," one who maintained his own convictions while trying to foster an atmosphere that encouraged debate.[13] As contemporary ideologies sought to control minds through uncritical assent, Bainton doubted that any set of answers was definitive. He considered it more important to preserve a setting where people could formulate their own affirmations, not force them on everyone else. In his view history vindicated an attitude that accepted differences and "assumes a measure of variety in human behavior, honors integrity, respects the dignity of man, and seeks to exemplify the compassion of God."[14]

To be sure, church history was full of examples to the contrary. Dominant ecclesiastical parties had persecuted dissenters for centuries in the name of dogma and behavioral uniformity. Some argued that Christian theology demanded an enforced orthodoxy; others held that suppressing differences among people violated biblical principles. Bainton took the view that any attempt to control the search for truth defeated gospel teachings. No matter how repression was justified, "any theology which justifies the sacrifice of Isaac, the burning of Servetus, or the incineration of a hundred million persons in an act of massive retaliation has gone wrong somewhere along the line."[15] Contemporary uncertainties made it imperative to identify a consensus in historical experience that fostered an open-ended search for truth as different people perceived it.

Bainton thought the modern tradition of intellectual freedom had begun with medieval mysticism and Renaissance humanism.

Mysticism nurtured the validity of private experience and resultant ideas. Renaissance humanists espoused free inquiry into all topics. Open inquiry rested on the fundamental notion that one could arrive at truth through investigation, criticism, and revision. This frame of mind never held ideas sacrosanct enough to be placed above reexamination. Using this approach initially with documents, scholars eventually applied their perspective to beliefs, and there Bainton found the tradition finally operating as he wanted it. Minds were untrammeled when

the creedal formulations of the Church come to be regarded as tentative, and the historic statements of faith as only adumbrations of ultimate truth and as subject therefore to modification when fresh light should break from God's word. This whole attitude, which defines the faith less as a deposit than as a quest, makes for tolerance at least toward all the varieties of Christianity. . . .[16]

During the Reformation, antagonists argued bitterly over doctrine, and Bainton admitted that Renaissance liberty had yielded to dogmatism. But after the sixteenth century, a more open-minded perspective began to prevail because Christians "had come to esteem honest error as a stage toward truth, and even to conceive of themselves as possibly mistaken."[17]

This sketch is at best a superficial interpretation of complex intellectual currents. It is important to notice Bainton's historiographical orientation to see how he could write history the way he did. While chronicling the tradition he favored, he paid little attention to the social circumstances that affected it positively or negatively. Bainton treated ideas as forces that transcended cultural contexts, capable of affecting practical situations but not shaped in turn by their environment. His primary interest lay not in accounting for the rise of ideas by referring to their context. Rather, he was driven to find historical precedent for principles that could benefit contemporary believers and reinvigorate cultural values.

Bainton favored movement toward truth rather than possession of it, and in an aside, he commented on what this implied for ecumenism. Whenever addressing the subject of institutional concord, he was more concerned about tolerating differences than reconciling them in some comprehensive union. He favored a spirit of unity, but Bainton was ambivalent about structural mergers because people would always differ over particulars. His support for ecumenism was limited to ideas: "Latitude for diversity in the life of the Christian community is to be safeguarded, but no one polity will automatically insure or preclude it." He wanted to preserve freedom of expression for all varieties of Christian life and experience. Ecumenical attitudes were good when they broadened minds, and as long as the movement supported an irenic search for truth, he favored it. "Let us indeed preserve the ecumenical tradition, but not the code of Justinian with its death penalty for denial of the Trinity."[18]

Freedom among religions depended on similar freedom in the state. If modern civilization was to succeed in preserving a consensus of values, people would have to reject all models where states invoked divine law. Bainton observed that freedom suffered when people ruled as if their policies directly affected the majesty of God, the salvation of souls, or the stability of Christendom. Against that insidious notion, he argued that "the noblest achievement of the Western world has been the conduct of controversy without acrimony, of strife without bitterness, of criticism without loss of respect." Confidence in the free exchange of ideas could help revitalize European and American culture. Bainton did not fear contradictory propositions. He worried instead that an ideological deadlock would create a climate of opinion that stifled diverse ideas. The antidote to mind control was a liberal tradition that valued free expression for its own sake: "Balance and again balance is what we need." Bainton the historian doubled as cultural libertarian, observing that "one word may be extricated from the long travail of liberty in the past and made a watchword for the present, and that word is 'reasonableness.'"[19]

If friendly discussion could not resolve arguments, Bainton prescribed his third and finest historical principle: toleration of religious differences. Religious liberty was a cornerstone of healthy social interaction, and Bainton spent most of his scholarly career surveying the foundations of that ideal. He specialized in Reformation personalities such as Sebastian Castellio, David Joris, Bernardino Ochino, and Michael Servetus. These particulars gave him the basis for broader observations, and one observation isolated the elements necessary for persecution. This formula has now reached the status of a maxim, useful as an interpretive guideline and a gauge for anticipating further change. "The prerequisites," he said, "for persecution are three: (1) The persecutor must believe that he is right; (2) that the point in question is important; (3) that coercion will be effective."[20] Bainton spent a great deal of time explicating specific arguments in support of religious freedom, but he was more interested in tracing the decline of oppression. He hoped his special studies would bolster liberal policies that could keep bigotry at bay in modern life.

Chronicles of violence for religion's sake abound, but Bainton related only enough of them to depict their unrelieved cruelty. He was more concerned to use persecution as a foil and show that it was not only ineffective, but a tactic that caused people to seek freedom instead. When officials used force to vindicate God's honor, Bainton reported the replies of those who said God could maintain His dignity without having people burned. When authorities persecuted dissenters as a means of saving souls, he pointed to those who answered that salvation depended wholly on God and that constraint was futile. The consensus drawn from six-teenth-century experience and bequeathed to modern times was that human violence did not glorify God, nor could it preempt divine initiative in spiritual experience. God's transcendence and the primacy of individual responsibility combined to defy programs that presumed to dictate uniform responses to ultimate questions.

Religious liberty also benefited from new ideas about churches and society. Ecclesiastical authoritarianism had been plausible when people regarded one church as the ark of salvation and its sacraments as the only means of grace. But when congregations began to view themselves as collections of sinners saved by free grace, their separate organizations could no longer impose universal demands. Bainton noted that this more sectarian conception emphasized morality more than sacramentalism. This stress on personal purity made churches give up all designs for controlling the whole population. A similar change occurred regarding the idea of a united Christendom. Medieval patterns had envisioned a singled society, knit together by a common faith. In such a society, religious dissent would not be permissible because it threatened social stability. Sixteenth-century Protestants tried to reinforce those patterns as strenuously as their Catholic counterparts. But social fragmentation worked against the unitive concept, and by the early 1600s, pluralists abandoned the ideal of Christendom with a unified church-state. Modern societies came to see diversity as wholesome to all facets of life. They appreciated the value of competition in political, economic, and religious spheres as contributive to the freedoms undergirding their culture.[21]

Some defenders of Western civilization held that democracy was essential to religious liberty. Bainton did not agree that only one form of political organization could be tolerant. He pointed out that in Cromwell's day, a dictatorship had granted tolerance, and enlightened despots such as Frederick the Great had removed religious restrictions. It was possible for religious liberty to exist in different governments, but Bainton still thought a democratic society was where religion flourished best and without interference. He considered democracy a way of life, not a form of government, a perspective based on ideals that went beyond constitutions. One of those ideals took government to be an instrument of justice, upholding the dignity and rights of citizens. A second required respect for the convictions of others despite disagreement with them. One of the most important corollaries of this attitude was that "majorities should not ride roughshod over minorities." Toleration succeeded only when people embodied "breadth of spirit and a readiness to treat many matters as nonessential and therefore open to variety."[22] The third principle insisted on morality in public affairs because integrity was essential to sound statecraft. These beliefs, Bainton suggested, could sustain American citizens in times of ideological conflict. Even if their ideals were only imperfectly realized, the traditions of democratic life and religious liberty had a valid core that survived historical variation.

This belief synopsis telescopes all of Bainton's work on persecution and religious freedom. He was not interested in comprehensive or exhaustive analyses of factors in historical development. For him it was more important to pinpoint emergent results and recommend their application to contemporary crises. At times the student in Bainton gave way to the pastor and homilist. At times he could only lament events rather than explain them. He regretted, for instance, that Martin Luther had agreed to persecute Anabaptists on the grounds of sedition. He thought the early reformer's fulmination against Jews was such a "vulgar blast," that he could wish "Luther had died before ever this tract was written."[23] Studying Calvin led Bainton to similar lessons for current application. "The story of Calvin and Servetus should," he warned, "demonstrate for us that our slogans of liberty need continually to be thought through afresh." Stressing the importance of human life then and now, he wondered how "we are today horrified that Geneva should have burned a man for the glory of God, yet we incinerate whole cities for the saving of democracy."[24] Such moral object lessons could be quoted ad infinitum. One more will have to suffice, and it lays bare the essential Bainton: someone who ranged over the field of church history for principles that might strengthen religious affirmations in his own time. Bainton wrote, "Deeper than all the arguments bandied back and forth by a goodly company of advocates was a deeply rooted conviction of the incompatibility between the cross and the stake. Suffering is the lot and the mark of the Christian. He must be as the sheep and not as the wolf. If he is to follow the Master he must ascend Calvary and not the judgment hall of Pilate or of Herod."[25]

CONSENSUS FROM MAINSTREAM PROTESTANTISM

Winthrop S. Hudson was another scholar who emphasized the importance of traditional principles in modern times. His teaching and writing flourished from 1947 to 1980 principally at Colgate Rochester Divinity School, and, happily, his researches have continued after retirement. When consensus history was in vogue, Hudson's work resonated within that idiom remarkably well. But he never ceased growing, and several of his later publications such as the compact *American Protestantism* and the comprehensive *Religion in America* defy easy categorization. Still, his early work was part of the immediate post–World War II era, and it clearly used a selective reconstruction of the past in attempts to meet contemporary needs. Readers seemed to need reminding that their culture had distinctive Christian roots, and Hudson devoted much of his scholarly career to that purpose. Like Bainton, he grounded much of his perspective in the Reformation period, English Puritanism in this case. He also emphasized freedom and toleration as important ideals, giving those culturally beneficial traits a notably religious origin and significance.

Signs of the times at midcentury convinced Hudson that "the basic problem confronting mankind today is a spiritual problem." From his perspective this meant especially that "a day of reckoning has come for the churches." The situation was acute because Americans seemed to have sold their birthright and forgotten their heritage. Citizens had become "increasingly illiterate religiously," he thought, having reached the point where they were "largely ignorant of theology and have little or no awareness of belonging to any historic religious tradition." Hudson determined to rectify this state of affairs with sound history. By subjecting the past to "a frank re-examination and reappraisal," he hoped to bring durable values to public attention again. He thought historical awareness could galvanize the American people, particularly its Protestant majority, and reinvigorate their affirmation of basic truths that were rooted in collective precedent.[26]

Present-day culture had apparently lost its sense of direction. Hudson knew that beginning a new search for consensus would involve "certain uncomfortable conclusions" about the aimlessness of modern life, but he thought such a return to basics would prove beneficial. Viewing the past as a heritage capable of rectifying current ills, he maintained that "the 'lessons of the past' must be taken into account in the formulation of any positive program which will give real hope of bringing about a renewal of powerful, ethical, and spiritual religion in our time." These lessons could not ignore the religious roots of social freedom that had been transplanted from England to American soil. History could inform citizens about how national character had developed around "a robust faith in a living God (judging, correcting, disciplining, guiding, and directing the American people)" as one of its central features. It could also show how traditions had "eroded and [were] reduced to the pale affirmations" found in twentieth-century expressions. Suitable lessons of the past could both warn and stimulate, judge by contrast and encourage through example.[27]

Hudson became interested in relationships between religion, political thought, and social freedom while still a graduate student. His doctoral dissertation focused on John Ponet, a sixteenth-century churchman who advocated limited monarchy through constitutional principles sensitive to popular welfare.[28] Later Hudson surveyed the general decline of British authoritarianism and the rise of representative government, charting this process alongside a corresponding growth of Protestant beliefs. As social freedoms developed through the time of Oliver Cromwell, Puritan influences were increasingly influential in securing greater liberty.

Puritan doctrines about God's sovereignty and human sin led to convictions that visible churches should be voluntary and independent. Politically, this required the state to be neutral, allowing churches to pursue visions of the holy commonwealth on their own. Hudson thought left-wing Puritans had been notably effective because they would not rely on civil authority to reform society. They relied instead on "the power of a godly public opinion created by the preaching of the Word. Persuasion rather than coercion was the means upon which they depended to attain their end." This basic attitude informed "the heritage of the Cromwellian period," and as a "legacy to the future," it posited four great ideals: liberty of opinion in religious affairs, voluntary formation of churches, tolerance of different organizations, and separation of church and state.[29]

When colonists brought these ideals to the New World, voluntary religious affiliation became "the chief glory of the American Republic." Hudson described this achievement at length, stressing the view that "a carefully defined equilibrium of church and state has been the great tradition of American religious and political life." Free religious association without state interference was something the churches claimed for themselves. Hudson did not agree that dominant churches had independence forced on them from outside, nor did minority churches seek it on purely expedient grounds. Ecclesiastical leaders wanted liberty for solid, orthodox religious reasons. Hudson's analysis occupied a long historical perspective designed to observe ideas permeate culture. In that sequence he noted how "the subsequent development of the free church system was made necessary by convictions which were implicit in the thought of Puritanism from the beginning. The complete voluntarism of the Cromwellian era was a foretaste of what could be expected when the strength of the Puritan movement was transplanted to American soil."[30]

American freedom grew from concerns about a Christian society which Puritans developed during the time of the Commonwealth. Later generations of reformers, especially left-wing groups who did not compromise their ideology, persisted in calling for a broadly representative frame of government. As church architects, they advocated something other than simple democracy, recognizing that any majority could become tyrannical. Hudson argued that Puritans gave highest priority to allowing individuals to preach the Word as they understood it. This led evangelicals to champion a spectrum of human rights including the freedoms of speech, assembly, and the press, plus guarantees against arbitrary arrest. These combined liberties helped overthrow absolutism in both civil and religious contexts. For Hudson, this tradition grew directly from theological affirmations. He acknowledged that some rationalists had advocated separation of church and state in a mild way, but their skeptical orientation raised serious doubts about their Christian status. So, while not altogether dismissing those he called "extra-church liberals," Hudson gave little credit to their activity. In his zeal to link political liberty and Protestant belief, he event went to the point of claiming that Thomas Jefferson "drew his ideas from the political Calvinism of Milton, Locke, and [Algernon] Sidney."[31]

Admittedly not all Puritans had advocated broad freedoms. Hudson duly noted that America's first Congregationalists and Presbyterians clung to the ideal of a church recognized by law. Their attempts to fashion a new Zion in the wilderness left no room for dissent, only liberty to vacate a district where the right kind of church enjoyed support and protection from civil authority. New England Congregationalists had been able, for a time at least, to translate their dream of a godly society into a confessional state. When such conservative colonists spoke of religious freedom, they really meant freedom for only themselves with no toleration of alternative viewpoints. Aside from a few exceptions, early colonial policies did not accommodate religious differences because leaders in church and state valued uniformity more than unrestricted theological expression.

Hudson's treatment of these colonial theocracies discloses an important aspect of his thinking about causation. For him the key element in historical change was the force of ideas. Basic libertarian principles eventually triumphed over minority control because powerful elites could not withstand the internal momentum of a great heritage. Right-wing Puritans found themselves in "a particularly vulnerable position" defending governments where only the saints ruled and yet where voluntary churches exerted only limited influence. He considered the more consistent sentiment of left-wing thinkers to have been "the dynamic religious force in colonial society, and it exerted an increasing influence within all the Protestant churches." Such influence stemmed from "greater consistency in following out the logic of assumptions shared by all." In this interpretation, reasons for accepting the

voluntary principle were "reasons drawn from the common trea-
sury of Reformation faith." Hudson's respect for the force behind
an effective tradition was confirmed by the process where "such
formerly right-wing groups as the Presbyterians, Anglicans, Lu-
therans, Reformed, and even the New England Congregationalists,
driven by the logic of their own fundamental affirmations, . . .
ultimately accept[ed] the left-wing point of view."[32]

Theological tenets derived from the Reformation eventually
worked themselves to the surface of Puritan values and culminated
in the separation of church and state. Hudson viewed this as
vindication of Protestant affirmations, and subsequent events in
American life underscored their importance for cultural development. He observed that churches, once deprived of state support,
were placed in the healthy position of maintaining themselves on a
voluntary basis. All religious groups were free to express themselves, and as a result, pluralistic church life "became strong and
vigorous, being based upon personal conviction rather than nomi-
nal adherence." Post-Revolutionary decades witnessed "a new
surge of spiritual vitality" that stimulated denominational competition and spurred missionary outreach. This energy

brought the gospel to every settlement established in the westward march of
the American people, sent missionaries into every corner of the earth, and
created colleges and hospitals and charitable foundations. Nor were the evils
of society forgotten. Reform movements of every kind and description began
to flourish. Slavery was abolished, temperance became respectable, wages
and hours and conditions of labor began to be regulated, and legislation was
adopted to improve the lot of the wards of society—the blind, the fatherless,
the mentally deficient, the prisoner, the indigent.[33]

More important than these tangible benefits, a mutually supportive pact emerged between religious influences and civil liberties.
Hudson pointed out that social freedom permitted believers to
embrace religion voluntarily and avoid the old pitfalls of enforced
worship. And in turn spiritual freedom engendered a respect for
the common good and prevented citizens from reverting to anar-
chy and despotism.

History contained many illustrations of what happened when
spiritual and political interests worked against each other. Hudson
chose modern Roman Catholicism as a case study of church-state
antagonism. Using official documents from 1870 through 1954, he
depicted a system of ideas that contrasted sharply with the Protes-

tant heritage. Less than a decade later, the Second Vatican Council invalidated much of his analysis, or at least made it obsolete. But Hudson's critique is still helpful as another demonstration of his reliance on doctrine as the essential factor in historical causation. He was convinced that the character of institutions and cultures derived from fundamental ideals. These in turn drew upon beliefs regarding God and human existence. Faith led to practice, and church historians needed little else to explain behavior. Theology and social policy were always part of a single fabric for Hudson, and he thought pre–Vatican II pronouncements were instructive as warnings. Catholic history could show what happened when civil and religious freedoms were not properly balanced.

Hudson was interested in questions about how power was exercised in areas of religious identity and personal initiative. Questions of this general sort help explain why he defined a Catholic as anyone who submitted to Roman authority. He listed, only to dismiss them, other definitional features such as veneration of saints and relics, belief in purgatory, attending private confession, performing stations of the cross, and using incense, holy water, and rosaries. Those pious practices did not constitute Catholicism for him; what counted was accepting "the Roman obedience," allowing hierarchical officials to control individual conscience. Defining Catholicism this way and focusing on all the power concentrated under Roman jurisdiction pointed up exactly the kind of absolutism that British and American Protestants had been fighting against for three centuries.

For Hudson, the basic difference between Catholicism and Protestantism lay in the extent of their respective freedoms. Catholics were free at only one point: they could accept or reject obedience to Rome. If they submitted, they had no further initiative. Issues were settled by ecclesiastical authority, not by private conscience, because every participant was in the custody of a confessor. Church members were not free to seek new insights, consider other perspectives, or choose different alternatives. This meant that Catholics were "able to participate only to a limited extent in the discussion and debate of the democratic process."[34]

Roman absolutism reached its zenith in 1870 when the First Vatican Council endorsed papal infallibility. Thereafter Catholics had to acknowledge the Roman pontiff as capable of giving the authoritative interpretation of Scripture and thereafter of defining

dogma. But more significant for Hudson, *Pastor Aeternus* central-
ized all legislative, executive, and judicial power in one office.
Matters of discipline and government as well as questions of faith
and morals were to be settled exclusively by the bishop of Rome. As
supreme ruler of all the faithful, the pope had full authority to
direct followers in what they must do and what they must believe.
"He alone is declared to be the judge of everyone; he alone can be
judged by no one."[35] Such power to command assent and obedience made Hudson doubt whether it was compatible with the
American tradition that safeguarded voluntary belief and action.

Judging from its internal authority structure, Catholicism left
little room for personal initiative. Restrictions of that sort presented a marked contrast to Protestant emphases on debate and
free choice in religious affairs. Then in 1885 Catholicism showed its
true colors regarding political theory in the papal encyclical *Immor-
tale Dei*. That general pronouncement, stated broadly enough to
cover Catholics and non-Catholics alike, defined government as an
agency committed to the welfare of all citizens. But it also held
that, since God was the ultimate source of authority in government, every properly constituted state should foster the religion
which God had established, viz., the Catholic church. Hudson
concluded that such reasoning made popular sovereignty impossible. A theory that derived authority from God rather than from
the people was incompatible with any government that ruled by
popular consent. States that showed religious favoritism eventually erred, he claimed, "by firmly rejecting the pernicious notions
of freedom of religion, freedom of spirit, freedom of assembly, and
freedom of the press." So Catholic political theory was at least
consistent. Once it established the transcendent superiority of
Christian priorities, all implications for ordering political life followed in logical sequence. And Hudson found its specific tenets to
be "far removed from what is commonly understood by democracy."[36]

It was true, Hudson admitted, that popes in recent times had
announced they did not condemn democracy per se. But he suggested that basic propositions in Catholic constitutional theory
made any prodemocratic statement highly suspicious. Roman
authorities said only that it was not wrong to prefer democratic
government, but then they added that states should maintain
Catholic doctrine and protect the church. Hudson argued that the

terms of such a proviso were mutually contradictory and violated "almost every basic democratic doctrine." Papal declarations promised that the church could adjust to republics and reconcile itself to the rights of citizens. But Hudson insisted "this is quite different from providing a positive foundation for a democratic society." In the Roman scheme of things, a concern for liberty involved special privileges for the church; freedom meant accepting the divinely instituted inequalities found in social stratification. If the church denounced absolutism, it focused on governmental interference with ecclesiastical prerogatives, not on citizens' rights. Hudson agreed that Catholic democracy was theoretically possible in contexts where these priorities held sway, but he thought it could provide only "government *for* the people, . . . not necessarily *of* and *by* the people."[37]

Few events in twentieth-century Catholicism prompted Hudson to revise his assessment of nineteenty-century policy statements. Recent papal allocutions only confirmed his thinking that doctrine took precedence over social need. He knew that individual Catholics occasionally challenged papal authority and spoke their minds on controverted issues. But on the whole, Hudson detected no real change in the church. Official pronouncements were more important in his eyes than any dissent or nonconformist activity. If actual practices contravened official manifestors, he viewed them as aberrations rather than clues to more complex realities under the surface. Instead of seeing any latitude for the faithful to interpret beliefs for themselves, he emphasized incidents where the papacy condemned liberalizing tendencies and called for strict adherence to official teaching.[38] Many Catholics lived in hope of attaining more freedom, but Hudson thought their position was mixed with pathos and tragedy. Nothing they did, he held, could transform the church's essential character.

After portraying Catholicism as authoritarian in religion and restrictive in politics, Hudson added some further comments in a postscript. These judgments are pertinent to historiographical analysis because, by criticizing the Catholic perspective, he could indicate through contrast which ideals were crucial for the democratic process. At bottom Hudson found Catholicism inimical to civil and religious liberty. Its vision of society was naively utopian, depending too much on revelation and not enough on the way people actually behaved. Its concept of group cooperation was paternalistic, assuming that people needed only to obey papal directives because the church had all the answers. The ecclesiastical structure subordinated believers to an ideal that assumed perfection. Such pretensions failed to see "that our understanding of God's revelation may be partial and even perverted by self-concern, . . . that the church in any of its institutional forms wears the countenance of a sinner and stands under judgment, . . . [and] that only proximate justice and harmony can be secured by various devices of checks and balances."[39] Admittedly some modern Catholic leaders were encouraging greater initiative among laypersons. But Hudson maintained that the basic ecclesiological system still confined the apostolate to the hierarchy. As long as the laity accepted such discrimination, this shackled their individual freedoms, and democracy could not flourish there.

While attacking modern Catholicism for its basic structure, Hudson also charged Protestantism with failure to sustain its once-effective heritage. Churches had developed great strength in this country because voluntarism forced them to rely on their own resources. Such conditions gave religious groups a better sense of identity and mission, and this in turn benefited the moral and physical welfare of all citizens. But success proved the churches' undoing. After attaining a measure of reform in slavery, education, and temperance, Protestant institutions seemed uncertain about what else to do. Hudson characterized this modern impasse as one where churches had become "complacent and satisfied" with their past victories. They confused religious and cultural responsibilities to the point where it made no difference whether secular or ecclesiastical organizations performed further tasks. As a result, "the distinctively Christian character of the culture began to be dissipated and its vigor and vitality tended progressively to diminish." In the current situation, Hudson observed, churches had relinquished those duties which once defined their worth. Programs for cultural improvement could not survive for long without the religious impulses that had created them. Deprived of spiritual energies, cultural institutions operated on nothing better than habit and an ebbing moral sentiment.[40]

By the mid-twentieth century, American Protestants no longer defined themselves along lines that had once made them so effective. They no longer possessed inner integrity and a clear sense of purpose. Discipline had declined because membership standards meant little to adherents. Liberal theology had mixed too freely and compromised with modern intellectual trends. Evangelistic zeal had waned because religious groups transferred the bulk of their activity to nonchurch agencies. In aligning Christian practice with secular standards, "the churches succeeded only in demonstrating that they had little of consequence to contribute and that the person outside the church could justifiably remain indifferent." The progression of American decline was "clear and remorseless": "Discipline disappeared, evangelistic fervor faded, faith lost its force, and the churches, living at peace with the world, lost their sense of a distinct and special civic vocation in society and devoted their energies to social activities, humanitarian enterprises, and the building of costly edifices."[41] The perils of success and acculturation had, in Hudson's view, produced a situation where the great principles of Protestant heritage faced possible extinction.

Obviously Protestantism needed revitalization in order to recover its inner strength and sense of purpose. One suggestion frequently made in modern times was ecumenical merger, but Hudson was dubious of any real help from that direction. As a student of Christian history, he knew that people would always differ over polity and liturgy. Such diversities were healthy, he thought, and these different expressions of the faith would atrophy in a single organization. Authoritative control would eventually supersede private judgment, he suspected, and this type of ecumenism harbored the same threats as those in the Catholic system. Uniformity was too costly at such a price. It closed off religious growth and vital interchanges that might "lead to profitable and fruitful discussion out of which a fuller apprehension of truth may emerge." Institutional changes did not foster this kind of search, "since no church has a final and unambiguous grasp of divine truth." Hudson penned his own convictions as well as his view of history in saying "the true Church of Christ can never be fully represented by any single ecclesiastical structure. God is not the exclusive possession of any church, and the existence of different churches . . . serves as a constant correction to the pretensions of all churches." Contemporary lassitude needed correction, but tinkering with externals did not get to the root of the problem.[42]

Efforts to reinvigorate a listless Protestantism would be better advised to concentrate on its core, Hudson thought. Churches could have more impact on modern life if they recovered a theological identity and distinguished between themselves and secular institutions. History taught an important lesson: "Churches in a democratic society must stand for something definite and specific if they are to avoid surrendering to the dominant cultural tendencies of the times." If Protestantism hoped for new strength, it needed to acquire a more coherent perspective and institutional integrity. Doctrinal reaffirmation and renewed discipline would help achieve those ends.

As a historian, Hudson pointed to the need for retrenchment, but he was noncommital about which doctrines and discipline needed to be emphasized. He thought the Protestant message should have "some normative content," but historians like himself had neither the duty nor capacity to "define the theology that is needed if a quickening of the spiritual life is to take place within the churches." Fresh ideas about identity and mandate were best "determined by the churches themselves through procedures of democratic discussion." The essential factor worth safeguarding was to give all believers freedom to seek the truth and to express their convictions in public. The best Hudson hoped for was continuing religious ferment within and between diverse denominations, not an inclusive creed or a comprehensive institution. The real Protestant tradition flourished where people were free "to achieve disciplined communities of Christians who seek to bear witness in their corporate life to the demands of an Eternal God in the midst of changing circumstances."[43]

Protestantism rested on a consensus of values that also supported social stability. Its influence on the political order was "determined by the success of the churches in creating an informed and committed electorate." Churches helped preserve democracy best when they could "stand apart from the culture with something to say that is distinctly its own." Protestants could bolster cultural vitality by developing "procedures for group discipline to form a corporate conscience on specific issues, and . . . an aggressive missionary spirit which will serve to extend its influence." Hudson admitted there were no guarantees that churches would remain true to their high calling: they might enshrine social gods on their altars as some had in the past. But the American experience proved that religious liberty had released churches from local customs and allowed them to pursue lofty ideals. In contemporary life, where secular standards appeared to be so dominant, Hudson thought Protestantism should return to the role it played in securing democratic freedoms. If churches could regain their theological integrity, citizens might draw strength from their heritage again and work to achieve "a reasonably Christian democratic society" through voluntary cooperation.[44]

CONSENSUS NEEDED FOR THE AMERICAN EXPERIMENT

A third scholar who contributed to consensus history was Sidney E. Mead, who held professorships from 1940 to 1974 at the University of Chicago, the School of Theology at Claremont, and the University of Iowa. Mead achieved renown as an essayist, and his pithy contributions were often more valuable than the volumes his colleagues produced. Many of his studies emphasized similar points and involved some repetition. But there is a tenacious consistency to his treatment of several basic themes. These carefully crafted writings disclose a vigorous, independent mind that concentrated on central religious features in American culture. Mead's distinctive interpretation of those features is still something to be reckoned with as today's students seek to decipher the past.

Mead was troubled and frustrated by the religious scene of his day. He spent the better part of forty years tracing the roots of a dilemma and urging others to recognize its importance. The basic problem, he found, was that Americans tried to function with "bifurcated minds." They tried to be good citizens and good church members with different sets of ideas. There was an unresolved tension between the theology that legitimated religious freedom in republican government and the theology generally professed among denominations in the United States. Mead often used strong language to startle Americans into seeing that they had not come to terms with disparate elements of their heritage. The lamentable fact was that "at dominant important points the basic principles and premises of the dominent religious establishment are at war with the fundamental principles and premises of the civil order in which the church-member-citizen lives." This syndrome showed signs of "endemic mental abnormality" in present culture with "attendant psychogenic oddities" found among its participants. Trying to live with unreconciled perspectives resulted in "split minds" and "religious leukemia," an "anemic condition" that plagued most theological enterprises. Failure to solve the problem made religion a superficial quotient in the nation's common life, an ineffectiveness that amounted to "wasting sickness evident in the inclusive society." Mead's historical essays concentrated on helping citizens and church members understand the roots of their two traditions. Knowledge might help resolve tensions and bolster the proper kind of religious activity in contemporary culture.[45]

How had Americans acquired a bifurcated mind-set? Mead hoped theologians could reconcile the principles that tugged people in different directions, but first they needed to understand how the problem originated. In this modern approach to history, he went far beyond the old scientific ideals, recognizing that every scholar worked with "presuppositions and ideology largely absorbed from the dynamic community in which that mind has been nurtured." He knew that every person's work was affected by perspective, and each investigator "picks from the past what will bring his story to the culmination to which he is committed."[46] With this modern viewpoint, Mead concentrated primarily on the meaning and consequences of religious freedom in American life. He considered separation of church and state to be the nation's outstanding religious accomplishment, while theological irrelevance was its cardinal failure. Those twin themes intertwined throughout a single historical continuum. Every discrete essay added pieces to a mosaic that depicted America's potential for, and frustrating inability to, achieve social and religious harmony.

As contemporary participant and observer, Mead never ceased calling for intellectual coherence and logical consistency in religion. He wished church leaders would ignore trivial matters and concentrate on the main issue of Christian identity and republican citizenship. But he did not invoke any "high" concept of the church, declaring instead that "my primary interest . . . is not what religion *is*, but what it *does*. From my perspective, the definition of what religion is, is a matter for sectarian insiders to quarrel about." As a nonsectarian outsider, then, Mead said the historian's purpose was "to delineate the effect religious beliefs and convictions have had upon what people did and the way they did it." He made it his duty as a trained observer to expound all the ideologies of America's pluralistic culture. So historical knowledge about competitive ideas "in the free market of the institutionalized sacred" was preliminary to creative thinking in contemporary times. This understanding of the historian's task lay behind Mead's announced intent to "attempt to delineate the religion of the Republic and to point out how it differs from the religions of the denominations exemplified in their institutional forms, theological and practical. I have hoped thus to prod competent theologians," he continued, "into seeing the theological issue between the two (or more) religions."[47] This might seem a modest goal, but it aimed at nothing less than assigning proper order and proportion to elements at the heart of American life. Creative theology could then refurbish contemporary culture by supporting the consensus that sustained it.

Mead thought American religious history had produced an unprecedented institutional pattern, but churches neither recognized their unique situation nor adjusted their thinking to it. This failure was crucial to understanding how churches subsisted in the new setting without participating in any dynamic way.

Before the American experience, Christian establishments had been accustomed to fourteen centuries of exclusive power. Of course the earliest gospel messengers had not used force, but "when in the fourth century Christians entered . . . a disgusting alliance with Constantine, 'Christendom' was born." Mead distinguished between *Christianity* which depended on the sword of the spirit and *Christendom* which wielded a sword of steel. In this distinction he pointed out that, "contrary to what some always held to be a central principle of the Gospels," defenders of Christendom "freely used coercion to defend their orthodoxies and to hold the wavering faithful in line." Using blunter language to describe this "institutionalized salvation that left such a trail of suffering and blood behind it," Mead charged that "anyone who judged its defenders by their record thereafter might decide that they confronted those who disagreed with them, not with their professed Master's advice to 'Love your enemies,' but with the cruder and earthy battle cry, 'Kill the bastards!' "[48] This attitude permeated medieval practice where divine grace was monopolized by a self-perpetuating priesthood that exercised considerable power over social and political affairs as well as religious ones.

But a conceptual revolution attended modern times. Mead traced its rise in the Reformation defense of private judgment regarding the Scriptures, then to respect for private judgment without any concern for biblical authority. Those attitudes set the stage for an intellectual breakthrough, but early American colonial forces held it in check. Ecclesiastical bodies in the original plantations used coercive power to defend their version of orthodox belief and practice, often applying "every weapon in the arsenal of physical violence against the heretic, dissenter, or schismatic person." Such policies did not prevail for long, however, because many heterodox churches flourished in the heterogenous colonies. By the time a nation emerged, civil leaders realized it was both impossible and undesirable to establish the old Christendom ideal of a national church. The situation constituted what Mead called "a strange new commonwealth" where Christians had to adapt their institutions and ways of thinking "to meet the exigencies of a world they did not make and only grudgingly permitted to be born." This sort of pluralism may have resembled conditions in the pre-Constantinian Roman Empire, but it appeared "to be so new in America that the founders defended it primarily as an experiment worth trying." The lively experiment in America was essentially an attempt to see if a commonwealth could exist while granting full liberty to multiple religious groups, knowing that most of them still claimed in traditional fashion to be exclusively *the* church.[49]

Mead's interpretation of the American heritage pivots on the eighteenth century because the most influential components of national character emerged during that period. As political leaders fashioned arguments to defend political independence from Britain, they also developed an appeal for toleration and cooperation among American religious groups. This aspect of the Revolutionary era figured heavily in Mead's treatment of subsequent events. It is important to recognize the nature of what he called "rationalism," its role in achieving religious freedom, its fate at the hands of orthodox churches, and its continuing significance for bifurcated minds in the twentieth century.

For Mead, the most notable feature of rationalism or Enlightenment, terms he used interchangeably, was its theological content. He judged rationalism to be a genuine religious alternative to confessional Christianity. This aspect took precedence over any consideration of its epistemological framework, humanistic priorities, or sociopolitical orientation. Rational religion undergirded national consciousness, Mead insisted, giving it tangible form and legal structure. He characterized the Enlightenment viewpoint chiefly "as a radical monotheism," and for those who shared its tenets, God was "an unquestioned presupposition." Rationalists chose to learn about God from the book of natural creation, not restricting themselves to special revelation in the Bible. They regarded Jesus as an unparalleled moral teacher, not an embodiment of Deity. Such a redefinition of Christian premises eventually brought rationalists into conflict with orthodox opinion, but despite later charges against them, Mead declared emphatically that "whatever else they may have been they were not atheists."[50]

Correlative to ideas about God as Creator and Governor of the Universe was a conviction that humans as creatures were limited in scope and ability. For Mead, this meant that "finite man could not have absolute assurance or final knowledge of anything, even of the existence of God, and his own salvation." Such modesty led to tolerance of varying opinions. Every isolated truth was relative to a person's vantage point and powers of observation. If one granted that human intellects were limited, then everyone should be free to express opinions about religion, just as they were free to advocate viewpoints on other topics. Enlightenment theology insisted that "man is not 'saved' by knowledge and must live by faith in the Creator and His Providence."[51]

Rationalism allowed great latitude for differing ideas about God and moral obligation. In doing so it still tried to reach general agreement on divine providence, the reward of virtue and punishment of vice, the existence of human souls, and life beyond the grave. Rational religion plumbed for universals, distinguished between substance and form, separated basic truths from the idiosyncracies that pitted sects against each other. Mead held that this comprehensive theology was the only one compatible with a pluralistic commonwealth because it was deliberately antiparticularistic. It offered a cosmopolitan, inclusive theology that incorporated "the essentials of every religion." Enlightenment religion affected political theory by insisting that only what was common to all religions could be worthwhile in a nation of many churches. "It was this theology that made theoretically acceptable the scandal of Christendom at the time—acceptance by a nation of religious pluralism and the consequent multiplicity of independent religious groups." Indeed, in commenting on the centrality of rationalist religion in the Constitution and First Amendment, Mead found that "national religious freedom and separation of church and state were conceived in actual religious pluralism and were dedicated to the proposition that all religions are equal."[52]

Enlightenment convictions were basic to accommodating confessional diversity, but there were not enough rationalists to put the plan into practice. Mead found that two other factions pooled their interests with rationalists to help achieve separation of church and state in America. One group was pietistic. Some pietists represented separatist movements from continental Europe, while others had deserted right-wing colonial churches due to heightened emotions during the Great Awakening revivals. Pietists of various origins and placement appealed to common spiritual experience as more important than the formalism of ecclesiastical establishments. Their religious priorities were different from rationalists, but they shared an antipathy to churches that wanted to enforce uniformity. Those who championed unmonitored private experience "concluded that the difference over which Christians had battled and bled for a millennium were immaterial between those of like heart."[53] The other group was composed of conservatives who favored establishment of a state church but lacked sufficient influence to prevail. Such people differed over granting religious freedom to others, "but all were practically unanimous on one point: each wanted freedom for itself." In a classic case of political compromise, churches in this third bloc provided the swing vote because "by this time it had become clear that the only way to get it for themselves was to grant it to others." Unlike Bainton's golden humanitarian thread or Hudson's celebration of dynamic Protestant values, Mead's assessment of this tripartite coalition was that "the true picture is not that of 'triumph,' . . . but rather a mingling through frustration, controversy, confusion, and compromise of all the diverse ecclesiastical patterns transplanted from Europe."[54]

A complex alignment of forces during the eighteenth century resulted in separation of church and state at the national level. Mead's evaluation of the factors involved left no doubt as to which of them he considered most important. "Most of the effectively powerful intellectual, social, and political leaders were rationalists," he declared, "and these men made sense theoretically out of the actual, practical situation which demanded religious freedom." To him it was a fact of lasting significance that civil, not religious, authority had set limits on the absolutist tendencies inherent in most churches.[55] The American heritage embraced a precedent fraught with consequences when neutral governmental officials

acted to prevent any sect or combination of them from monopolizing definitions of the truth and imposing a particular set of
behavioral standards on all the people.

But the very success of this rationalist-pietist-pragmatist alliance removed the primary bond that had held it together. As he
surveyed the events following the Revolution, Mead pinpointed
how the American character became saddled with antagonistic
components. The unresolved tension in national life was due to the
fact that "churches, each intent on its own freedom, accepted [the
alliance] in practice but without reconciling themselves to it intellectually by developing theoretical defenses . . . that were legit-
imately rooted in their professed theological positions. And they
never have."[56] Confusion resulted from intrasigence, and this fed
controversies in the aftermath of freedom. In the ensuing decades,
pietists and conservative pragmatists realigned themselves with
traditionalists against their erstwhile rationalist allies.

During the struggle for religious liberty, rationalists accentuated
their common goal with many church groups, and while differences between them existed, they went largely unnoticed. Some of
the differences were these: Rationlists were detached and cerebral;
church members were zealous and attuned to spiritual experience.
Enlightenment thinkers reasoned about God from the created
order that was open for anyone to investigate; church members
were content with exclusivist ideas about God derived from special
revelation in Scripture. Rationalists found religion useful for public morality and social harmony; church members embraced religion for the salvation of souls. Jesus, for rationalists, was an
exemplar of ethical perfection; for church members he was the
divine and loving Savior. These differences became clearer as the
eighteenth century drew to a close, but basic issues were ignored
because debaters squabbled over superficial points. Orthodox
church leaders began to attack Enlightenment theology as "infidel"
for the aforementioned reasons. As momentum gathered, an increasing number of pietists and conservative pragmatists joined
the attack against rationalism because they noticed the denial of
biblical authority and rejection of trinitarian formulae. Excitement
over trying to decide what was Christian and non-Christian kept
many of them from seeing that rationalism had solid religious
content and that religious freedom was its paramount achievement. In one of his more compelling metaphors, Mead captured

the irony on all sides when the shift in sentiment occurred. Pietists and pragmatists eventually discovered their

latent incompatibility with rationalism and arrange[d] a hasty divorce in order to remarry traditional orthodoxy. American denominational Protestantism is the offspring of this second marriage living in the house of religious freedom which was built during the first marriage. The child has always accepted and defended the house with fervor, if not always with intelligence. But it has commonly exhibited great reluctance to own up to its rationalist architect and builder.[57]

Mead held that ecclesiastical developments in the early national period were responsible for twentieth-century religious ineffectiveness. He indicted churches for not treating rationalism as worthy of respect and for failing to articulate a set of theological principles common to every religion in the republic. As things turned out, these items on the national agenda were never discussed. They were subordinated to Second Great Awakening revivals, fears about the French Revolution and possible social upheaval, and increased competition among evangelical denominations. But Mead's treatment of such events never lets the reader forget the sour taste that lingers after religious leaders turned away from the real American experiment. He pointed out that the theological issues between rationalism and other religions "was all but lost sight of in the excited attack on infidelity." Those who opposed Enlightenment thought resorted to moral and political accusations instead of debating theology on its merits. They asserted that rationalism led to personal immorality and social chaos, claiming that orthodox Christianity was the only sure foundation for good morals and sound government. They rarely discussed the crucial differences between natural and revealed religion. Calm appeals to reason fell victim to a flood of demagoguery. So American churches turned their attention to the practical problems of evangelism and "laid much intellectual business on the table." But success in revivals did not make the problem go away, and Mead located the origins of bifurcated mentality in the fact that "the major piece of the churches' unfinished business . . . is religious freedom." American Christianity succeeded in shouting down the Enlightenment, but it "has never developed full-blown theoretical justification for its most distinctive practice."[58]

Enlightenment statesmen based the republic on cosmopolitan theological convictions, but after 1790 churches rejected them.

Instead of encouraging denominations to accept rivals as equals, religious freedom spurred them to compete among themselves, each one stressing the superiority of its own doctrines and institutional forms. In a culture that recognized no difference among them, churches heightened their sectarian claims to gain advantage in the free market of souls. The American experiment called for new thinking about religion in a republican setting, but church leaders "turned back to preeighteenth century theologians, or to the theologians of Europe's Established churches." Mead lamented the split between ideals undergirding common life in the nation and those that sustained church membership. "Cosmopolitan principles were opposed to tribal principles," he pointed out, "widening the gulf between being Christians and citizens of the Republic."[59] And instead of bridging the gulf, believers exhibited a fatal tendency to keep salvation and social responsibility in separate compartments.

Once diverted from serious theological activity, nineteenth-century Christian intellectual capacity declined, Mead held, because of pragmatic revival techniques, moralistic activism, and scholastic attempts to control humanistic learning. In the process of such decay, churches adopted ecclesiastical systems that were "at war with their social system." In retrospect they had "divorced 'salvation' from responsible involvement in the society in which they lived." It was sad enough that most groups abandoned theological rigor and settled for conversions based on an effective sales pitch. But this shortsighted emphasis also prevented people from thinking of their local group as part of God's eternal Kingdom. "Any one 'church' in our society is too small," Mead pointed out, "too circumscribed in time and space, too droopy in its thinking, too competitive, too involved in its own survival, to offer any plausible claim to even point to the transcendental community" that had inspired Christians in previous centuries.[60]

Worse than this parochialism, though, churches lost their appreciation for civil neutrality in their all-or-nothing drive to defend their particularities. Mead found that groups in competition with each other also competed with the openhanded policies of national government. They disapproved of any cultural orientation that did not embody some species of orthodoxy, saying that a noncommittal society was "infidel," "godless," or "secular."[61] Sectarian attempts to permeate society criticized republican antiparticularism because church leaders thought the state had to embrace orthodox Christian principles or collapse. Churches that argued in this manner abandoned their democratic responsibility, in Mead's estimation. The ideas and practices they manifested under the aegis of religious liberty were a denial of the conditions that had allowed them originally to flourish.

Religious groups acting under American toleration had, in Mead's homey phrase, "put themselves into a bind." Rationalists had put religious freedom on a solid theoretical basis, but churches accepted separation of church and state without resolving attendant intellectual ambiguities. This discrepancy required people to choose between church and public service, or at least hold separate duties in precarious balance. To "become American" meant accepting the cosmopolitan creed "and to renounce traditional particularity along with the devil of sectarianism and all his works." Ecclesiastical advancement involved emphasizing what a group held particular to itself, even though its distinguishing features were irrelevant to the general welfare of the commonwealth. Unavoidably then, "the issue with which religious freedom confronted the churches was an issue between two religions," Mead insisted, "theirs and that of the Declaration." This continuous tension juxtaposed public welfare and denominational ideology, each claiming supreme allegiance. "Church members in America have always been faced with the necessity to choose, . . . between the inclusive religion of democracy and the particularistic Christianity of their sect." As a step toward gaining a new consensus, it was important for citizens to recognize that the unsettled dilemmas associated with religious freedom were a veritable "Trojan horse in the comfortable citadel of denominationalism . . . in the United States."[62]

Mead found tragedy as well as irony in American church history. Religious leaders were not only unable to deal with separation of church and state theologically, few of them perceived what would happen to churches when they endorsed a particular cultural arrangement. American Protestantism was permeated by pietism, and Mead noted that its intellectual naiveté lent itself to activism bound by certain socioeconomic problems and their solutions. In this equation churches gradually abdicated their role as culture critic and endorsed the prevailing code of acquisitive nineteenth-century society which they helped create. Mead remarked with puckish humor that "Protestants, in effect, looked at the new world they had created, . . . and, like Jehovah before them, pronounced it very good. A widespread complacency, a smug self-satisfaction with things as they were (or as they were supposed to be), settled upon them as soot settles on Chicago."[63] The end result was that American denominations found themselves as completely identified with their country's dominant cultural patterns as had ever been known in the more blatant days of Christendom.

Mead's analysis of more recent American religious life touched the same problem that fascinated Hudson. Both historians were concerned about the cultural captivity of Protestant churches and their inability to deal with public issues on an independent basis. But where Hudson urged churches to reassert distinctive beliefs and discipline against secular society, Mead suggested the opposite. He disagreed that the current anemia in Protestantism was due to its loss of particularity, and he argued against sectarian distinctiveness as a remedy. America was not in a "post-Protestant" era, he said; it had never been wholly Protestant before. The challenge at present was for churches to base themselves more adequately on the "religion-in-general" substratum of the national Constitution. Churches needed to accentuate their positive contribution to the inclusive theology of the Republic, not shore up their denominational particularities. Open toleration had manifest virtues, Mead held, and "the gates of hell have never prevailed against the church's vision of the universal." But America's lively experiment faced an obstacle that could prevail against the vision, viz., "religious particularity possessed of coercive power."[64] In Mead's anticipated consensus, it was the duty of church members as well as citizens to resist particularity for the good of all. As far as he was concerned, it was sectarianism rather than any imagined secular influence that threatened to undermine a healthy society.

Sectarianism made churches ineffective in republican life. Religious pluralism had produced conditions genuinely different from the old framework known to Christendom, and ecclesiastical thinkers needed to formulate an accommodating rationale. Mead wanted them to recognize that in the American setting no group could aspire to be anything more than equal with all the others, and none should accept being anything less. During the past two centuries, most church leaders had resisted the implications of this principle of equality. For their own sake and for that of society as a whole, they had to face reality. And in adjusting to these circumstances, the intellectual challenge was to create a theology that transformed sectarian mentality into affirmation of one cosmopolitan religion for all churches in the country.

Mead clarified this primary focus in an early collection of essays: "My point," he said, "is that there is an unresolved issue between 'America's two religions' . . . that contributes to the anxious misery inside our society; and my purpose has been to prod some who are theologically more hip than I am into taking it up at the point in our history where it was laid on the table and largely forgotten." Over the years, though, he seems to have been undecided whether there were two religions or just different forms of one with intermingled emphases. Either way, they functioned as separate ideologies. Mead identified one of these sources of misery as church religion, "commonly articulated in the terms of scholastic Protestant orthodoxy and almost universally practiced in terms of the experimental religion of pietistic revivalism." The other pertained to religion in a democratic society. This second belief system had always been "rooted in the rationalism of the Enlightenment . . . and was articulated in terms of the destiny of America, under God, to be fulfilled by perfecting the democratic way of life for the example and betterment of all mankind."[65] As uncoordinated perspectives, these religions made conflicting claims on popular loyalty. As components of a possible synthesis, their emphases held some promise of a consensus beneficial to both religious and social vitality.

Despite his frustration with the persistence of traditionalist thinking, Mead remained hopeful that new theological activity would occur. The institutional matrix for such thinking already existed in denominations, entities which fit neither classic definition of a church or a sect. Denominations were, he held, the pragmatic result of conditions in democratic society. As the product of new conceptions about identity and scope of action, they made no exclusivist claims about being *the* church. They acknowledged each religious group to be "a visible but finitely limited part of the church founded upon imperfect knowledge, appreciation, and exemplification of the gospel."[66] Denominations did not absolutize or try to universalize any of the particularities that distinguished one version of Christianity from another. In Mead's estimation it was possible to reconcile a Christian defense of pluralism with inherited concepts about Christendom. This new sort of ecclesiological thinking could become one of the most durable features of religion in the New World.

Republican government corresponded to denominationalism in that its religious principles also mitigated absolutes in the earthly sphere. But according to Mead, a general belief in God lay at the heart of American character, and this kept the nation from being merely a secular or thisworldly entity as well. The key was that republican affirmation of the Infinite necessarily implied limitations on human beings as finite creatures. "That is the premise of all democratic institutions. It is the essential dogma of the religion of the Republic." As those theological convictions worked themselves out in church and state, the lesson of America's authentic heritage became clear:

> The primary religious concern in our nation must be to guard against national idolatry; against the state becoming God. . . . The founders sought to incarnate such a guard in the legal system of the new nation, the spiritual core of which is a theonomous cosmopolitanism. The constitutional structure was designed eventually to deny the traditional resort to coercive power to every religious sect, while protecting the right of each freely to compete openly with all the others. In this situation the sects "correct one another" for the civil authority by curbing all of them, [and] encourage each to tell "the other that he is not God."

Opposed to such freedoms were people Mead called "temple-ists" who disregarded human finitude and insisted that everyone must perceive and worship God in a prescribed manner. Democratic beliefs kept temple-ists from monopolizing religion, however, and denominations flourished where tolerance supplanted coercive power as each sought truth in its own way. Denominations curbed each other under republican conditions, restricting institutional pretensions with common deference to the Almighty.[67]

These were the elements that made it possible for denominations to flourish in free society. Mead despaired over recalcitrant churches that failed to see they had changed into denominations. At the same time, he hoped historical experience could stimulate theologians into recognizing the limits imposed by freedom. He studied the historical process in order to show Christian groups how they might avoid the pitfalls of exclusivist thinking. Such information illuminated the folly of separating salvation from social and political responsibility, of choosing between being a faithful church member and a loyal citizen of the Republic. Knowl-

edge might, he hoped, arrest the continued proliferation of bifurcated minds. If this trend were reversed, theologians might once
again serve effectively in society at large. These expectations led
Mead to search historical byways for the consensus he prescribed,
for signs of "a heightened theological consciousness, a willingness
to re-examine the traditional content of the Christian faith . . .
and positive attempts to revitalize the life of the denominations."
So these were the issues, and this was the consensus Mead
thought lay at the core of American life. As a final challenge, he left
the option up to citizens who might choose to accept it:

The practice of religious freedom has always been in conflict with the
distinctive theology of right-wing Protestantism [and this] enables one to
diagnose Protestantism's present sickness as a psychosomatic indigestion,
resulting from an inability either to digest the theology on which the practice
of religious freedom rests or to regurgitate the practice. . . . I do not think
Protestantism can give up the practice of religious freedom which it has
accepted. Therefore, I conclude, if it cannot learn to digest the theory on
which such freedom rests, the prognosis cannot be a happy one.[68]

In each of these three cases, church historians fashioned distinctive views of the past in order to counteract problems in the
present. Bainton drew lessons from what he took to be primitive
Christian ideals and bolstered them with concentrated study of the
Reformation period. His findings on religious liberty, pacifism,
and the evolutionary process of spiritual discovery constituted an
attitude he wished present churches would support. Part of Hudson's vigorous scholarship reflected an emphasis on consensus,
and that segment tried to buttress democratic values as grounded
in modern Protestantism. His studies of theology and political
theory pointed to strong links between free church traditions and
the practices that distinguished Western culture from other orientations. Mead was driven by similar concerns, but his analysis and
prescription differed considerably from Hudson's. He thought
contemporary religious ineffectiveness resulted from a preoccupa-
tion with ecclesiastical particularities rather than from a lack of
them. His exploration into national experience reaffirmed the
positive value of religious freedom which Bainton and Hudson
also endorsed. But Mead's detailed scenario for a new American
consensus went largely unheeded. Many historians accepted his
depiction of ideas and events involved in the separation of church
and state. But few shared his passion for theological renewal or

agreed that ideological particularism was a problem they should address. Still, all three of these church historians provide typical examples of efforts at midcentury to make scholarship relevant by using previous experience to address contemporary questions.

5
Intellectual History
and the History of Ideas

Historians in this century gradually abandoned the ideal of detached observation. They rejected old models of scientific method as inapplicable to their profession and assimilated easily with the current paradigm that discerns presuppositions in all forms of human inquiry. After 1930 a number of perspectives emerged to replace the one that had dominated procedures for so long. Discussions about method faded into the background, and considerations of personal interest, subject matter, and interpretive viewpoint took their place. Historians grouped themselves into clusters notable for particular interpretive emphases or topical priority that made their treatment distinctive. These rather forthright expressions of special interest arose in no developmental pattern. They existed alongside each other and attracted scholars who shared an inclination toward some preferred topic or approach to the material. As overlapping subgroups, these schools of thought provided contemporary investigators with multiple options.

Earlier in this century, traditional tastes in political and military history began to make room for a wider range of topics. As horizons broadened, a few voices called attention to the importance of ideas in historical experience. In 1900, for instance, Edward Eggleston urged his colleagues in the American Historical Association to include ideas in their coverage of cultural developments. A decade later James Harvey Robinson publicized the relevance of ideas in history, especially those which contributed to social progress. By 1930 progressive historians and advocates of New History discussed ideas as a factor in cultural improvement.[1] After that, investigators began to mention the role ideas played in

historical events, whether conservative or progressive, obstruc-
tionist or innovative. As progressivist attitudes waned, intellectual
history acquired a more mature outlook. Historians learned to see
ideas as an essential ingredient in explaining human experience,
not necessarily emancipating current readers from the past but at
least helping them to comprehend more fully the motivations that
stimulated earlier activity.[2]

In recent years historians have usually treated ideas in one of
two ways. There is no uniform terminology for identifying these
separate approaches, but two generic labels provide some guidelines in a confusing field. "Intellectual history" studies ideas as
causes, as an instrumental factor in human action. The "history of
ideas" approach appreciates systems of thought in and of themselves. This latter viewpoint does not value ideas for their functional capacity but for their intrinsic merit, and this alone is enough to
make knowing about them worthwhile.

Intellectual history came into its own when students recognized
that thinking was a basic component in social existence. Ideas
needed to be understood before social history could adequately be
explained. As one analyst of historical trends put it, "How could
the fortunes of any social group or movement or period become
truly meaningful without an appreciation of its characteristic aspirations and attitudes? In facing these questions, a handful of social
historians [let] intellectual history in through the back door." Once
the door was open, historians searched more systematically for
connections between bodies of thought and related areas of collective action. Many scholars produced valuable findings on the way
ideas and institutions supported each other. In trying to "grasp the
purposes that induced men to combine in the way they did rather
than some other way," they perceived more clearly "the human
aims (often diverse and clashing) that the institution served."[3]
Social history led to intellectual history as a means of accounting
for human action. So ideas were important because people held
them and put them to use. Intellectual historians concentrated on
understanding how ideas "shaped historic developments by setting the terms in which groups or generations of men conducted
their lives." Or, in the words of another analyst, they tried to
"recapture the meaning of ideas in history by seeing how they
function in their pragmatic social settings and by following their
course of development in periods of social change."[4]

If social history paved the way for intellectual history, literary criticism nurtured the history of ideas. Here scholars were fascinated by ideas in and of themselves. Instead of trying to show which conceptions stimulated action, they studied how ideas fit together in systems. This focus helped them understand various mind-sets and see how those changed over periods of time. In order to grasp central features of a previous age, historians with this orientation often concentrated on "a single idea or cluster of ideas in its successive formulations, treating it in virtual isolation from other aspects of history." Assuming that "pervasive symbolic expressions represent the ways in which any people confronts experience," they scrutinized documentary evidence to locate the most pervasive and telling expressions of an era.[5] Close attention to texts enabled historians of ideas to sift through ambiguous symbols and reconstruct their meaning. Interpreters hoped they could understand how previous mental constructs had existed, what dynamism made them appealing, and why they eventually changed.

Historians of ideas appreciated thought for what it was, having little concern for what it did or did not do. For them ideas possessed a quality that made understanding them inherently worthwhile. As one exponent of this perspective averred, "the speculations of a serious and competent . . . thinker have an intrinsic worth that has nothing to do with their direct impact upon politics or programs."[6] Some historians may have been attracted to a study of isolated ideas because they recognized that philosophical tenets were durable, intricate, and subtle. Others may have been drawn into the ranks after they grew away from progressivist history and gained greater respect for the tragic and ironic elements in human experience. Once their naiveté faded, historians could realize that ideas expressed both the aspirations and losses of an era, the intractable dilemmas as well as the hopes of every age.[7]

Many church historians pursued either intellectual history or the history of ideas. They were much more numerous than those who worked with a high-church perspective, and they outnumbered the ones who wrote consensus history, too. Church historians had traditionally given doctrine an important place in their treatment of religious affairs, and this old preference made them compatible with the new trend. One observer thought the recovery of religious history in this context was one of the most significant professional achievements at midcentury. "Puritanism, Edward-sean Calvinism, revivalism, liberalism, modernism, and the social gospel," he declared, "have all been brought down out of the attic and put back in the historical front parlor." Even cultural historians who did not find religion intrinsically interesting had to admit that it was a necessary part of explaining the past. Church historians capitalized on these newly sympathetic attitudes regarding their field. Their work coincided with "studies of American religious thought which assumed that ideas themselves were interesting and of intellectual worth, in addition to possessing certain causal power in the environment."[8]

The general profession once again defended religion as a factor too important to be ignored in cultural experience. They gave fresh support to scholars who had been emphasizing the centrality of beliefs and theology for quite some time. So church historians acquired a new legitimacy, less through their own argumentation than because secular investigators rediscovered their field. One disgruntled beneficiary, James H. Nichols, noticed this nonchalance among his colleagues and chided them for not taking more of a lead in exploring religious topics. Studies in literature and art, he said, led historians to seek the ideas behind creative activity. And so studies in religion should produce even bolder searches for the ideas that gave voice to belief. To his dismay, this had not occurred. Puritan studies, for example, were currently exhibiting a remarkably renewed energy, but, he grumbled, not a single church historian had contributed to this renaissance.[9] It was also true that church historians did little to argue for the respectability of studying ideas. Perhaps they felt no need to defend traditional ways, and some must have had a sense of déjà vu about the whole vogue of intellectual history. Few were led by contemporary debates to do anything new in an orientation they had found congenial all along. Serving as exemplars more than protagonists, many church historians have functioned since the 1940s with this now thoroughly legitimized perspective.

The work of two secular historians is a better indication of when the general profession began giving increased attention to ideas in history. In 1940 Ralph H. Gabriel published a survey of American democratic thought, and religious ideas received considerable attention throughout the study. Gabriel wrote at a time when cultural values were being threatened by totalitarian regimes in

Europe. He thought that Americans had lapsed into uncertainty about basic aspects of their heritage, and much of his analysis emphasized the ideological features that supported a free society. With this consensus motivation for writing history, he treated ideas as important forces in cultural formation. Religious thought was significant for larger social questions, he thought, because it affected the values and ethics that were integral to cultural cohesion. Three years later Merle Curti produced an overview of the growth of American thought. He regarded ideas basically as expressions of social, economic, and political interest groups. Rather than seeing ideas as causal agents in history, he considered them rationalizations best interpreted by the interests they served. Curti wrote from a generally progressivist stance, viewing intellectual history as liberation from old absolutes, as movement toward pragmatic or functional skepticism. Of course religious thought played a part in this scenario, but here doctrines gradually gave way to science because secular guidelines promised a faster rate of human progress.[10] But while these texts were gaining respect among secularists, several church historians produced sophisticated and appreciative studies of religious ideas.

CHURCH HISTORY AS INTELLECTUAL HISTORY

H. Shelton Smith

H. Shelton Smith was an oustanding example of those who focused on the ideational underpinnings of past experience. After holding several posts in northern cities, he spent the bulk of his career from 1931 to 1963 teaching at Duke Divinity School in North Carolina. There, he worked to improve academic standards for ministerial training, and he helped build a university graduate program that was unequaled elsewhere in the South.

In his earliest published work, Smith analyzed trends in religious education, especially the influence of liberal theological emphases on immanence, growth, and goodness in human nature. He found those motifs to be unrealistic in contemporary times and called for curricular reforms based on a revised theology. But more interesting to the historiographical analyst, Smith forecast the rest of his scholarly agenda in that single book. He noted in it that one of the major themes in American religious thought was that the doctrine of original sin had gradually been revised; thereafter he devoted many years to chronicling its changing definitions. Smith also recognized that racism thwarted the ideal of a comprehensive Christian community; his final lengthy project concentrated on religious attitudes about this aspect of American culture.[11] All these studies stemmed from a genuinely professional concern to understand the way ideas had affected historical events and were in turn shaped by their cultural circumstances.

Smith investigated theological anthropology or the intellectual history of original sin because he thought contemporary culture needed a less naive conception of human nature. And before tackling modern complacency about sinfulness, it was important to know how Protestant doctrine had changed over the course of time. Starting with Puritan affirmations as the dominant intellectual position, Smith noted how strongly it underscored guilt and depravity in human nature. The federal doctrine of original sin held that all of Adam's descendants were guilty because everyone participated in his first sin and because Adam as representative of humanity had failed to honor his covenantal obligations. Using ideas of direct and representative participation, Puritans "sought to fix a double grip" on convictions about the inability of people to reach God through their own efforts.[12] This was no lifeless theory, embalmed in the Westminster (1646) and Savoy (1658) Confessions. It remained a vital element in Calvinist preaching for over a century thereafter, and it still reflected majority opinion when the Great Awakening revivals occurred in the eighteenth century.

This early formulation attracted many who defended its accuracy regarding fallen human nature. One of the more creative protagonists was Jonathan Edwards whose venturesome metaphysics held that humankind formed one moral whole wherein all posterity shared in Adam's first sin. But Smith pointed out that Edwards made little use of federal or convenantal theory in his argument, even though he defended the doctrine of imputed guilt through direct participation. This modest shift inaugurated a long process of theological revision. As a result later Edwardseans eventually ceased believing that all of humanity had sinned in Adam, and they abandoned the notion of imputed guilt altogether. Samuel Hopkins, for instance, was a disciple who unintentionally weakened the foundation of ideas about innate depravity. Neither he nor other followers retained the metaphysical basis whereby all people were identified with Adam. Using no explanatory process to sustain their position, Smith said they simply "asserted some sort of unalterable connection between Adam's first sin and the existence of a depraved nature or sinful affection in his descendants."[13] Their arid tomes did not explain how such a state of affairs could be true. They merely reiterated that everyone was corrupt upon entering the world because of a divinely established constitution.

The stern decree of original sin attracted critics as early as Edwards's day, and their number increased thereafter. Smith singled out Englishman John Taylor for asking how imputed guilt could be reconciled with the goodness, holiness, and justice of God. Traditionalists answered that it was a natural consequence of Adam's fall from grace for all persons to be corrupt and therefore face eternal misery. Members of the clergy like Charles Chauncy of Boston also found the imputation theory to be both irrational and immoral. And to make matters worse, he thought it mocked divine justice because it depicted a God who brought children into the world destitute of virtue and then condemned them for their moral failure. Jonathan Mayhew, another liberal of the day, echoed the view that such a perspective made God unspeakably cruel. Samuel Hopkins perpetuated Edwards's conclusions while not using his argumentation, but, Smith pointed out, "the new cultural and moral climate supported Mayhew, not Hopkins." He observed that "affluent Bostonians might continue to repeat the federal doctrine of original sin on Sunday, but they felt more at home with Mayhew's conception of man on Monday."[14]

Controversies over human worth became more widespread during the early nineteenth century. In 1805 Henry Ware emerged as a leading critic of traditional orthodoxy, proving that his nascent Unitarian denomination existed primarily to sustain convictions about human goodness, not to dispute arithmetic in the Godhead. Ware articulated a popular theory of human nature that set the tone for subsequent debates. He also succeeded in focusing on the moral capacity of children as the area where Calvinists had to make their case. Within this context, Nathaniel W. Taylor modified Puritan tenets to preserve their core. People sinned, he maintained, with a regularity that made it seem inevitable, though there was no supernaturally imposed tendency toward depravity. People had the power not to sin, but they did so with distressing regularity.[15] In restating what he considered the essentials of doctrinal probity, Taylor's moderating position caused outcries from conservatives as well as liberals. He alienated those to his right by denying that Adam's posterity entered the world as sinners or that God punished them for inherited sinfulness. His viewpoint disappointed those on his left because it still found human activity sinful and divine intervention necessary for redemption. Even though Taylorism tried to preserve continuity with earlier statements about sin and salvation, its departure from traditional categories was itself part of liberalized thinking. As such it only partially helped the older position and could only temporarily hold back greater changes.

Debates about fundamental religious issues were not confined to rarefied levels inhabited by cloistered combatants; rather, they had a direct bearing on important features in American culture. Contrary opinions about human potential occasioned fights over professorships in universities. These debates figured in the establishment of several new seminaries, Andover being the first in 1808. Varying perspectives caused long and bitter controversies in Calvinist circles, especially among Congregationalists and Presbyterians. Theological differences generated stormy exchanges in tracts, journals, and books. Within Presbyterianism, tensions between old school and new school attitudes led to heresy charges that split the denomination in 1837. As revivals mushroomed in the Second Great Awakening, debates about salvation sparked factionalism in every section of the country. Religious periodicals begun at this time helped mold social and political thought for well over a century thereafter.[16] Smith reminded readers of these larger consequences to show them that ideas were not just parochial curiosities. They were packed with implications for a wider range of social activities.

By 1859 the Edwardsean version of original sin was faltering seriously, but it survived with an attenuated constituency. At that point, though, it faced what Smith called its "greatest challenge" in the form of Darwinism and new emphases on organic evolution. Findings in natural science prompted evolutionists to think of human nature as neither good nor bad, but as a neutral capacity that could gradually improve through development. Modern Christian thinkers found ways of reconciling their religious orientation with this optimistic view of human betterment: "Intellectual and moral progress became a basic presupposition of their social and religious thought," Smith wrote. The new theology attached high value to reason and accepted evolution as the method of creation. It perceived revelation in terms of a dynamic process where religious understanding moved to higher levels by means of progressive reconstructions. Theodore T. Munger, for example, regarded Scripture as a record of unfolding wisdom based on moral evolution. His theology included scant consideration of how people entered the world because he was more interested in urging them to develop the better qualities of their nature. Moral ascent was definitely possible in his view, and Christian preaching served this general tendency by pointing the way to spiritual progress.[17]

Lyman Abbott was another representative voice among late nineteenth-century liberals who abandoned the conception of inherited debility. According to his hypothesis, humankind had emerged from animal forebears, possessing at first only primitive mental and moral powers. At some indeterminate moment, people became aware that they had spiritual potential in addition to brutish tendencies. After that, one could call any yielding to lower promptings a type of sin. Such failures occurred, and biological reproduction perpetuated them, providing the occasion for further sinning. But Abbott did not emphasize the tenacity of sin in the human self because he was captivated by the idea of moral progress. His faith in spiritual improvement led him to magnify the possibility of increased goodness in people and to obscure any fundamental sinfulness in the human constitution. Not even the savagery of World War I persuaded him otherwise. Amid the fratricide of 1915 he clung to bland, reassuring platitudes: "The human race falls down occasionally," he mused, "bruises itself, and weeps some bitter tears; but picks itself up and goes on walking, and persistently in the right direction."[18]

Enthusiasm for inevitable progress was difficult to maintain in the twentieth century, however, and some Christian thinkers began to wonder if romantic notions about human goodness were hopelessly naive. Walter Rauschenbusch was one who defined sin as humanity's rebellion against God's plan for human happiness, thinking thus even before the Great War broke out. This less optimistic view allowed him to develop a theology that included not only individual revolts but also an interpersonal network of social sinfulness. Rauschenbusch remained confident that the

Social Gospel could rectify collective evil, but in the next generation, Reinhold Niebuhr was not persuaded by the hopeful esti-
mates of progressivist liberal theology. Niebuhr returned to a more
traditional emphasis on the failings of human nature, using
historical examples and contemporary observations to make his
point.[19] Like Rauschenbusch, he argued that groups were harder
to discipline with Christian ethics, but he had little faith that social
redemption was really possible.

Smith ended his study of this theme in American theology with
Niebuhr because he had come almost full circle. Most of American
intellectual church history featured a rejection of original sin as an
obstacle to natural progress and moral growth. But this ideological
trend had created utopian illusions about social betterment, and
they remained unfulfilled in contemporary experience. Smith
concluded with Niebuhr because in that towering thinker, he
found a modern voice which avoided the error of negating original
sin as part of reality. History seemed to prove that personal
sinfulness was an unpleasant but persistent fact that theologians
ignored to the detriment of society. Those living in modern times
could see from the cycle of historical experience that sin was an
integral category in concepts of salvation, and its residual presence
was indispensable to an adequate understanding of the human
situation in every epoch.

In a separate but related study, Smith concentrated on Horace
Bushnell, one of the most important figures in nineteenth-century
intellectual history. The Connecticut clergyman had been something of an enigma to his contemporaries because they had either
misunderstood or distorted his theological method. Smith took
great care to explain how Bushnell's christocentric thought included fresh insights into the intuitive aspects of religious thought and
the limited nature of theological language. Anyone willing to
apply his approach to disputes over trinity, incarnation, human
depravity, and Christ's redemptive mission "usually experienced,"
Smith promised, "an exhilirating liberation from an increasingly
scholastic orthodoxy." But Bushnell did not succeed in reconciling
the historic antagonisms between Calvinism and Arminianism,
faith and works, or fate and contingency. His mediatory example
did, however, point the way out of theological deadlock, inspiring
later thinkers to seek wisdom in comprehensiveness and spiritual
unity in inclusive affirmations.[20]

The other major task Smith set for himself was a study of racism, more particularly the ways in which religious thought had contributed to it. In his work on original sin, Smith viewed intellectual history with something of a jaundiced eye, describing modern optimism about human nature while not agreeing with it. In his examination of ideas on race relations, his interpretation reversed the pattern. He strongly disliked early racist attitudes and approved of changes that helped abolish slavery. And in decades of twentieth-century experience, he deplored those continuing defenses of injustice in a biracial society. His coverage of odious ideas portrayed them as reprehensible in their own right, and his running commentary occasionally flashed with indignation. Here, too, Smith was concerned to relate thoughts to larger cultural movements. When chronicling shifts in theological anthropology, he demonstrated their impact on religious institutions, ministerial activities, and national publications. In his analysis of ideas about black people, he also monitored their effect on practical action, depicting interaction against the backdrop of religious and social experience on this continent.

Smith set the stage for his last book with two strongly contrasting views. On one side he posited the general Christian idea that all persons are created in the image of God and as such deserve equal respect and goodwill. On the other hand, despite lip service to this general belief, Christians subscribed to ideas of Negro inferiority. Americans throughout the country, but especially in the South, abetted slavery, and after emancipation they resisted attempts to elevate freedmen to civil or political equality. These traditional patterns of white supremacy denied the egalitarianism derived from the biblical doctrine of *imago Dei*. Because they did, such perversions were the focus of Smith's historical interest. To identify the scope of his subject he declared that whenever "a person regards another race as an inferior member of the human family and seeks to deny it an equal opportunity for growth and participation in the common life, he is a racist." And going beyond definitional matters to lodge a normative judgment, Smith held racism to be evil for two reasons: "it impeaches the impartiality of God and, . . . it breeds social discord."[21] His critical review of racist ideas provided multiple examples of both observations.

To begin with, Smith surveyed attitudes regarding blacks in the American colonies. The earliest tracts and sermons on the subject showed with rare exception that New England Puritans, Catholics, and Anglicans alike condoned holding Negroes in bondage as compatible with Christian practice. Religious thinkers in all regions and theological traditions found baptism was no bar to slavery, and they argued moreover that Christian faith made for obedient servants.[22] Antislavery impulses did not begin to emerge until secular ideas in the Revolutionary era emphasized natural rights. This philosophy helped awaken the clergy to implications about freedom in their own gospel. Southern Methodists, Baptists, and Presbyterians opposed slavery for a time, but they did not exclude slaveholders from their communions and thus failed to sustain their protest. Quakers were the only group to purge their church of the practice, and even they did not eschew the spirit of racial discrimination. Acquiescent ministers consoled themselves with the thought that it was more important to save souls than to liberate people from earthly masters. As leading communions surrendered to proslavery sentiment, "antislavery in the South was thus a lost cause long before the rise of radical abolitionism above the Potomac."[23] Despite a few who refused to compromise with domestic bondage, southern emancipationism lost its vitality by the early 1800s, and the largest denominations became fatally entangled in racial servitude.

Northern clergy began criticizing the "peculiar institution" in increasing numbers after slavery finally ended in their region. Many of them held that no one could justly own another human being as a piece of property. As rational, moral, and immortal persons, so the argument went, all humans were created in the image of God. Slavery prevented people from governing themselves according to the divine laws written in the heart and recorded in God's Word. Others proclaimed slavery to be a collective sin for which the nation should repent. Using these arguments, sentiment in favor of abolition mounted in the free states. Meanwhile the southern clergy became embroiled in acrid debates to such an extent that three denominations divided over the issue by the middle of the nineteenth century.[24]

Religious thinkers in the South defended human bondage on several bases, the most important of which invoked biblical authority. The master-slave relation was explicitly sanctioned in both testaments, they said, and those who denounced slavery as sinful impugned the Word of God. Taking another line of defense, they upheld slavery as legitimate because it was adapted to the naturally inferior capacity of Negroes. Still others championed domestic bondage on the ground that it was the divinely appointed means of introducing Christianity to the African race. Variations on those themes tried to deflect criticism by contrasting the healthy condition of slaves with the miserable conditions that existed in their original homes. Apologists saw bondage as the chief means of lifting people out of the pit of barbarism. As such it was a temporary but essential step in improving the entire black race. Also, these defenders held that slavery, along with private ownership of property, operated as primary stimulants to social progress. An economy based on chattel servitude allowed white people to devote their superior talents to enterprises that would benefit culture as a whole.[25]

Abolition sentiment aroused the ire of the southern clergy, especially because its philosophy of natural rights opposed what they took to be the plain teaching of Scripture. When the Civil War broke out, church leaders were even more outspoken in defending slavery, claiming that those who attacked the practice contravened a divine institution and fought against God Himself. Prominent members of the clergy often led the way in generating secessionist enthusiasm while religious journals and major denominations heartily promoted political disunion. Their defiant apologetics insisted that God had appointed the South to preserve slavery as a means of redeeming Negroes. They also felt obliged to resist abolitionism because it replaced God's Word with an appeal to "higher law," a concept that subjected Christian faith to rationalist, atheistic assumptions. After 1860 religious influence was second to none in buttressing the struggle for southern independence. Ministers promoted morale in their parishes and sustained the Confederate cause. They often served as military chaplains while hundreds more enlisted in the ranks. Religious leaders were bent upon maintaining the white ruling class and black servitude. In their determination to perpetuate the status quo, "the South's most highly respected clergymen proclaimed the divine ordination of Negro slavery to the bitter end."[26]

Armed conflict settled the question of slavery, but racists who bent to overwhelming force did not change their fundamental convictions. Southern ministers again led the way in drawing the color line during Reconstruction, openly proclaiming the dogma of Negro inferiority and advocating racial segregation in churches. Ex-Confederate theologians also opposed postwar efforts to give blacks political and civil equality. They resisted parity even more strenuously in the area of social contacts. White religious leaders created the rationale for anti-Negro discrimination in schools and public facilities. Social equality was anathema to their thinking, and during postwar decades, they preserved the essentials of a racist creed to maintain white supremacy. Many of the old prejudices survived the war to appear again as Jim Crow legislation. Taboos remained in place so blacks could be subordinated to second-class citizenship. Added to the previous rationalizations for unequal treatment, Smith noted that "some prominent clergymen caught the Anglo-Saxon fever."[27] This new element provided one more ideological weapon with which to combat social change and to perpetuate self-serving policies based on ineradicable differences between the races.

In the early decades of the twentieth century, the southern social system made radical segregation even more inflexible. Habitual practices buttressed by laws replaced bondage as ways of keeping black people "in their place." Those who believed in Negro inferiority regarded social intermingling between blacks and whites as a species of original sin that would injure both races. So most church leaders in southern states defended separate public schools, no universal suffrage, no black testimony in courts, antimiscegenation laws, and even lynching. Preachers said those tactics represented the normal outcome of divinely implanted instincts. Smith observed that moderate clergy as well as extremists sanctioned this kind of discrimination. In the present century, major denominational leaders lost virtually all contact with their fellow Christians in black churches. Smith's concluding assessment of this lamentable segment of history contained irony spiced with justice: white theologians were themselves in bondage, "enslaved to the traditional spirit of color caste, and there was little prospect of their emancipation in the foreseeable future."[28]

Years of painstaking research went into each of Smith's histories. He based all his work on wide coverage of primary sources, and yet in each case, the finished product combined independent critical judgment with accurate reporting. Ideas about original sin and race relations were deeply embedded in American experience, and Smith's studies implied that one could not adequately understand the nation's past without knowing the thought patterns at work there. Interpreting cultural history satisfactorily depended on seeing how differing ideas about human potential and limitations affected action in society. In addition to identifying a component basic to historical explanation, Smith focused on anthropological and racial categories because he considered them important in modern life. Those themes were more than keys for unlocking bygone events; they permeated current problems and had to be taken into account if one hoped to influence present circumstances. So Smith proved himself to be an exemplary intellectual historian whose studies called attention to powerful ideas that affected the past and remained significant in his own day.

John T. McNeill

Another church historian who valued ideas for their influence on behavior was John T. McNeill. His career began with a decade of academic service in Canada and then continued from 1927 to 1944 at the University of Chicago, with a final stint until 1953 at Auburn and Union seminaries in New York. McNeill cultivated a lifelong interest in early Celtic Christianity,[29] but his better known publications defined him as a Reformation specialist with particular expertise in Calvinist thought. A closer look at his work shows involvement with a broad range of times and topics, including a recurrent focus on intellectual history. One can therefore classify him as this kind of historian, but his scholarship focused on other types of emphasis, too, proving that these historiographical categories are somewhat arbitrary and only partially accurate. McNeill blended a modicum of theological judgments with his research and produced some edifying narratives for a religious readership. He was also aware of environmental conditioning and incorporated secular causes in overall historical explanations. Some of his interpretations fit within a progressivist frame of mind while others pertained to a consensus orientation. In mixing these emphases, he always stressed the importance of religious ideas and their impact on personal experience, ecclesiastical patterns, and the larger cultural context. So one cannot characterize all of McNeill's complex interests and interpretations as fitting easily into one type of church history. For this reason his work epitomizes the multifaceted perspectives with which most modern historians have pursued their task.

When dealing with Calvinist ideas or other bodies of religious thought, McNeill did not analyze concepts for their own sake. He portrayed them rather as reflections on experience whose articulation helped direct subsequent human activity. Ideas were useful to increase spiritual resources or to nurture more creative imaginations. Theology consisted not of propositions but of insights to be tested in individual and institutional practice. From this point of view, Calvin was worth studying not as a formal theologian but simply as "a deeply religious man who possessed a genuis for orderly thinking and obeyed the impulse to write out the implications of his faith." Calvin's ideas nevertheless proved to have "notably affected the course of history, molding the beliefs and behavior of generations of mankind." Indeed, to one who surveyed the course of ideas over time, McNeill found it "remarkable" that Reformation emphases had lasted so long. Even in the twentieth century, his own "age of stress and perplexity," it was noteworthy that "Calvin's writings have been read with renewed attention and have vitally affected trends and movements in every sector of theological and Christian social thought."[30]

When McNeill launched his researches, standard outlines of Calvin's thought existed by the score, and he did not bother with adding another to the list. He discussed basic emphases found in the *Institutes* of course, but his central concern was to capture the religious spirit that motivated such lucid doctrinal instruction. In one of his more lyric descriptions, he characterized that religious impulse as

Calvin's world, from stars to insects, from archangels to infants, is the realm of God's sovereignty. A reverent awe of God breathes through all his work. God, transcendent and unapproachable in majesty and unsearchable wisdom, but also immanent in human affairs, righteous in all His ways, and merciful to undeserving men, is the commanding theme to which Calvin's mind ever reverts. The flame of worship to the eternal God is ever on the altar of his thoughts.[31]

With this initial affirmation as a guideline, McNeill then clarified how the magisterial reformer expounded divine sovereignty, human depravity, and the gift of unmerited grace. He set forth Calvin's ideas on the authority of Scripture, on the visible church as home to true preaching and valid sacraments, on discipline among the communion of saints, and on the full range of good works that spring from faith. These were not dogmas of timeless rectitude.

They were rubrics whose effectiveness could be measured by watching their impact on later religious and social constructs.

Another conception at the heart of reformist thought concerned tangible behavior, the way individuals and churches put transcendent standards into practice. Calvin wanted extensive reform in individual lives and ecclesiastical standards because he found human action sadly out of keeping with divinely established ideals. At the same time, he thought real change was possible. McNeill restated the reformer's critical-yet-optimistic attitude in less than crisp terms: "The spiritual qualities, which in the contemporary state of decline had seemingly passed out of the external and could be posited only of the unseen church, were to be given visibility again as the renovated visible society took on the character of the invisible model."[32] But then in clearer language, he pointed out how such a concept explained why Calvinists demanded rigorously monitored personal lives, rightly constituted churches, and Christian communities properly disciplined and instructed. Agents influenced by the Genevan model spread these stringent expectations through much of the continent. Calvinism was a body of dynamic ideas that affected Europe with emphatic doctrines about God and human response to Him. It sparked controversies over predestination and the Eucharist, and it insisted that governments inaugurate its version of reformed behavior in their various domains.

In addition to tracing the roots of Calvinist combativeness, McNeill tried to revise one-sided interpretations by pointing out lesser known irenic qualities in the religious system. He admitted that schism and disruption often followed in the wake of Protestant agitation, but he also argued that such results were unintended. In fact, mainstream reformers made the principle of unity a basic feature in their religious perspective. McNeill held that doctrines such as the priesthood of all believers were unitive rather than disintegrative in nature. Individual freedom led to communal obligations, not to self-serving license or indifference. The Protestant emphasis on personal initiative still "binds the individual to the group under inviolable obligations of love and service. It is a doctrine fundamentally unitive and in no sense divisive. It is a phase of communion, and the way of realizing it, while it is also a religious and ethical interpretation of everyday life and conduct."[33]

While stressing the principle of concord, McNeill acknowledged that Protestant history was nevertheless full of theological battles and institutional splinters. And he candidly described how factionalism diffused reform efforts that had stemmed originally from an ecumenical vision. But McNeill kept the ideal of union alive in his narratives, even in the most fragmented historical periods. His chronicle of events in Scotland, Canada, and the United States held out the possibility that modern Protestants might yet liberate themselves from atomism through wider fellowship in a reunited Christendom.[34]

Unlike Bainton and Hudson who saw danger in alliances between religion and culture, McNeill thought that when Christendom emerged it held some promise for improving the physical aspects of human existence. Of course the earliest forms of Christianity did no more than offer salvation from a doomed world. But this otherworldly attitude gradually changed to one where the church functioned as a beneficial leaven on social conditions. By the fourth century, a natural congruence of secular and ecclesiastical interests produced cooperative interaction. Between the years of Constantine and Theodosius I, Christians began to envision a new cultural unity wherein churches could apply spiritual values to temporal matters. Church leaders increasingly saw God's concerns as related to mundane affairs as well as to eternal ones, and their "attitude toward the social process became definitely positive and fundamentally optimistic." Instead of lamenting this altered viewpoint as Mead had, McNeill noted its potential for good: "Humanity and its government offered an inviting field . . . [and Christendom's] affirmation of God over against the world's confusion meant the validation of social and political hope and remedial effort."[35]

But gospel principles did not fully transform secular practices, and more reforms were necessary because human arrangements could never embody spiritual ideals satisfactorily. In medieval times, human life suffered again under grievous barbarities. Culture did not follow the more refined ideas of the clergy but instead was dominated by "a military aristocracy that was reckless, violent and uncouth." Nevertheless, clerical ideas were able to mitigate warfare to a degree by securing observances of the "truce of God" and the "peace of God." Despite the fact that mundane and ecclesiastical forces vied with each other to control medieval culture, McNeill found a sincere desire on both sides to improve conditions in the world around them. "Amid much deplorable wrath and suffering," he could detect encouraging signs which "bore fruit in arousing the Western mind to . . . sociological and political analysis and the quest of a better order of life."[36] Renaissance writers perpetuated the struggle between religious and secular perspectives in human affairs. Machiavelli showed how corrupt government could become if divorced from all spiritual values. Erasmus retained the higher ideal in his advice that Christian princes treat citizens equally before the law and protect the weak.

During the Reformation era, Luther and Calvin had to face political and economic issues in addition to their concern for religious renewal. Indeed, McNeill considered Protestant thought to be essentially positive in its orientation toward government and business. It anticipated "a revitalization of men and institutions through the human appropriation of divine resources."[37] And he credited Catholic reformers such as Bellarmine and Suarez with thinking of their rejuvenated faith as relevant to cultural matters, too. Early modern theorists in many confessions used the concept of divine covenant to sanction popular participation in government, drawing on natural law as well to buttress religious teachings about social responsibility. McNeill thought that, as a result of these developments, support for human liberty began to spread, even while theocratic regimes continued to flourish. And when nationalism burgeoned in modern times, Christian social ideas prevented irresponsible autonomy by reminding nations of their wider responsibilities. Prior to the emergence of completely secular theories of politics and society, the idea of Christian obligation to all of humanity stimulated politicians as well as church leaders to seek a world of international peace, welfare, and freedom.

In more recent times, religious influences on social development were not as easy to detect, although McNeill insisted that they continued to have a beneficial impact. Disagreeing with Bainton, he held there was "serious limitation" to the claim that Christianity promoted liberty in the modern world. Unlike Hudson, he did not see religious toleration and civil rights as direct results of church policy. Yet he did not dismiss religious factors as negligible. Church witness was an element to be reckoned with in struggles against unchecked mercantilism, industrial squalor, human slavery, and perennial matters of social justice. In his own day, McNeill observed that the old dichotomy between spiritual and mundane priorities had taken a new guise.

There is abroad a growing conviction that now, . . . a new and distinct era has begun. It was announced by a dazzling flash of light over the desert near Alamogordo at the dawn of a July morning in 1945. The scientific mastery of power has become potentially complete. . . . it would be a foolish pessimism to conclude that the new age will be characterized principally by dread of the destructive devices of science. It is, however, certain to be a time of rapid change, many perils, and much perplexity.[38]

But still he saw that religion had a fresh appeal to his perplexed generation. In an age dominated by technology, people could nevertheless see that secular patterns did not meet all human requirements. Questions about spiritual welfare and the need to pursue communion with God persisted, and these needs called for freedom of conscience to meet them.

But scientific materialism was not the worst problem. Of all the conditions that opposed a resurgence of Christian thought and values in contemporary life, McNeill judged fascist attitudes to be the most dangerous. Surveying the ideas of Nietzsche, Ibsen, and Spengler and watching how they were implemented in "internationally lawless governments" led by Hitler and Mussolini, he concluded that their viewpoint was "a philosophy not for men but for tigers." This beast-of-prey ideology had become popular to some extent because theological liberalism turned a blind eye to depravity in human nature. McNeill agreed with many others in calling for "a new appreciation of the old Christian sense of sin in the soul and of evil in the world" to counteract "the new barbarians." He welcomed the more realistic theologies of Karl Barth, Abraham Kuyper, and Auguste Lecerf because they placed sinfulness at the core of human experience again. Because liberal theology yielded diminishing returns, he thought Christianity should emphasize ideas that "contemplated man, the sinner, as capable of elevation to a state of grace or of sanctification and of participation in a society in which fair dealing, harmony, mutuality, charity and communion are predominant over greed and hate and violence."[39]

From McNeill's perspective, Christianity had leavened human societies with spiritual principles from the days of imperial Rome to the Third Reich. The course of Western civilization had taken unique directions because church leaders had advocated distinctive ideas regarding political theory, social welfare, education, liberty of conscience, and knowledge of the natural world. McNeill described the truly effective Christian intellectual as one not tied to particular shibboleths concerning doctrine, ritual, or polity. The genuine religious activist was "characterized by a combination of God-consciousness with an urgent sense of mission." This double orientation was "what makes him a reformer and a dangerous character to encounter on moral and political issues." The real intellectual was one who wanted "to bring to realization the will of God in human society."[40] McNeill was not a triumphalist in his historical studies of Christian ideas in action. He claimed no originality for seeing the impact of religious influences in cultural change. But he marshaled a great deal of evidence to sustain the view that Christianity helped resist absolutism, support republican government, denounce racism, and sanction the socioeconomic welfare of mankind.

CHURCH HISTORY AS HISTORY OF IDEAS

Perry Miller

Moving from intellectual history to a narrower concentration on ideas for their own sake, we find that Perry Miller excelled all others in this category. He spent his entire career, from 1931 to 1963, in the English Department at Harvard University, those years corresponding exactly to the ones H. Shelton Smith spent at Duke. Miller was interested in religious writings as works of literature. His orientation underscores the relationship between literary analysis and the inquiries that came to be called history of ideas. A few other scholars utilized this innovative perspective, too, but Miller's productivity outweighed them all.[41] His publications extended from colonial beginnings to transcendentalists in the early national period. In all these topics, Miller studied ideas as the product of earlier thought rather than the result of social circumstances. The impact of his work can hardly be overestimated; later generations still use his findings as a benchmark before trying to reinterpret a topic or period. His pioneering efforts defined New England's errand into the wilderness, the inner dynamics of Puritan thought, and the meaning of American jeremiads in terms that are still taken seriously today.[42]

When Miller decided to study Puritanism, the choice seemed a curious one in light of its generally negative image. But he hoped to counteract the popular misconceptions that stemmed from authors such as Vernon L. Parrington and James T. Adams by reading the evidence without prejudice. This emphasis on objectivity occurred before scientific ideals came under heavy criticism, and it allowed him enough leverage to give Puritan studies new respectability. Miller described himself as one who wanted simply to report events (or in this case, the expression of ideas) as they really happened. As historiography matured by accepting relativity and subjective insights, Miller's method became more sophisticated. Later self-disclosures announced an intent to "see underneath" the surface meaning of documents, to grasp the "real" issues that linked disparate sources. So Miller progressed with the times, and he capitalized on personal creativity to enhance the study of ideas in historical inquiry.

When we look back on the vast corpus of Miller's accomplishment, it is difficult to appreciate how much his perspective challenged the accepted wisdom of practicing historians. Asserting what many now take for granted, he began by laying himself "open to the charge of being so naive as to believe that the way men think has some influence upon their actions." And he further assumed that people in the seventeenth century took religion seriously. So he studied Puritan religious language "with an utter disregard of the economic and social factors." His concentration on intellectual life led to this epigram: "I have simply endeavored to demonstrate that the narrative of the Bay Colony's early history can be strung upon the thread of an idea."[43] Elsewhere Miller described his work as "a topical analysis of various leading ideas in colonial New England," an exercise that required "defining and classifying the principal concepts of the Puritan mind." Such analysis demanded an account of the origins, relationships, and significance of what early New Englanders took to be the truth. In that account he did not consider "chronology so much as structure, nor the morphology so much as the anatomy" of pertinent ideas.[44]

The only naiveté with which Miller might be charged is his claim to describe Puritan thought "in its own terms." At times he implied it was possible to grasp the meaning of Puritanism as its adherents had actually believed and articulated it. History seemed to be a mirror that could fully reproduce past events, and "in order that the texts . . . may be read for their proper meaning, it is necessary that the student divest himself as far as possible of those preconceptions which have been established only in later times, and approach the Puritans in terms of their own background."[45] This aspect of Miller's approach reflected a time when notions about impersonal observation were still in vogue.

But selectivity figured in historical investigation, too, and Miller used this subjective element to his advantage. "The history of ideas," he announced, "demands of the historian not only a fluency in the concepts themselves but an ability to get underneath them." So he endeavored to chart new waters by using two techniques: discussing primary source materials as flesh and blood realities rather than items "embalmed in a crabbed catechism." On the second, more creative level, Miller pursued the essence of Puritanism that lay behind its doctrines. He looked for vital energy that surged "inside the shell of its theology and underneath the surface coloring of its political theory." Miller was interested in more than antiquarian paraphrases of obscure texts. He wanted "to delineate the inner core of Puritan sensibility apart from the dialectic and the doctrine." Such a task required him to take systematic theology seriously because it gave Puritans symbols that dramatized their needs and satisfied their emotions. He found seventeenth-century theology expressive of something he sought in every great work of art, viz., "an urgent sense of man's predicament." At bottom he studied Puritanism because it was "yet another manifestation of a piety to which some men are probably always inclined and which in certain conjunctions appeals irresistibly to large numbers of exceptionally vigorous spirits."[46]

Piety lay at the core of Puritan life, and Miller prefaced his analysis of ideas with recognizing that fact. He thought it was necessary to understand the system's "Augustinian" roots before one could see how it utilized branches of scholasticism, humanism, and Ramist logic. Ideas stemmed from piety and then developed distinctive characteristics in areas like epistemology, natural science, anthropology, rhetoric, churches, government, and social order. Miller viewed piety as "the emotional propulsion . . . fitted to the articulated philosophy as a shaft to a spear-head." But this motivating force was only part of the whole. "Unless we consider the machinery of theory and demonstration which accompanied it," he insisted, "we can give no full account of Puritan thought and expression."[47] Faith as internal response was central; Puritan writings expressed that experience in an elaborate, meticulously worked-out body of ideas. And once articulated, ideas grounded in reason, together with arguments drawn from natural phenomena, developed a life of their own, even after religious impulses ceased to nurture them.

Miller was careful to avoid equating Puritans with John Calvin. He knew of course that they drew heavily on the Genevan Reformer, but subsequent generations of English theologians modified imported ideas enough to give them a distinctive character. They adapted the system to Anglo-Saxon culture and as a consequence, sometimes blurred its Gallic clarity. This English version of Calvinism was noteworthy, however, because it sought reasonable explanations for its beliefs. Calvin had been content with expounding the Bible, pronouncing basic doctrines without much concern about contradictions or dilemmas. The system originally put forth a God who did not need to be understood as long as adored, whose incomprehensible decrees required only obedience. But English recipients demanded more intelligibility in their religion. Seventeenth-century Calvinism took a new tack because it "needed amplification, it required concise explication, syllogistic proof, intellectual as well as spiritual focus. It needed, in short, the one thing which, at bottom, it could not admit—a rationale."[48] Pursuit of this rationale with all its widespread ramifications gave zest to studying Puritan ideas.

Convictions about divine sovereignty and human depravity were essential to any version of Calvinism, early or late. They supplied the foundation for everything built on it. Miller found little difference between continental affirmations of God's majesty and those voiced in New England. The first notable divergence occurred in dealing with human sin. Puritans confessed the Almighty to be ruler of all that existed, but they also considered human creatures guilty of their own perverse behavior. Jehovah did not mar His handiwork by creating people as sinners; their willful acts had caused reprobation, and so "the edge of the doctrine of innate depravity was made sharp on the whetstone of human responsibility." Puritan thought contained two apparently irreconcilable tenets: God's plan had not miscarried, even though subordinate creatures violated it. This complex doctrinal system avowed that man was independent enough to answer for his own actions, "even though all events, including his fall, had been predetermined and though without grace he was utterly incapable of virtue."[49] Contemporary psychological theory allowed Puritans to affirm the reality of human rebellion while not rejecting the perfection of either God's person or plan.

Calvinist thinkers drew the obvious conclusion that humanity could not save itself, enslaved as it was to sin and inadequate before a righteous God. Only an omnipotent being could cancel the effects of transgression, and impotent men could not initiate the process. God accepted or rejected persons according to an inscrutable wisdom, regenerating favored ones through grace and giving them a capacity to respond. Puritans went beyond this dictum and tried to preserve human agency in predestinarian soteriology. Drawing on ideas in faculty psychology, they argued that grace touched the soul through sense impressions. Human judgment apprehended this sensible experience the same way it discerned natural evidence. Grace thus cooperated with the human intellect instead of bypassing it. Redemption enhanced the faculties a person had before receiving grace and gave the soul additional ability to discern spiritual truths. By such tortuous reasoning, Miller claimed, Puritans materially softened the dehumanizing rigors of absolute predestination.

The spectacle of these men struggling in the coils of their doctrine, desperately striving on the one hand to maintain the subordination of humanity to God without unduly abasing human values, and on the other hand to vaunt the powers of the human intellect without losing the sense of divine transcendence, vividly recreates what might be called the central problem of the seventeenth century as it was confronted by the Puritan mind.[50]

Divine righteousness faced a hopelessly depraved humanity, and failure was the perpetual response to God's demands. Tension between these extremes stirred English thinkers to achieve what Miller called "the ultimate creation of the Puritan genius": a concept of covenant or doctrine of grace that undergirded the rest of their theological edifice. Covenantal categories were central to understanding salvation, and they conferred rational order on a universe otherwise considered whimsical and capricious. Miller regarded ideas flowing from the covenant of grace to be "the capital instance of the Puritans' deliberate effort to combine their piety with their intellectual concepts, to preserve the irrational force of revelation and yet to harmonize it with the propositions of reason and logic, of the arts and of physics."[51] Covenantal thinking also resonated against the realities of Puritan social experience, including specific economic and political standards and a particular understanding of common law.

If God were truly sovereign, able to disregard human necessity and logic, the problem facing Puritans was to establish a basis on which people could communicate with the Hidden and know what their obligations were. God Himself resolved this imponderable by providing the covenant, a contract in which divine power was limited by definite regulations. Put succinctly,

the idea of a mutual obligation . . . is fundamental to the whole thought. . . . In the covenant of grace, God . . . contracts with man as with a peer. But since the Fall man is actually unable to fulfill the law or to *do* anything on his own initiative. Therefore God demands of him now not a deed but a belief, a simple faith in Christ the mediator. And on His own side, God voluntarily undertakes, not only to save those who believe, but to supply the power of belief, to provide the grace that will make possible man's fulfilling the terms of this new and easier covenant.

The covenant recommended itself as both equitable and dependable. It did not subtract from God's absolute power or prescribe any limitations imposed by human requirements. At the same time, it assured believers of their salvation and reinforced their sense of moral obligation. Miller stressed this amalgam of Puritan ideas because he saw in it an entering wedge of reasonableness, if not of rationalism, whose tendency was "invariably in the direction of harmonizing theology with natural, comprehensible process."[52]

God spoke not in obscure utterances with confused intent but in terms of a compact that was decidedly reasonable. Miller found this concept intriguing because it acknowledged that "theoretically God is above and beyond all morality as we formulate it;" yet at the same time, "by committing Himself to the Covenant, God has sanctioned as His law not just any absurdity, but things which are in their own nature suitable, good, and fitting."[53] In the mutually binding covenantal pact, God had voluntarily agreed to observe regular, ascertainable procedures. Puritan thinkers expanded on this fundamental principle in their ideas about other categories. From divine self-limitation, they confidently affirmed the validity of human reason, the regularity of secondary natural causes, the harmony of faith and knowledge, the coincidence of enjoined and inherent human goodness, and the need for persevering moral effort.

The covenant of grace gave Puritans a sense of certitude. God was bound to fulfill His part of the agreement after initiating it with true believers. This allowed Puritans to combine arbitrary favor with free acceptance, predestined election with voluntary effort. Miller commented, "Once more we may marvel at the ingenuity of a contrivance which manages to demand what men cannot give and yet not punish them for failing, which forgives the wrong-doer and yet does not ask the law to go unsatisfied." Stating the position in a way farmers and merchants as well as university graduates could understand, Miller pointed out that the covenant

permitted man to conceive of divine grace as an opportunity to strike a bargain, to do himself a good turn, to make a sure profit, as an occasion that comes at specific moments in time through the agency of natural means, through the ministry and the plain, demonstrative sermon. Ergo, whoever does not close the deal when he has a chance cannot blame God for his own stupidity.[54]

This theory partially rehabilitated natural human ability and incorporated ethical reform as man's contractual duty. A moral code was evidence of sanctification, counterpart to faith as a sign of justification. Forgiveness as gift and holiness as duty were twin marks of the covenant.

With salvation at its core, Puritan thought expanded to consider humanity's place in nature and from there to theories of human association in church, state, and society.[55] Miller surveyed this architectonic and rang changes on the theme that dominated his analytic perspective. He found New England thinkers fascinating because they "had a particularly clear, an almost abnormally intense vision of man hemmed in between God and nature, at the mercy of malevolent forces and crushing objects." To him Puritans expressed the universal human condition, caught in circumstances beyond their control. Their system of ideas built around covenant theology was noteworthy because it defeated fear and made life secure. Puritans would not quail before a hidden God or admit an inability to influence the world around them. They "surrounded God with the integument of the Covenant" and "disciplined nature into conformity with a logical pattern of ideas."[56] Miller did not need to believe in the Puritan God or in salvation through grace in order to admire such ideas. He was intrigued by thoughts that clustered around the covenant, not for any existential value but for the vigorous way they confronted endemic dread and anguish.

The covenant served as template for social arrangements, the chief among these being proper ecclesiastical order. As regenerate persons, Puritans claimed liberty to organize churches among themselves, and they thought the Bible required all such groups to be autonomous. New England polity, generally known as Congregationalism, made each worshiping community free from intervention by bishops, synods, and neighboring churches. This "unique and distinguishing feature" set New World Puritans apart from Anglicans, other Puritans in England, and continental Calvinists. Churches were central to every phase of the salvation process because that was where grace most often touched human hearts. Puritan theologians discussed ecclesiastical structure at great length, and Miller once again registered his admiration for ideas that linked duty with freedom: "Along with a theology that conceived of man as a sinful creature who had mortally offended an almighty and irresistible sovereign, . . . the divines managed to erect a church wherein man was a responsible being, free and independent, who could not legally be compelled to submit to any exactions but those to which he consented."[57] Congregationalist polity freed churches from outside interference while its members pledged to observe internally generated standards of belief and conduct. It regularized the sometimes inconstant experiences of grace into orderly channels and then defended the autonomy of those routine forms because God had promised to work through them.

Covenantal thinking also affected government, holding that its highest priority was to protect lawful churches and to enforce a public code of ethics. The same dynamic that placed moral obligations on individual Christians also required all inhabitants of the state to observe minimal behavioral standards. One side of Puritan thought depicted the state as a theocracy. This meant that God was sovereign, and "His fiats were law and His wishes took precedence over all other considerations; the magistrates and ministers were His viceroys." In this context civil law was meant to proscribe evil as well as enjoin good. And as a theocratic state, Puritan government had "at the very beginning of its list of responsibilities, the duty of suppressing heresy, of subduing or somehow getting rid of dissenters—of being, in short, deliberately, vigorously, and consistently intolerant."[58] Mead had chafed at this uniformitarian ideal in Christendom, and Hudson labored to see in it the seeds of future liberty. Miller coolly noted that Non-Separating Congregationlists inherited and accepted the responsibility to wield unilateral power in the name of orthodoxy.

But there was room for change in Puritan political theory, and Miller located it in ancillary ideas that eventually reversed its original priorities. Alongside appeals to authority, revelation, and dogma, Puritans buttressed their conception of proper government with references to reason, logic, and the laws of nature. In thinking this way, they exhibited "the same dual tendency, the same confusion and latent contradiction," that had characterized their "attempt to reconcile piety and the intellect, spirit and reason." Puritans were satisfied with nothing less than preserving the Calvinistic sense of God's absolute sovereignty while maintaining a humanistic respect for man's dignity. The state, they argued, was created by a covenant of the people, and the scope of its powers was determined by those who agreed by compact to be ruled by its laws. Viewed in this way, magistrates were servants of the people, and Miller saw here the germ of future development. When theology declined, people used this secondary defense of politics and continued to think of the state as something created for a contractual purpose. "The divine ordinance and spirit of God, which were supposed to have presided over the political process, vanished," he pointed out, "leaving a government founded on the self-evident truths of the law of nature."[59]

But early New Englanders did not permit such polarizations to occur in their systematized thoughts about society. They held that when believers made a pact with God, they promised as part of their redemption to form a holy commonwealth in which everyone would obey divine commands. Moreover, church members would be the only citizens who could vote or hold office because only they had given proof of inward grace and visible sanctification. All inhabitants had to attend church, however, pay taxes to support the ministry, and conform to laws the saints considered necessary to their colony's sacred obligations. Miller did not waste time denouncing this "dictatorship of the righteous." He readily acknowledged that Puritans "confined the powers of legislation and election to a hand-picked minority of those who favored their own policies."[60] But in analyzing the way ideas fit into a self-contained system he was able to appreciate how an emphasis on God's arbitrary grace could proceed to gathered churches and legislated morals. Concepts of universal franchise and laissez faire among the unregenerate were unthinkable in their system.

As long as piety motivated Puritans, their attendant ideas gave meaning and purpose to everyday life. Once that basic impulse began to fade, theology took different directions, and Miller faced the task of charting New England's transformation from colony to province. In this phase of his analysis, he noted cultural factors that encouraged change, but Miller still spent most of his pages describing new ideas for their own sake. Puritans entered the eighteenth century confident that their theological concepts provided answers to every contingency. "But the one thing they had not foreseen, nor could their compendia possibly have foreseen," he observed, "was that experience in the New World might pose problems . . . which appeared to have no rationale whatsoever."[61] Among those unsettling events was increased economic success in which acquisitiveness threatened to supplant concern for salvation among the saints. Another was a series of attempts to overturn the ecclesiastical and social elitism that was embedded in the New England way. To make matters worse, there were also unexpected difficulties in perpetuating conversions and adequate support for churches among the Puritans' descendants.

New Englanders who became absorbed in business and politics were less willing to endorse the theological and social covenants they had inherited. General prosperity seemed to ease the cares which earlier Puritans had felt about their destiny. The social structure refused to stay fixed, and "pious industry wrecked the city on a hill, in which it had been assumed men would remain forever in the stations to which they were born." Worse than that, apparently few baptized children of Puritan communicants cared about progressing to full church membership when they came of age. So many ministers supported the Half-Way Covenant, a compromise that lowered admission standards by offering baptism to third-generation Puritans. For Miller, an important intellectual era was coming to a close because saints in later New England could not sustain the thought patterns bequeathed to them. Most distressing of all, the English clergy began advocating toleration of religious differences. This contrasted starkly with local enforcement of rigid standards for faith and practice. Congregational leaders railed against all these threats with litanies of faultfinding and calls for repentance. In this manner the jeremiad emerged as a ubiquitous vehicle for haranguing public shortcomings. And yet by turning in on itself to protect the status quo, "New England became not the vanguard of Protestantism, but an isolated remnant." New ideas and circumstances called for flexible adjustment. When the beleaguered Puritan commonwealth remained "faithful to its radical dedication," it became not a vigorous society but "a stronghold of reaction."[62]

The clergy produced sermons and religious treatises at an undiminished rate in the eighteenth century, but there was little creative theology in the doctrine they served up for popular consumption. Miller commented on how derivative Puritan discourse became and noted that its topics narrowed to a shallow range of immediate concerns. "The vast inclusive framework of the New England mind, spread out in architectonic perfection, . . . disintegrated speedily after 1690, and by 1730 was virtually dead." He found few writers of the period other than Solomon Stoddard who put forth any venturesome ideas. By contrast, he thought that Samuel Willard's immense tome simply codified doctrine which had accumulated, and atrophied, since 1630. Most clergy were busy with what Miller called "incessantly calling the people to reformation and thundering at the lassitude of the baptized." It seemed that ideas were not synchronized with the times, and heedless Puritans continued to invoke an outdated metaphysics. Miller's final assessment was that covenant theology became passé, "not only because it was incompatible with . . . a Newtonian universe, but because it had become unendurably dull."[63]

But taking a much longer view, Miller judged later Puritan ideas to be part of a transitional phase rather than symptoms of utter collapse. He described the eighteenth-century terrain as "a parched land crying for deliverance from the hold of ideas that had served their purpose and died." But even though he said the times introduced "a complex of tensions and anxieties," compounded by "an intricate system of interacting stresses and strains," he knew that a monumental intellect emerged to rejuvenate Calvinism.[64]

Jonathan Edwards introduced significant new developments in the history of ideas, and (as with previous mental giants) Miller found him interesting because he was "one of those pure artists through whom the deepest urgencies of their age and their country become articulate." Edwards was intriguing, too, because he returned to the fundamental issues that had engrossed early Puritans. Miller saw Edwards as augmenting God's sovereignty while rejecting human dignity, that conceptual counterbalance which earlier thinkers had labored so hard to maintain. This controversial interpretation of the Northampton clergyman held that he "came to feel that rationalism and ethics had stifled the doctrine of God's sovereignty and dethroned the doctrine of grace, [so] he threw over the whole covenant scheme, repudiated the conception of transmission of sin by judicial imputation, declared God unfettered by any agreement or obligation, made grace irresistible, and annihilated the natural ability of man."[65] Regardless of how accurate Miller was regarding Edwards's use of the covenant, he recognized that Calvinistic Protestantism received a strong restorative impetus from this latter-day Puritan and that his ideas influenced generations of Americans for quite some time thereafter.

Of course Miller's interest in American ideas extended to many fields beyond Puritanism. His oeuvre exhibits a great variety of literary analyses and historical studies. No single professional definition is broad enough to do him justice, but his detailed work with Puritans justifies our considering him a church historian of high caliber. And his pioneering ventures into the history of ideas adds even greater dimension to his labors as church historian.

Herbert W. Schneider

Herbert W. Schneider was another scholar interested in the history of ideas. His career in the Philosophy Department of New York's Columbia University lasted from 1918 to 1957, forming a rough equivalent to those of Smith, McNeill, and Miller. In several publications, he touched on ideas that Miller treated in greater detail, but Schneider preferred to depict them with broader strokes on a larger canvas. This more generalized outlook on American ideas was part of his comprehensive concerns that included political philosophy, morality in public life, and the various ways religious values were expressed in cultures around the world.[66]

Schneider based his perspective on the relativism that was basic to modern historical understanding. Ideas had some intrinsic value, but he found them worth studying only when they applied to specific situations. He recognized that attitudes about the past changed over time and produced divergent interpretations. Those who investigated earlier epochs were "compelled to interpret a more or less alien past by the categories of the present." This modern outlook no longer expected to find a single standard for truth or significance. Schneider's voice bespoke the new age in saying, "the final history of anything cannot be written." He knew all his work had limited value because "whatever outline history may have at present will sooner or later be lost in favor of new outlines, for it is the ever-changing present and not the past that gives form to history."[67]

At first glance it appears that Schneider did not consider Puritan thought worth much attention. The New England tradition had all but disappeared, he observed, and new categories drawn from different intellectual languages had replaced it. A sense of irreversible transition led him to declare that "our grand-parents are aliens in our country and we in theirs." But students might benefit from exploring strange terrain, glimpsing bygone phenomena in the same manner as when they "occasionally visit the monuments and tombs of a buried antiquity."[68] Aside from their curiosity value, ideas could also highlight earlier mistakes. When previous thought patterns had been inept, historians could mark them as errors henceforth to be avoided. In Schneider's judgment, one such wasted effort was the body of religious thought that followed Jonathan Edwards. He deemed it "one of the most intricate and pathetic exhibitions of theological reasoning which the history of Western thought affords." Mincing no words, he found that

the dialectic involved is so replete with apparently meaningless technical distinctions, and the literature of the movement is so controversial in spirit, that the few theologians who have taken the pains to pick their way through this desert have merely succeeded in convincing others that there are no signs of life in it. And modern Protestants are so thankful to be rid of the Puritan incubus that they point to these post-Edwardeans as the death agony of a monstrous theology which should never have been born.[69]

This ruthless summation underscores both the relativism and the progressivist spirit that operate so widely in modern historiography.

Schneider derived lessons of another sort by distilling what he called illustrations of universal themes from historical data. He noted for instance that, whenever people saw themselves as sinful, their self-reliance failed, and they fell back on piety for consolation. Schneider differed with Miller on the importance of piety in early New England, holding that Puritan humility was an example of human doubt and timidity. The other side to this recurrent pattern was that, when descendants became comfortable with privilege, their piety faded, and they externalized customary morals, polity, and creed into rigid laws.[70] Schneider hoped that his abstracts of historical experience would help present-day readers cope with contemporary problems. History for him was an aid to understanding how previous ideas had emerged and why people who used them found them so valuable. But the past was not binding, and one need not adopt earlier systems in their entirety. "These lives were not ours," he insisted, "and nothing is less enlightening than to attempt to estimate the ideas of other men and ages as though they were made for us." So Schneider concerned himself more with the facts of prior thought than with its truth. He considered Puritan theology to be hopelessly antiquated, but the old system was still worth studying. Careful analysis had merit because even though the form was dead, "the issues and motives which dominated the struggle are still alive." In sum, he said the historian's task was to serve as "a kindly, clinical observer," trying to glean something useful from the "perennial interplay between moral ideals and dialectical justification, between faith and reason."[71]

Giving Puritan thought its due, Schneider covered all the major emphases on divine sovereignty, human sin, predestined election, and covenants of grace for individuals, churches, and the public realm. His succinct expositions were always models of fair representation.[72] In addition to appreciating ideas for their content, he also gauged their practical application. After expounding the ideal of a community of saints, for instance, he then went on to see whether that concept actually worked in concrete situations. It did not, and Schneider was not surprised. He thought any social program based on religious authority was bound to collapse because human imperfection could not bear the weight of such uncompromising standards. The weight was so heavy, "no one can live long in a Holy Commonwealth without becoming sensitive, irritable, losing his sense of values and ultimately his balance." Slight offenses became disproportionately large because the saints viewed them as sins against Almighty God. Dissenters in church and state were charged with blasphemy, innovators with heresy. As a result Schneider noted that theological factionalism "spread like infectious fevers" through a social fabric that expected nothing but docile conformity. But attempts to enforce orthodoxy could not repress the tensions between practical experience and theological absolutes. The inevitable outcome was that "the Holy Commonwealth was literally exploded by the force of its own religious passion."[73]

Puritanism eventually succumbed to spiritual atrophy, an element more telling in its decline than factionalism. Schneider did not hazard a guess as to why personal zeal decayed, but he was careful to monitor this transformation of a people "from the elect of the Kingdom of God into the elite of New England." In his view the concept of a holy commonwealth never achieved reality. It was only the ideology of a small minority "surrounded by . . . unregenerates over whom [it] attempted to tyrannize." Such power contained the seeds of corruption, and belief in God's sovereignty declined until it "ceased to be the spontaneous product of . . . pious imagination and became the instrument of oppression in the hands of an ecclesiastical oligarchy." Some of the clergy tried to keep their social order aligned with its impossibly high ideals. The Mathers, for example, were particularly notable for vain efforts to awaken in others a sense of sin that was quite lacking in themselves. But by the 1720s, Increase and Cotton Mather clung to an ideology that was past its prime. Society had, Schneider declared, simply moved beyond the theocratic blueprint they espoused. Their dated ideas made them "sour old men" who amused the public by heaping invective on every departure from the old ways. As an observer, Schneider's epitaph might have been clinical, but it was scarcely kind: "with them died the last and most pompous incarnations of the political theocracy."[74]

Agreeing with his contemporary Perry Miller, Schneider prized the creative and dynamic innovations which Jonathan Edwards set forth. He found this rejuvenated version of Calvinism especially attractive because it concentrated on inner experience, precisely the area that had declined so markedly since the early days. Edwards thus spoke for latter-day Puritans who took traditional doctrine seriously. He and others concerned about individual spiritual renewal articulated a rationale for the Great Awakening that was couched in the old theological categories. But Edwards's triumph notwithstanding, Schneider once again stressed the inevitability of intellectual transition. The Awakening was fleeting, he observed, because it was psychologically impossible for such emotional tension to exist for very long. And in the aftermath of revivals, Puritan ideas sank to an even lower status. "New England, instead of making religion the business of life, gladly returned to the life of business," Schneider noted, "and has ever since kept itself comparatively aloof from great awakenings."[75] Later generations not only failed to see the power and beauty of Edwards's intellectual effort, they grew more detached and cautious about all religious affections.

The final irony in Schneider's chronicle of Puritan thought was not that ideas became outmoded but that their impulse survived under different auspices. As a case in point, expressions of human dependence on an omnipotent deity became virtually irrelevant to later New England experience. But preachers continued to intone the stock phrases, and laypersons to hear them, not because anyone affirmed the idea any longer but because they cherished familiar emphases. Schneider's musings on universal themes in history reached the level of aphorism: "Beliefs seldom become doubts; they become ritual." Explaining how ideas permeate culture, he said, "They become intrinsic parts of the social heritage, themes of public celebration. Thus the sense of sin became a genteel tradition, cherished in the imagination long after it had been surrendered in practice." Even more epigrammatically, "the Puritan insistence on human depravity became the compensatory justification of Yankee moral complacency." In light of repeated historical experience, thought patterns did not disappear but rather took new shape. Puritan benevolence had found its object in the excellence of God, for instance, but two centuries later benevolence itself had become deified. And over the same course of generations, the God who had been sovereign changed into a repulican, devoted like his people to human happiness.[76]

Schneider found the historical study of ideas useful for meeting present-day intellectual problems. He thought acquaintance with previous ideas and recurrent themes could give his contemporaries both balance and perspective for meeting new challenges. Like Miller, Schneider contributed to church history as an exercise in the history of ideas. But he also resembled Smith and McNeill by viewing ideas as important causes in human events. These two approaches about the importance of past thought—"intellectual history" and "history of ideas"—cannot be separated into neat compartments, as the work of these four scholars demonstrates. But their efforts provide stimulating variations on a basic conviction: ideas, including religious ones, are an essential component in adequate historical explanation.

✒6
Syntheses and New Explorations

By midcentury a great deal of monographic research in religious history had accumulated. Much of this material focused on either the institutional, social, or intellectual aspects of church life. Other treatises defied easy classification because they cross-matched categories in unique ways. Studies from all these perspectives became so numerous, correlating them posed a formidable challenge. Several scholars tried their hand at integrating the best data and insights into comprehensive narratives. A half dozen such efforts appeared within a twelve-year period. Between 1960 and 1972, these overviews synthesized much of what had been accomplished during the previous two generations of historical scholarship. It was clear from these summaries that church history, at least the subsection dealing with American topics, had reached a plateau. It was also clear that much of the story had been left out, and since 1970 the most innovative students have investigated new topics to rectify that imbalance.

THE CONTRIBUTIONS OF CLIFTON E. OLMSTEAD

Clifton E. Olmstead made the first modern attempt at synthesizing accumulated information about religion in America. When his overview appeared in 1960, it was the first serious rival to William W. Sweet's narrative which had been composed three decades earlier. Olmstead's book signaled the end of Sweet's dominance in American church history. It put forth a complex interpretive pattern and included a more comprehensive view of pertinent data. Olmstead said he did this because he wanted "to set the story of American religion within the broad sweep of political, economic, and intellectual history." He also stated in a prologue that he would give as much attention to theology as he would to social action. Apparently he thought contemporary readers were as interested in intellectual history as they were in the impact of religion on American culture. And he thought both ideas and action were best understood within "the vast interplay of forces which have acted upon and through ecclesiastical institutions."[1]

A focus on institutions was characteristic of Olmstead's investigative technique, and it proved to be restrictive. Another limitation derived from his chronological priorities: twenty chapters totaling 400 pages were devoted to colonial and early national periods; only nine chapters totaling 175 pages covered post–Civil War topics. Events following World War I received notice in a mere seventy-nine pages. Given that allocation, however, the author provided a wealth of information about denominational growth, missions, interchurch agencies, and new religious expressions. In an effort to combine diverse materials, Olmstead simply lumped different perspectives together. Some of his references to the frontier carried Turner/Sweet overtones, while others echoed progressivist motifs that emphasized improvement through conflict. At times his institutional history stressed the impact of religion on society; at other times it demonstrated how cultural conditions had influenced the shape and content of religion in America. This first modern effort to write an overall American religious history included all the interpretive viewpoints to date; it did not, however, integrate them into a coordinated account.

Despite his announced intention of highlighting theology as much as other aspects of religion, Olmstead's preference for tangible organizations made ideas secondary in his church history. He dealt with religious thought at some important junctures—the 1740s, 1830s, and 1890s—but his discussion followed a history-of-ideas format instead of an intellectual-history format. He did not link ideas with other facets of this country's church life or general culture. When mentioning ideas Olmstead sometimes resembled consensus history, alluding to shared values in national development. But he did not use those general references as unifying themes, and he always reverted to specific denominations in order to let them speak independently on given topics. His major contribution to historiographical synthesis, then, lay in recognizing the plurality of American religious institutions more clearly than previous authors. And in expressing this, he strove to be comprehensive, going beyond mainstream Protestants, Catholics, and Jews to cover denominational splinter groups including such special orientations as Mormons, Christian Scientists, and Jehovah's Witnesses. But even here all he did was to list them as catalogue items instead of blending data into a single narrative context.

As one greatly interested in colonial beginnings, Olmstead gave the Puritans ample room in his text. At times he wrote admiringly of their zeal and doctrine, saying that they imported new principles such as freedom of conscience based on Scripture, rule by law, and government by consent of the governed. "When broadened and liberalized," he predicted, "these ideas would exercise a profound influence on the shaping of American democratic thought." But on the other hand, he was not blind to less attractive practices in Puritanism. Religious liberty and individual freedom were not, in all candor, part of the Puritan vocabulary. "Dissenters of any kind," he remarked wryly, "were as welcome as a northeaster." Neither did racial parity rank high among them. Mincing no words, Olmstead said that the average New Englander "regarded the aborigines as objects to be pitied, more frequently despised . . . as ignorant, shiftless, depraved savages." Furthermore, Puritans were not opposed to slavery. Even clergy members owned black slaves and found the institution consistent with the Bible. In Olmstead's judgment, slaveholding waned in northern regions only when it became economically unfeasible; it did not decline because of religious or moral reasons.[2]

Revivalism was another facet that loomed large in American experience, and Olmstead recognized its pervasive importance. But he did not regard evangelicalism as an unalloyed boon. Awakenings helped mold a theology for the American environment, he acknowledged, nurturing humanitarian impulses and aiding ecumenism by diluting denominational peculiarities. They stimulated an increase of faith after periods of spiritual decline and appreciably expanded church membership. He noted, too, that after experiencing personal salvation in revivals, people usually embraced a program of social reform. However, Olmstead was apprehensive about the lack of balance in revivals of his own day. His judgment of a leader in the latest Awakening remained tentative and noncommital:

[Billy] Graham presented his listeners with a compelling but simplified pietistic Gospel which emphasized individual salvation through decision and public confession of one's faith in Christ. The Christian life was conceived largely in terms of daily Bible reading and prayer, winning other souls to Christ, and adherence to the well-established pietistic virtues. There was little if any evidence of social discernment and certainly no effort was made to relate the Gospel to the highly complex problems of contemporary society. On the whole the Graham revivals . . . constituted a pep rally for that segment of the population which tended most to be identified with formal religion. To what extent the revivals stimulated a continuing Christian experience is difficult to say.[3]

Olmstead saw evangelism as a tangible and perennial force in American religion, but unless personal salvation led to efforts to reform society, its effectiveness was blunted.

Olmstead's concern about the general quality of religious life became increasingly apparent as he discussed more recent times. There he couched critical observations and accurate analysis in his subtle wit, providing some of the most striking phrases in the book. He depicted, for instance, the representative churchgoer after the Civil War as one for whom religion was a matter of respectability: "He might be careless in his orthodoxy, slovenly in his worship, and indifferent in his attitude toward social ills; but he was anxious not to be denied a reputation for piety, charity, and unimpeachable conduct. . . . Orthodoxy was his profession; activism was his life. If the two elements suffered from incompatibility this did not concern him, for logic was not his forte." Olmstead frequently referred to social progress in terms of building the Kingdom of God, and he saw the average church member as one who wished to hasten its realization. "He crusaded against sin, blissfully neglecting the complex and demonic forces which contributed to public corruption and social upheaval. He supported the church as a cause worthy of his backing and regarded his Sunday attendance as being as much a favor to his pastor as a benefit to his soul."[4]

By his own day, churches had acquired more members and displayed less spiritual leadership than ever before. Theology had atrophied in clashes with modern science. Olmstead wrote that liberal adjustments had diluted doctrine to the point where "God was conceived as being so immanent that He became a naturalized American, while religion became a social activity, a form of cultural amusement." Ecclesiastical institutions reduced their ideals to complacent humanitarianism and expended their energy on collecting pennies for missions, settlement houses, and Thanksgiving baskets. "It was all most commendable," he quipped, "none were more aware of that fact than the donors."[5]

There were, however, a few encouraging signs in recent events. The Great Depression had deflated the more naive aspects of trust in human perfectibility. Suffering on a national scale had caused religious thinkers to reassess progress in light of the persistence of sin. After a spate of hot and cold wars, Olmstead found that people were once again serious about eternal truths. "Never before had the relativities of life seemed so complete, certitude so uncertain, disaster so imminent. Everywhere the cry went out for security. . . ." Olmstead found religion in general without promise and had no hope for a nondescript faith based on sentimentalities. But he discerned glimmers of hope among those who blamed America's religious malaise on having made temporal expedients into absolutes, like another golden calf. He agreed with this vague definition of secularization and criticized it in eloquent terms. At the end of his magnificently detailed narrative of institutions, he held out for something intangible that lay beyond them. Thus he aligned himself with those who "stress the truth that above the relativities of history abides the living God. . . . They cannot identify America with the Kingdom of God, but they trust that in spite of human fallibility they can work for its coming. . . . in loyal devotion to its appearing they make ready for the next brave step into the unknown."[6]

SMITH, HANDY, AND LOETSCHER'S OVERVIEW

The first half of a two-volume classic edited by H. Shelton Smith, Robert T. Handy, and Lefferts A. Loetscher appeared the same year Olmstead's book was published. These three outstanding church historians produced a magisterial overview that correlated the best of recent scholarship in judicious interpretive essays. That work and its companion volume appearing in 1963 also supplied a total of 187 representative documents, giving students a better feel for primary source materials. This combination of expository writing and illustrative documents proved how richly diverse religion had been in this country from the beginning. Its author-editors shared the conviction that all the "sharp crosscur-rents" of religious activity had to be "explored in their full dimen-sions" before students could "understand the moral and religious phenomena of modern American culture." By summarizing mono-graphic research up to that point, they also hoped that their work might "stimulate others to undertake still further exploration in the history of American Christianity."[7]

Editorial decisions about covering time periods and various topics were judicious and evenhanded. Beginning with English colonization in 1607, but acknowledging prior Spanish and French activities, the documentation proceeded in equitable distribution to the 1960s. In a departure from convention, the editors did not follow standard periods of American history that were based on wars or political epochs. Except for noting the Civil War as a traumatic spiritual experience, they constructed a new time frame-work that drew its rationale from religious developments alone. This new chronology did not revolutionize American church histo-ry, but the editors' independent thinking indicated how seriously they thought ecclesiastical data need not conform to secular cate-gories. These volumes featured two main emphases: religious thought and the impact of church activities on wider aspects of American culture. The editors did not stress consensus history, but continual references to "churchly traditions" apprised readers of values that persisted over many generations. Neither did the editors view materials with an exalted, theologically based concep-tion of their subject. Still, constant attention to internal develop-ments showed they understood churches to have functions beyond those of social institutions.

A concern for church traditions allowed the editors to touch upon interdenominational themes as well as those pertinent to single denominations. But as the title *American Christianity* indi-cates, neither volume ventured beyond Christian topics. Coverage was limited to mainstream churches with their many dissenting bodies and minority viewpoints. This overarching representation of Christianity in American life recognized a predominance of Protestant voices in past centuries while noting the longevity of Catholic presence alongside them. The editors provided for a wide range of expressions to exhibit the pluralistic character of religion in this country. Of course the two volumes did not depict American Christianity as a homogenized entity, but they stopped short of displaying all the ethnic, regional, and theological variegation that it actually contained. While demonstrating the complexity of various confessions, liturgies, and polities, they nevertheless featured documents that portrayed religion as essentially a white, male province.

The critical narrative in these volumes deliberately incorporated a wide range of viewpoints in historical explanation. Each editor was responsible for major sections of the project, and all of their interpretive essays were notably comprehensive and free of special pleading. They recognized several factors in the struggle for religious freedom, for example, and they did not grant decisive influence to any one of them. No simple explanation of such a significant development was adequate. The authors mentioned geographical, economic, political, and philosophical aspects of the situation in addition to theological ones as pertinent to increased religious freedom. They included practical considerations such as economic necessity and political compromise plus Enlightenment ideals and principles drawn from Reformation heritages.[8] Reading these volumes on any given topic made students aware of how complex historical realities had been and how multifaceted an adequate explanation of them had to be.

Revivalism had become a perennial American phenomenon by the early 1700s, and the editors of these volumes duly noted its importance. Here, too, they treated this country's inclination toward evangelism within a complex interpretive pattern. More interested in effects than causes, they pointed out that revivals acquired numerous converts for churches and democratized Christianity by making it a religion of the common people. They noted also that inner religious experience often quickened wider moral concerns and stimulated philanthropic programs in society. When theology shifted to Arminian convictions in the nineteenth century, churches amenable to emotional religion grew, while those which prized creedal precision failed to keep pace. Revivals continued to support programs of missionary outreach and benevolent action in communities at large. Through all these considerations, the authors discussed American revivalism in the context of transatlantic, especially British, influences, humanitarian concerns stemming from the Enlightenment, increased theological compatibility among Protestant denominations, and the generally optimistic expectancy with which Americans regarded their place in God's plan of salvation.[9] No single explanation could account for revivalism as a whole. Taken together, they helped students see that a realistic grasp of church history had to be textured with many nuances.

As one might suspect in an undertaking where Smith had a hand, theology was integrated with other aspects of religious life in every historical period. These volumes displayed religious ideas in all their dynamic intricacy and motivating power. The authors provided a balanced account of both steadfast traditions and those which altered markedly under changing cultural conditions. They were especially judicious in their treatment of recent intellectual developments, showing no dismay at liberal responses to modern questions, new platforms based on social conscience, or radical speculations that departed noticeably from traditional concepts. Instead of despairing over such innovations, the authors pointed to neoorthodoxy as an encouraging return to Christian values that would not compromise with secular trends. They also suggested that Adventist-Holiness thought had emerged in the twentieth century to become a third force alongside Protestant doctrine and the outlook preserved in Eastern Orthodox–Roman Catholic communions.[10] This appreciative chronicling of rich theological activity, blended with sophisticated understanding of churches as a force in society, provided a synopsis of lasting scholarly importance. It portrayed Christianity as an identifiable historical dimension in the American experience, interacting at all times and places with other aspects of national life.

WINTHROP S. HUDSON'S SYNTHESIS

Two years later Winthrop S. Hudson added another text to the list. In keeping with his interest in consensus values, he offered this book with the view that "there is knowledge to be gained and lessons to be learned from the American past." This general overview included denominational history to some degree, but it often synthesized the American experience in an attempt to "depict the religious life of the American people in interaction with other dimensions of their experience, and to depict the unity American religious life exhibits as well as its particularities."[11] In this depiction, he did not overemphasize any special era or topic; balanced chronology matched inclusive subject matter in equitable correlation.

Using the consensus theme, Hudson had a unique way of both organizing materials and interpreting them. When treating colonial society, for instance, he could admit that several European cultures had influenced it and still call the result "limited pluralism." Several church traditions had admittedly coexisted there, but he thought that such "diversity was primarily ecclesiastical, a variety of forms within the context of a common religious faith." Viewed thusly, early American life was "largely homogenous, sharing common assumptions and common patterns of behavior."[12]

In the nineteenth century, religious freedom permitted a great deal of denominational fission, and immigration added ethnic differentiation to the mix. Regional and racial divisions placed further strains on an imperiled Protestant homogeneity. Yet Hudson did not view American culture as exhibiting "rampant pluralism" because "at a deeper level of the American experience there remained an underlying unity." He pursued the same theme with twentieth-century materials, too, going beyond the churches to point out "a national faith—a belief in providence and the mission of America" that was affirmed by Protestants, Catholics, and Jews alike. Black Americans also subscribed to this faith, despite slavery and then segregation. "Though sorely tested, often perverted, and increasingly diluted, this national faith retained sufficient health . . . for Martin Luther King to be able to touch the conscience of much of the nation by reminding Americans of their common national faith."[13]

Seeking an even larger unity, Hudson viewed American experience as the western segment of a transatlantic community. Indeed, he held that life on this continent could be properly understood "only as an integral part of a larger European society." Hudson regarded the Atlantic as the mare nostrum of European colonizers, with America constituting half of its linked symmetry. "In almost every respect, we have been and are part of Europe; and this is true in religion as it is in literature, law, philosophy, art, or science."[14] This was not an original observation, but it served as a valuable corrective to overblown ideas about America's unique importance that often lurked in the consensus perspective.

Intercontinental awareness shed new light on revivalism, an aspect of church history which many considered peculiarly American. Hudson pointed out that such phenomena occurred not only here but in England, Scotland, and Wales. Spiritual awakenings coincided with pietist movements in other parts of Europe, too, and they should be viewed as a whole. But this commonality notwithstanding, revivals provided an important common denominator for most forms of American Christianity. Churches of all denominations had been affected by religious fervor; new preaching dominated pulpits and altered the structure of public worship. Revival experience became the most widely accepted way of introducing people to the Christian life, and "the ultimate consequence was to mold the various denominations into a common pattern, to subordinate differences, and to make possible wide-ranging cooperative endeavors." Hudson termed this consensus of values and behavior a "functional catholicity," and he saw voluntary associations for moral reform as its most practical outlet. Evangelical Protestants banded together to support missions, education, and a host of other charitable causes. Revivals released fervor; voluntary associations channeled the energy. So "Protestant churches jointly addressed themselves to the task of spreading churches and schools across a continent while devoting themselves, at the same time, to reforming the nation."[15]

In Hudson's view the tide of evangelical reform crested in the latter half of the nineteenth century. It ebbed after that because multiple challenges from science, immigration, urbanization, and industrialization challenged traditional piety and demanded changes. As a result Americans lost much of their previously concentrated purpose. By the beginning of this century, citizens supported many progressivist reforms with revivalist ardor. But in Hudson's estimation "progressivism, like the social gospel, was almost exclusively a manifestation of middle-class idealism [with] no consistent philosophy and . . . a miscellaneous collection of reforms."[16] Diffused as they might be, those efforts at reform could marshal popular forces enough to support drives for women's suffrage and Prohibition. Those two causes were the last ones, though, that succeeded in uniting American religious zeal with a concern for broader social issues.

New problems and contemporary disarray did not deter Hudson from treating American religious history from a consensus viewpoint. Neither did increased pluralism. He knew that the massive waves of immigration had sharply modified the nation's religious configuration. By 1920 Catholicism had reduced Protestant numerical predominance considerably, while large increases in Jewish and Eastern Orthodox populations had created other significant communities to be reckoned with. In addition to that, "marked Lutheran growth, the emergence of new 'disaffected' Protestant groups, and the growing strength of Negro churches had [also] altered the Protestant spectrum." Hudson called the decades between the world wars ones of "drift and indecision," a period of "disarray and disaffection." Religious groups were unsure of their proper orientation and vocation. Despite those uncertain times, Protestant revivals in the 1950s and Catholic rejuvenation after Vatican II hinted at a renewed sense of purpose. Jewish congregations acquired a stronger identity because of Israel's struggles in the 1960s. Eastern Orthodoxy and Negro churches also found strength in rededication to basic traditions and the unfinished agenda of social justice.[17]

One of the best features of Hudson's book is that he continually revised it, staying abreast of the latest research and contemporary events. Now in its fourth edition, it has integrated current religious movements and recent trends of historical investigation. But to end at the beginning, it is worth noting that an added chapter in his latest version is entitled "New Pluralism and the Search for a New Consensus."

EDWIN S. GAUSTAD'S GENERAL HISTORY

In 1966 Edwin S. Gaustad added another title to the list of general histories. In it he described the roles which religion had played in American life, preferring to follow the contours of national history instead of charting the rise and progress of ecclesiastical bodies. Gaustad chose that larger context because he was convinced that religious influences had contributed significantly to American culture. Careful inquiry into past religious activity was as vital and legitimate a form of historical investigation as any other. Indeed, he argued that "religious history, while admittedly complex and controversial, cannot be ignored without doing violence to the integrity of the American experience." Gaustad enhanced interest in his book by including a rich display of illustrations. More than 300 plates graced the text. Another winning feature was the incorporation of 224 excerpts from original sources. This documentation preserved "the temper and testimony of earlier witnesses" in their native vigor and allowed readers to see how varied the American religious experience had actually been.[18]

As far as method was concerned, Gaustad addressed that question in a separate publication the same year, articulating there the standards that had become operative in modern church history. The study of religion, he confirmed, had "cast off its beleaguered defensiveness and has come to terms more openly with the contemporary, secularized, pluralistic society." Church historians now concentrated on institutional, social, and intellectual themes without special pleading and utilized them through "the scholarly, candid, open examination of ecclesiastical traditions." The best students of religious groups and ideas could place their findings alongside those from other investigations in hopes of achieving a shared result: "sound and analytic history superseding parochial or defensive polemic."[19] Gaustad admitted that the diversity of definitions and interpretive insights in modern scholarship had resulted in "a fuzzier, uncertain philosophy of history." But he saw strength in variety and welcomed "a broadening of both the scope of the investigation and the ranks of the investigators."[20]

In constructing his comprehensive text, Gaustad combined documents and pictures creatively with the narrative. In apportioning time periods and topics, half the book was devoted to a developmental account and half to descriptive analysis. Historical coverage began with colonization, "the discovery and settlement of a continent," while the rest succinctly recounted "the birth and growth of a nation." The final 237 pages attempted something genuinely new: a synthetic discussion of worship and religious values found among the American people at large. This overview described how citizens drew on common "aims and aspirations" while basing their conduct on durable reference points such as Scripture, theology, liturgies, evangelism, education, and philanthropy. They found application in a host of causes aimed at social justice, welfare support, peace and war, and a search for better understanding of human rights in a complex world community. It constituted probably the most original effort since the 1890s to categorize American religion in a fresh way.[21]

On the historical side, Gaustad condensed the results of earlier monographic researches with workmanlike dispatch. He noted Puritan restrictions on toleration, for instance, and rang all the changes on revivals, perfectionism, millennialism, and the resultant concerns for social reform. He wrote appreciatively about achievements in religious freedom while admitting that Protestant cultural dominance had an ugly side to it when "nativism fed on fears, biases, and aspirations that marched under the banner of religion."[22] Touching intellectual history, he included it in a curiously reverse manner, pointing out what people thought only by showing what they did. Not content with describing ideas found in formal argumentation, he showed what belief systems meant by describing how adherents lived by them.

In a survey of more recent times, Gaustad remained balanced and undismayed. He noted that some religious institutions had faltered since World War II, but others flourished in their stead. Ethnic, gender, and sexual revolutions had altered many traditional practices. New theologies and moralities were disquieting to prevailing conceptual structures. Gaustad regarded all these as signs of spiritual vigor that sought new forms of expression. As evidence of continuing energy in religion, he pointed out that "Jesus movements and spiritual communes multiplied, while pentecostal and charismatic excitement erupted in unexpected places;" even "Oriental religions [have become] a sidewalk commonplace."[23] So while some contemporary observers were pessimistic about recent trends, Gaustad knew that religious expressions were simply changing direction, not declining in vitality or fascination. Someone such as he with the longer perspective that history afforded could detect many possibilities for personal meaning and social relevance in the many religions of the republic.

MARTIN E. MARTY'S PERSPECTIVE

In 1970 Martin E. Marty composed an overview of American Protestantism that qualifies as synthesized research in church history. He said that in this attempt to cover the whole Protestant story he was willing to risk "his credentials in those circles which believe that all history should be highly specialized and monographic." Building instead on those more narrowly focused works by others, he wove their data into a distinctive interpretive pattern of his own. Marty thought Protestant history had not received sufficient attention, a serious lack since more than sixty percent of Americans in his day fit that category. He might also have announced that few others dared to treat the subject with such sweeping inclusiveness as he would. As with most other surveys of American religion at midcentury, this one also chose to avoid institutional confinements in order to view "the whole Protestant complex, particularly insofar as it had public and extra-ecclesiastical impact." His graceful prose and compelling insights assayed "all the people somehow called Protestants," their internal struggles as "mainliners versus outsiders, fringe-group members, latecomers, etc.," and their external programs through which they sought to "define themselves over against and to relate to non-Protestants in America and the larger world."[24]

In the early years of national life, white Anglo-Saxons had been "statistically the overpowering force" in the country, and Marty noted that this large segment of the population harbored a religious objective. They wished nothing less than to create a righteous empire, to develop a spiritual kingdom by converting all inhabitants to common beliefs and by influencing their activities through a legal infrastructure. As colonies became states in an atmosphere of free religion in a free society, Protestant spokespersons adapted their goals to those conditions. Voluntary churches flourished in a competitive ethos and found new agencies for perpetuating the old objective. In this regard Marty pointed out that evangelical leaders wanted to do more than save souls. They viewed holiness as a necessary second step in conversion; changed hearts produced changed behavior. This twofold conception of reform was a dominant cultural influence in Protestant America up to the Civil War. Evangelical proponents continually sought to "complete the reformation of manners and the reformulation of morals" which undergirded the lives of all citizens.[25]

As time went on, though, many nonwhite and non–Anglo-Saxon Protestants added new elements to the dominant religious persuasion. Challenging uniformity even further, non-Protestant groups such as Roman Catholics increased their numbers dramatically. Industrial urbanization placed additional strains on the concept of one spiritual hegemony. Varying responses to these factors caused sharp disagreements among Protestant leaders, and this inaugurated what Marty called the "two-party system." His bipolar characterization was particularly useful for grasping the fact that two noticeably different religious orientations have existed alongside each other for the past hundred years. No single term or label can define either party adequately, but Marty used some adjectives in tentative, suggestive ways. One point of view was notable, he said, for emphasizing "individualistic" or "private" religious concerns while the other gravitated toward "social" or "public" issues. Along the same set of priorities, one sought to "rescue" people from worldly affairs while the other worked to "transform" conditions in the world around them. These delineations were not mutually exclusive, of course, and persons could adopt varying attitudes without institutional interference. But individual Protestants generally tended to cluster around one or the other party's emphases on opposite sides of a spectrum.

On the end where private concerns held sway, Marty declared that people "accented individual salvation out of the world, personal moral life congruent with the ideals of the saved, and . . . rewards or punishments in another world in a life to come." By contrast, he portrayed the other focus to be "public insofar as it was more exposed to the social order and the social destinies of men." Each party used words like "evangelical" and "gospel" to fit their respective contexts; one cherished revivalism and sought "conversions and reaffirmations of faith" while the other gradually lost confidence in revivals and "worked instead with techniques and processes which strove for some transformation of the world." Marty also pointed out that this bifurcation within Protestantism "did not follow the base lines of denominationalism." Members in every church separated into clusters according to their notions as to whether religion should address public or private issues. Those with differing answers had more in common with like-minded members of other denominations than they did with opponents in their own. Some people in every branch of Protestantism were pessimistic about changing society and concentrated on saving individual souls. Others in those same churches were optimistic regarding social transformation and, though they did not neglect the individual, concentrated their efforts on community issues.[26] Each side claimed its religious priorities to be classic and normative. Their coexistence has maintained both diversity and vitality in contemporary Protestantism.

Marty kept his eye on both parties as the twentieth century displayed its unhappy sequence of wars, economic depressions, racial strife, and failed crusades. During this time church membership increased steadily, but it seemed to grow in proportion to lowering standards. The positive thinking and moralism so widespread in churches apparently could not deal effectively with the basic problems of national life. Even though "the Graham rallies came to be racially integrated," he quipped, "the Second Coming did not occur." When Protestants reacted to the cultural unrest of the 1960s, the two-party template continued to help classify their varying responses. Few Protestants viewed their country with imperial ambitions any longer, but Marty thought their collective influence was still notable. One important change was that, after having battled secular alternatives since the age of Enlightenment, Protestants seemed finally to have developed an ability to live with secularity.[27] So Protestant influences had been strong in America's past, and they persisted in modern times because church membership was still high. Whatever the future might bring, it seemed certain that Protestantism would continue to be an important historical force through the two parties and their separate emphases.

SYDNEY E. AHLSTROM'S VOLUME

In 1972 Sydney E. Ahlstrom distilled several decades of personal inquiry and reflection into one massive volume. His narrative epitomized the genre that synthesized known material and freed church historians to concentrate on monographic research again. This monumental synthesis profited from several types of investigative techniques, and it featured a more inclusive range of topics than any previous publication. Ahlstrom sustained his study of phenomena spread over five centuries with "the firm conviction that the moral and spiritual development of the American people is one of the most intensely relevant subjects on the face of the earth."[28] He knew, as did all compilers of general texts, that Christianity had not been the only factor in American religious history. And he was more determined than the rest to present materials from a broader viewpoint, one that went well beyond the familiar traditions of Judeo-Christian heritage.

As many did before him, Ahlstrom addressed the question of method, and he, too, articulated guidelines which virtually all church historians have followed in modern times. He held that his field of study had to be "placed squarely within the larger frame of world history." Embodying the view that separates modern scholars from earlier generations, he said church history "no longer enjoys any rights of sanctuary." Students of religious topics "cannot claim supernatural or divinely inspired sources of insight," because their work "is allowed no immunity from the demands of evidence that historians generally make." In a corollary observation, Ahlstrom held that the "old fence" around his subfield was gone; church history had become more broadly conceived. In an overview of religious impulses, all viewpoints which affected morally serious lives deserved notice. And as church historians thought more inclusively, they had to admit the existence of a "radical diversity of American religious movements." They could no longer speak of a single religious tradition that dominated national life. Beyond this, historians could study religions best when they were operating in social contexts. People's faiths and values found expression in human communities. The place to see religion at work was amid the demographic, economic, political, and psychological dimensions of social existence.[29]

Just as Ahlstrom typified modern church history in his ideas about method, so he did with regard to complex subject matter. He began his survey of the American experience by using a tenth of the book to explore European roots in medieval Catholicism and Reformations of the sixteenth century. Thereafter he followed all major branches of Christendom to the Western Hemisphere and recounted the events that enriched American life by their "sheer multifariousness." From colonial plantings to contemporary times, he traced patterns of Protestant influence, watching old establishments and dissenters meld into a quasi-establishment that for more than a century after the Revolution shaped America as a nation with the soul of a church. He gave full play to evangelical Protestantism, its revivals and social programs which dominated national culture from the Great Awakening to the 1920s. Intellectual history was a strong interest, too, and in this sprawling account, Ahlstrom allowed more room for theological developments than had any previous author.

There are actually three separable themes in Ahlstrom's integrated treatment of religious history. On one level he discussed religion that was identified with tangible institutions. Spiritual life often centered on organized groups, and a great deal of church history involved denominations, hierarchies, and other aspects of straightforward associative bodies. On a second level, Ahlstrom discerned religious sentiments that had been expressed outside normal ecclesiastical channels. Many Americans had voiced spiritual concerns and followed courses of action unconnected with formal institutional patterns. These less tangible currents were legitimate manifestations of religious sensibility that lengthened the list of topics to cover in a comprehensive history. In addition to organizations and impalpable options, the book featured a third emphasis: the way in which religion interacted with the socio-political sphere. It was important to see how spiritual promptings sought practical outlet in the larger cultural nexus and how in turn the social milieu affected religious priorities. Pages devoted to this reciprocal process helped round out a comprehensive overview whose scope surpassed all others.

These three emphases enabled Ahlstrom to conduct a thorough-going canvass of religious activity in the United States. His volume contained a panorama of imperial ambitions and countervailing forces, ennobling ordeals and faltering crusades, with a supple prose that rewards close attention. On the whole, the result of his labors was a triumph. But success brought no lasting sense of accomplishment because, as his work reached completion, the author found that contemporary events were making his viewpoint obsolete. He was sure that at least one of his findings was accurate: "The pluralistic character of the nation is a fact. The Protestant establishment in its historic form is no more. The Puritan spirit, together with the revivalism and the legalism that informed the mainstream denominations, is being pushed into the backwaters of American life."[30] But even as he wrote this, he knew that churches were undergoing profound changes, and American religiosity was moving in unexpected directions. Ahlstrom's interpretive insights, acquired over a lifetime, could not explain the new forms of American religious expression.

Issues in the 1960s had raised questions for a new generation of historians to answer. It was clear to Ahlstrom that the decade of John XXIII, John F. Kennedy, Martin Luther King, and Malcolm X had "revolutionized the church historian's general situation." This meant that the melting pot was smashed, the old landmarks were gone, and America's destiny was uncertain. Facing these unsettled conditions, Ahlstrom said, "It is this new present . . . to which our historical explanations must now be related." But what new configurations would call for attention; what interpretations would need revising? The only response that seemed clear in 1972 was that of greater inclusiveness. As fresh religious expressions created new perceptions, "many types of subjects now lost in the shadows cast by past historians will be raised up for examination." Contemporary developments produced a new social and intellectual environment, and this made historians aware of poorly understood topics whose origins and previous experience needed to be ascertained. The problem confronting church historians was the same as that challenging all students of the past: "to find a new plot, a new rationale, a new set of priorities, and new angles of vision."[31] Investigators needed to look at many more neglected antecedents before they could account for how America had evolved into a post-Puritan, post-Protestant, post-Christian, post-WASP culture.

Ahlstrom never claimed to be writing from such a new angle of vision. He knew that later church historians would eventually acquire such a perspective, but all he could do was point out the need. Writing at the end of a "momentous decade," he sensed that he stood at a "turning point in American history," at a time when cultural ideals subsumed under terms like "Protestant establishment" faced a moment of truth. Before the 1960s, all minority elements in American society—Catholic, Orthodox, Lutheran, Jewish, infidel, red, yellow, and black—had to relate in one way or another to a pervasive ideology derived from the "great Puritan epoch." After that turbulent decade, the old rules did not apply, and groups no longer conformed to dominant cultural standards. Racial strife at home and inept military campaigns abroad created anxieties that dissolved social bonds and rejected traditional religious activities. The postwar revivals of the Eisenhower years had "sputtered out," and the nation was experiencing a crisis of conscience "of unprecedented depth." It seemed to Ahlstrom that the recent turmoil had "committed a kind of maturing violence upon the innocence of a whole people." Some new formulation of spiritual values would emerge, he thought, but it was impossible to anticipate what it would be or when it might appear. Standing on the threshold of an age when new awareness would supplant earlier perspectives, he offered his book to readers with the hope that they might glimpse "something of the vitality and diversity of the religious commitments that over the years have brought the American people to their present engagement with the future."[32]

INVESTIGATIONS FROM NEW PERSPECTIVES

For a time it seemed that these general surveys would suffice. Readers could consult at least a half dozen of them to see how the best of earlier research had been synthesized into overviews of the American experience. But others continue to appear, lengthening an already crowded list. Three notable ones have begun treating American religion from self-consciously contemporary perspectives. Earlier generations of church historians could only anticipate revised interpretations; these up-to-date authors have begun to furnish them.[33]

When Ahlstrom alluded to "neglected antecedents" in American life, one of the subjects that needed to be understood more fully was the contribution blacks have made in this country. The need was clear because a few pioneering studies had already whetted scholarly appetites. The sustained vitality and increased activism in Negro churches called for thorough study and incorporation into the pluralistic kaleidoscope. Afro-American energies in recent civil rights movements made it all the more urgent to understand the religious motivations behind such activity. Innovative and probing investigations have produced a great many excellent monographs on black Christianity.[34] These valuable additions to knowledge have expanded the trickle of earlier works into a widening stream, much to the benefit of future synthesists who will one day achieve a richer and more balanced overview.

Another major topic that has been neglected for too long is women's studies. As with blacks, so with women. Everyone knew vaguely that women played an important part in all aspects of religious life, but full and specific information was one of those subjects "lost in the shadows cast by past historians." Simple justice required a more adequate representation of the evidence. Contemporary developments in feminist consciousness called for revising both language and interpretive schemes that overemphasized male leadership patterns. For these reasons and many more, a great number of first-rate studies have appeared recently in this area.[35] They have supplied much needed information in familiar categories, and moreover many of them explore fresh topics in creative ways. Encouraging as it is to see overdue materials finally receiving more attention, a fact of greater significance is that women are now entering the church historical guild themselves.

Their intelligence, industry, and new perspectives will make the profession's future accomplishments better than anything produced thus far.

Several familiar topics continue to receive a great deal of attention by specialists. Sophisticated investigations help maintain high quality in Puritan studies, for example, already a cottage industry earlier in this century.[36] Flowing naturally from that field of concentration, other students pursue new researches into religious influences and eighteenth-century colonial life.[37] Religious factors were crucial in nineteenth-century national culture, too, and new monographs probe those relationships with increased insight.[38] Regional studies persist as well, and investigations into a subculture's religious underpinnings have yielded much appreciated information, especially regarding that of the antebellum South.[39]

As befits the largest denomination in America, scores of researchers have pursued new topics in the immensely complicated story of Catholicism. Whether concentrating on clergy or laity, on individuals or special groups, these studies shed light on important areas, revealing at the same time that there are many more questions that need to be answered.[40] Catholicism has been labeled an immigrant church through much of its history in this country, but in fact all Americans are products of that demographic theme. Recent publications in immigration patterns continue to highlight their role in everyone's religious heritage.[41]

In church historiography up to midcentury, revivalism was analyzed and described to excess, probably attracting more attention than the Puritans did. Since then studies of revivals have decreased in number but increased in sophistication.[42] Researchers are asking new questions, and their work brings fresh insights by looking at known data from different angles of vision. Another topic of continuing interest has to do with the interpenetration of religion and politics. Each of these spheres of human activity is perennially important; neither can remain untouched by the other. New publications about this fascinating relationship remind us that there is more to know in this area.[43] Many new monographs concentrate on religious thought, a stock-in-trade among church historians for quite some time. Contemporary researchers expound the ideas of neglected theologians, relate bodies of thought to larger contexts, and in many ways, show us how ideas make a different in cultural experience, past and present.[44]

Recent scholarship has produced a variety of valuable books on more discrete themes. While not focusing on huge institutions or national movements, several works on Quaker life rest on the highest standards of excellence in contemporary study.[45] Alongside them stand exemplary investigations into nineteenth-century phenomena such as Mormons and other groups that emerged when utopian expectations were strong.[46] Studies of Eastern religions have made their way into church history, too. Their influence needs to be assessed whenever one tries to fathom the depth and measure the currents in all of American religion.[47] Finally, and perhaps most importantly, in light of possible future developments in religious practice, valuable new research is being published on the Pentecostal-Holiness aspects of Christianity.[48] These emphases have a long past and a promising future. Historians are beginning to show in better detail how that past and the present are connected.

The preceding paragraphs refer to one hundred titles which have appeared since 1972, the year Ahlstrom's volume climaxed a period of generalized overviews. As a sketchy survey of recent monographs, this does not do justice to the wealth of new material and viewpoints that actually exist. Scholars have pursued specialized studies in church history all along, and the dozen-year period used in this chapter is only a convenient device to separate earlier work from more recent efforts. The profession is strong, energetic, and increasingly complex. More historians than ever before are now studying religious phenomena, asking new questions of old data and opening new fields hitherto unexplored. Many of these investigations were influenced by three experts whose labors epitomize the best traditions of modern church historiography. It will be useful to look in greater detail at their careers that culminated in this, the next to last, decade in the century.

ᴂ7
Exemplary Scholarship
in the Penultimate Decade

While synthesized texts and narrowly focused research projects appeared during the 1960s and 1970s, three church historians introduced their own publications which enhanced their already distinguished careers. One of these historians was Robert T. Handy, professor at Union Theological Seminary in New York from 1950 until his retirement in 1986. Handy acquired some notice as a synthesist, too, collaborating with H. S. Smith and L. A. Loetscher. But he was more interested in raising new issues and revising old viewpoints. Though he kept his eye on larger interpretive schemes, the main point for him was to bring additional elements of historical experience to light.

Handy was primarily a narrative historian. Above all, this meant that action was the essential ingredient in recounting the past. He spent relatively little time expounding systems of ideas or analyzing trends. Policy statements and religious manifestos seemed less important than the real accomplishments of ecclesiastical institutions. What mattered to him were specific activities which led to tangible results. Whenever he considered the intellectual aspects of events, Handy usually referred to ideas as motivations for behavior. Bodies of thought were also helpful in explaining the ideological conflicts within groups which led to schisms and alternate patterns of activity. Action began when a single individual responded to a religious experience; this in turn led most often to affirming some credo held with others in an institutional setting; in this manner, churches produced general religious influences in culture. For Handy, this relationship of the individual to national life helped historians understand the way personal activity affected society at large.

Handy's writings also ranged freely over a spectrum of times and topics in ways that encouraged others to do the same. Of course he favored some themes over others, but compared to W. S. Hudson and S. E. Mead, scholars of comparable age and reputation, Handy's perspective was more diversified. Instead of tying himself down to a single era or subject, his interests ran the gamut from religious among aboriginal Indians to prospects for churches in the 1990s. Moreover, he paid great attention to Catholic and Jewish experience in addition to Protestant activities. Black churches received much notice, too, as did the many types of immigrants who increased extant denominations and gave such venerable traditions as Eastern Orthodoxy a new start in this country.

None of Hardy's interpretive theses were unique, but he applied them with rarely matched sophistication. One thesis had to do with the importance of pluralism in American life, an old standby among church historians for decades. Handy rang changes on this theme better than anyone else. His appreciation of its complexities seized on the fact in greater detail, and his depiction of its role in achieving religious freedom was more realistic than any other effort in that direction.[1] He knew its existence was ancient and pervasive: "As far back as records run, the American religious experience has been a pluralistic one." If one wished to comprehend the whole story of religion on this continent, it was necessary to begin with Native Americans because they inaugurated the phenomenon, embodying a great many different faiths and rituals. White colonists then brought virtually every European version of Christianity to these shores. Jews also arrived to amplify pluralism, so its main outlines were set by the end of the colonial period. Later immigration increased the number of competing groups, while black churches, splinter groups, and indigenous forms such as Disciples, Mormons, and Jehovah's Witnesses added to the mix. Handy based all his work on the conviction that "any effort to understand what religion has meant historically on the American scene must assess what influences the pluralistic setting has had on the religious life and thought of individuals and groups—both those involved in organized religion and those not." Supporting his treatment of particular topics is the notion that "the pluralistic style of dealing with religion has set its stamp on both the spiritual life and the religious institutions of the American people."[2]

That stamp on life and institutions could be discerned in four notable characteristics. Handy was not the first to point these out, but here, too, he discussed them in ways that suggested additional interpretive possibilities, opening avenues for further investigation. For one thing, he saw pluralism as a major factor behind the practice of religious freedom. If such a relationship meant simply that no single church had been strong enough to force its will on others, it raised the question whether freedom was the result of a pragmatic compromise, and was thus vulnerable to cancellation, or whether it was based on durable principles. Freedom had led, secondly, to voluntary methods of winning converts and to a stress on activism in the American religious style. Further, these evangelical efforts internalized differentiation, and churches subsequently tolerated diversity within their several communions. Handy opened new lines of inquiry when he proposed that such an obscuring of differences among denominations was a crucial factor in ecumenical understanding and activity. He also explored new ground by putting forth the idea that internalized pluralism "has been part of the reason why religious bodies find their sense of identity and purpose blurred in the later twentieth century." At present this view seems as plausible an explanation of contemporary religious ineffectiveness as those which emphasize ecclesiastical decay or fatuous leadership. Younger historians will probably also probe the ramifications of Handy's observation that "interreligious endeavors themselves illustrate the pluralistic style, for they take many forms, are devoted to religious liberty, use voluntary means, tend to be activistic, and themselves internalize much of the pluralism with which they seek to deal."[3] Reference to these characteristics can explain a great deal regarding dialogue across Catholic-Protestant and Christian-Jewish lines as well.

Another theme which Handy considered important had to do with religious concern for social problems. In looking at church influence on everything from family life to voting, he touched upon such topics as education, temperance, and abolition, culminating with the Social Gospel activities that flourished in cities at the turn of this century. He considered the multifaceted aspects of urban reform efforts to have been the "most conspicuous phenomenon" in a long history of attempts to apply religious principles to cultural problems. Even after it virtually disappeared in the 1940s, "its legacy of social thought and tradition of involvement . . . continued to be evident in many ways in American life."[4] This was so because churches in quite different theological settings remained committed to the fundamental contention that religions must recognize and deal responsibly with social and economic questions. And, taking ecumenical concerns into account, various gospels of social relevance were additional stimuli to interdenominational cooperation. Ecumenical activity increased when churches pooled their resources to affect all human concerns with their witness.

Historians are usually content to study materials within a single country, but Handy investigated religious experience in both the United States and Canada. In each case he acknowledged the integrity of separate histories, succinctly representing prominent individuals and movements on both sides of the border. But even more instructive was the way in which he used balanced judgment in pointing out parallels and contrasts. He noticed differences right away, beginning as early as the colonial period. Whereas American churches moved fairly quickly away from uniform patterns to a system of competitive denominations, Canadian churches clung more tenaciously to European ecclesiastical traditions. Churches in northernmost British America yearned less for new departures, and no major Canadian group claimed, as did many south of them, that they were recapitulating elements of Christianity which had been forgotten since the first century.[5]

Revivals and revolution shaped American religion along distinctive lines. Handy thought the bonds of national feeling and unity as a people were affected by the shared warmth of eighteenth-century religious enthusiasm. Evangelical stress on universal sin and widespread opportunities for grace had underscored a common experience, thus enhancing the basis for democracy. So in the United States, liberal democracy and evangelical piety were seen as compatible, supplementary elements. New ecclesiastical institutions rose on the foundations of representative democracy, and popular government was thought to work best when citizens affirmed common religious principles. So, "the pragmatic quality of American life stems in part from the partnership between democracy and the churches struck during the revolutionary epoch."[6] Canada, however, experienced tensions rather than consolidation. There were massive differences between the large bloc of Catholics in French-speaking Quebec and the Protestants of all sorts elsewhere. In the latter category, political and religious factionalism further divided groups of English, Scottish, Irish, German, and American origin. Intense struggles occurred between those committed to some form of religious establishment and those who wanted religious liberty and only voluntary support of churches. When diversity defeated privilege, government still assisted denominational educational programs, and "in Canada religious institutions were not so sharply differentiated from the major institutions of the culture."[7] The American image of a "wall of separation" between church and state did not seem relevant there, nor was it invoked.

Handy pointed out other features worth pondering for purposes of comparative interpretations. Americans adjusted rather willingly to increased diversity among Protestants, for instance, but they reacted violently to Roman Catholic growth. In Canada a powerful Catholic presence precluded nativist vehemence, and so a bilateral religious context promoted tolerance of other church groups. Moreover, the Enlightenment spirit was largely suppressed in Canada, and as a result, there was never much emphasis on civil religion as an alternative to confessional allegiance. Unlike the American amalgamation of piety and government, Canadians recognized the secular origins of their state, and thus they supplied no religious interpretation of national purpose.[8] Then, too, American churches have not gone far in ecumenical endeavors because of their sectarian pluralism. But Canadians point to the United Church of Canada which in 1925 marked a distinctive achievement along these lines. With the confluence of Methodists, Presbyterians, and Congregationalists, "three streams of tradition flowed together in one of the most significant church unions since the Reformation."[9]

When considering questions of acculturation and religious identity, Handy noticed a curious reversal of experiences in the two countries. On the American side, evangelicals had sought to convert individuals while trying to permeate the whole country with their values at the same time. Local congregations, church assemblies, and interdenominational councils may be divided by polities and confessions, but all are agreed on the goal of making America a Christian nation. "Denominational pluralities could be accepted comfortably," he noted, "because there was an overarching frame of reference provided by the nation which was confidently given a Christian interpretation." As a result, the different communions became interchangeable agencies, competing to achieve the same end. After the Dominion of Canada was created in 1867, churches stepped up their efforts to influence broad cultural questions, but they never agreed on a single vision of national purpose. Catholics were rent internally by tensions between liberals and ultramontanists. Protestants were divided by problems that stemmed from ethnic and theological sources. Industrialism and immigration contributed more difficulties as Canada grew from an agricultural society to one with strong urban centers. All these factors challenged ecclesiastical effectiveness and caused churches to stand apart from larger society while still trying to assuage its ills.[10] Yet in face of these difficulties, Handy expected future events to be as interesting as those which had produced present conditions. The past disclosed resilience in response to reverses, revival and renewal in the wake of controversy and schism. He indulged in no "post-Christian" gloom but put forth critically appreciative views on religion in culture. These views will stimulate further research by later church historians in both countries.

Of all the suggestions put forward in his work, none have attracted more attention than Handy's ideas about "Americanized Christianity." They stem from the fact that, throughout the American experience, evangelical Protestants have referred to civilization during the course of their preaching. Handy investigated ways in which religion and culture have related to each other in this country's development. More specifically, as a historian he looked for common denominators among "English-speaking evangelical denominations which thought of themselves as comprising the religious mainstream of the nation and which believed themselves to be especially charged with making America a Christian nation." In such a context, Handy did not probe for consensus in American culture, nor did he lament any decline from earlier standards. He sought to understand historical patterns rather than solve moral or theological riddles. The subject was important to history because, as it explained earlier activity, it could also shed light on more recent questions about the role of religion in contemporary culture. "The Protestant dream of Christian civilization and the actions which stemmed from it must be taken seriously," he insisted, in any "attempt fully to understand the American experience."[11]

Even before Europeans colonized the New World, they had long thought it proper to have a mutually supportive alliance between culture and the Christian faith. Those ideas crossed the sea and flourished where Protestantism dominated the middle part of North America. Anglicans as well as Congregationalists took steps to establish a religious civilization, by law and at public expense. This method of enforcement was largely rejected by the end of the revolutionary epoch, but Handy noted that even those who worked for disestablishment shared one conviction with their opponents. All of them assumed that "society needed a unifying religious perspective and a broadly accepted morality," if it was to prosper in the future. Early in the nineteenth century, Protestants learned to rely on persuasion instead of laws and public monies to advance their cause. But while using voluntary rather than governmental means, most "still looked for a Christian America and worked toward that end." Revivals and various missions movements caused churches to grow faster than the increase in population, and this encouraged the conviction among evangelical groups that the nation would prosper as long as it rested on the Protestant virtues of its people. It was axiomatic that civilized life needed some kind of religious base, and this early vision of a healthy America made evangelical Protestantism essential to its moral and social strength. "Though the means for attaining the long-desired goal changed, the hope for a Christian America glowed with a new intensity."[12]

Such a vision emphasized broad areas of agreement among evangelical groups. Most early national denominations accepted a variety of features among themselves because they felt there was so little difference beneath the surface. Interdenominational agencies also contributed to the shared ends of religious fulfillment and civic success. Even millennial expectations of the time enhanced the idea that Christianity would display its greatest blessings in American achievements. Handy acknowledged the strength of this consensus, but he pointed out that it excluded other religious elements that were also part of national life. Protestants denied Catholics a place in the vision because of ancient controversies, Mormons because of recent ones. They left most immigrants out, too, in favor of native-born WASP constituents. To those excluded from the dream, and to historians who looked at it later, "fateful limitations in the search for a Christian America were painfully disclosed." Most leaders in their zeal "failed to sense how coercive

their efforts appeared to those who did not share their premises."
Perhaps the most telling omission in this regard was black Christians. Hopes for a Christian America made relatively few references to Negro life, its strong religious base, or the question it
posed for social harmony. Antebellum religious leaders did not
make room for slave or free black Christians in their plans for a
religious nation, and abolition did little to correct this myopia.
Handy assessed these limitations and found that "idealistic and
well-intentioned white Protestants moved in an atmosphere tainted
by racism and imperialism." Those obsessed with Anglo-Saxon
superiority cut themselves off from an increasing number of fellow
citizens. Their tunnel vision prevented contact with those who
might have helped them see what could happen as a result.[13]

Exclusion of groups from the evangelical core was, in Handy's
estimation, symptomatic of a more complex historical phenomenon. That larger transformation involved a subtle reversal of priorities, the reversal of hopes for a Christian America into the lesser
reality of an Americanized Christianity. Efforts to wed religion
and civilization perpetuated habits of thought and language, but
late nineteenth-century leaders made the advancement of civilization the greater good. In perhaps its most succinct form, the
"Handy thesis" holds that

in many ways the image of a Christian America in the Gilded Age was much
like that held widely among evangelicals in the first half of the century, but one
very important shift in overall perspective was taking place. . . . In the earlier
period, the priority of the religious vision was strongly and widely maintained; it was Christianity *and* civilization, Christianity as the best part of
civilization and its hope. In the latter part of the century, however, in most
cases unconsciously, much of the real focus had shifted to the civilization
itself, with Christianity and the churches finding their significance in relation
to it.

After the Revolution, a resurgent Protestantism set out to make
America a Christian nation, not with the old methods of force but
by voluntary means. In a democratic setting, the new nation was
imbued with the religion-and-civilization aspirations of its dominant inhabitants. Protestantism became so welded to its cultural
vehicle in the process, most citizens could not separate the two
thereafter. As a result, Handy observed, "Instead of the church
having Christianized civilization, they found that the civilization
had captured the church."[14]

From a historian's perspective, there were positive and negative aspects to this amalgamation, a religious culture or acculturated religion. On the positive side, Protestants could share a type of unity despite their otherwise overwhelming diversity. Faith compartmentalized into churches that were also divided sectionally and racially could still grasp a common ideal by stressing the Christian character of American civilization. But the negative side eventually proved more influential than longings for Christian wholeness. Protestants failed to see that their attachment to an idealized America had deleterious effects. As they allowed cultural standards to define their religion, they associated the product with a narrow range of economic and social interests. They viewed the whole nation from a religious frame of reference, but their identity with middle-class mores made then uncritical defenders of the status quo. Moreover, attachment to particular social forms made it difficult for Protestants to accept further change, which was bound to occur sooner or later. This adherence to a single cultural standard caused them to react negatively and ineffectually to the influx of immigrants, to mushrooming growth, and to radical innovations in science and philosophy. Handy noted how churches had come to court worldly approval, and he utilized a quote from George Santayana to limn this reversed priority. Far from "prophesying its end, or offering a refuge from it, or preaching contempt for it," he found that churches in modern times existed "only to serve [the world] and their highest divine credential was that the world needed them."[15]

Twentieth-century historical realities posed a serious challenge to evangelical expectancies. The consequences of industrialization, urbanization, immigration, and intellectual revolution had been superimposed on the rural setting that originally nurtured the hopes for a Christian America. Some leaders accepted the shift from rural to urban patterns and tried to influence the new environment with revised patterns of thought, organization, and action. Their emphases on social gospels and cooperative Christian efforts found common cause with the more familiar strains of Bible-centered, revivalist, missionary-minded behavior. Consequently, Protestant campaigns to influence temperance, Sabbath observance, and public education were still strong in this century's early decades. A few activists sensed that "there was uneasy recognition that forces were at work in society which were threatening Protestant values, "but the momentum of traditional views seemed invincible to most. In Handy's view, even though some might be worried, "the anxieties and perplexities were seen to be molehills beside the towering mountain of hope."[16]

That mountain eroded after World War I, and Protestant ambitions lapsed during the "religious depression" of the 1920s. Their strength ebbed further in the 1930s because of decreased membership, reduced budgets, closed churches, and dismissed ministers. Evangelical Protestantism also lost its place as arbiter of the nation's values and behavior patterns. Handy found that the enthusiasm and confidence needed to sustain the crusade had flagged. "The confident belief that America was basically Protestant and was progressing toward the kingdom of God had been an important foundation for evangelical Protestant crusading. But that foundation was crumbling under the pressures of population shifts, intellectual changes, and increased pluralism." Some outward vestiges remained in place, but the realities had changed enough for some observers to call it the "second disestablishment" of religion in American history. Taking the long view, Handy regarded this eventuality as the natural outcome of Protestant choices. "What is being emphasized here is not that the Protestant churches were lethargic and inactive, for they were not, but that their special identification with American civilization was drawing to an end." To this, he added that a significant phase of national life had passed, and "the rhetoric of a Christian America was increasingly out of place."[17]

Many of Handy's writings contain topics and interpretations that will lead to further research. In addition to their content, these works encourage further inquiry because of the fundamental attitude that underlies them. For instance, while investigating the "second disestablishment," Handy did so as a historian, not as a theologian or a disgruntled churchman. Rather than delivering critical or approving comments about contemporary times, he tried to interpret them in light of preceding events. He sought understanding, knowing that conditions would change over and over as events continued to unfold. The wisdom that undergirded his professional activities was perhaps best expressed in these words: "Significant changes in any of the nation's major religious subcultures are important, not only for those who belong to it, but also for the life of the nation as a whole. Either to mourn, to praise, or to condemn indiscriminately what has passed is not as helpful as an effort to understand it for what it was and for what it tried to do. . . ." With that attitude uppermost in his mind, Handy argued that accurate information was always useful. "The recognition that an era did come to an end some years ago can be liberating for all. The passing of the Protestant era has allowed many to see more fully the meaning of the highly pluralistic character of American religion." Protestant crusades to create a Christian America have largely ended, and Handy thought the beneficial result was that now everyone can more easily recognize the Catholic-Jewish-Orthodox-Protestant-Mormon-Pentecostal-New Thought-Humanist nation that has emerged. The successes and failures of Protestant crusades left America with "the same basic problems of religion and society which they encountered." Still from the historian's point of view, "From [those] successes and failures there is much to learn."[18]

THE MATURATION OF CATHOLIC STUDIES

Catholic historical scholarship reached high levels of sophistication and balance in the modern period through the works of several investigators. These efforts are perhaps best reflected in John Tracy Ellis, whose researches and qualities of mind adhered to the standards esteemed in the profession at large. Ellis said that he decided to become a historian while still in college. That decision preceded his commitment to the priesthood and at times seemed firmer, but at length the two vocations happily coincided. After earning a Ph.D. in the 1930s, teaching undergraduates for some years, and at one interval, studying theology part-time, Ellis received ordination in 1938. By 1940 he was both a priest and an instructor in history at the Catholic University of America. "Thus began," he said in retrospect, "my truest professional life."[19]

Ellis's formal training had concentrated on European history, and he preferred to teach in that broad field. But in 1941 university officials chose him to succeed Peter Guilday, and Ellis dutifully accepted appointment to the relatively unfamiliar field of American church history. He also edited the *Catholic Historical Review* for the next twenty-two years and directed graduate students in advanced research. Those experiences and plain hard work made Ellis master of his new subject matter. He brought a wider chronological and geographical perspective to American topics, and his accomplishments were the culmination of a notable historiographical development that began with John G. Shea, improved with Peter Guilday, and has matured in contemporary times.[20]

It struck Ellis that writing Catholic history was particularly rife with difficulties. To begin with, Protestant and Catholic polemics had perpetuated mutual antagonisms for generations, and "the most devastating of all the pitfalls that [church historians] have had to encounter have sprung from the internecine strife that for centuries characterized the various branches of the Christian family." Ellis determined to overcome those entrenched biases. He wanted to move "out of the darkness and shadows created by the religious wars of the sixteenth century," though he knew that "prejudice, and the suspicions bred by prejudice, die hard." So as a step toward overcoming such prejudice Ellis set out to "shake off a minority-group apologetic mentality" because he thought the efforts of conscientious scholars were too often "open to suspicion by reason of their affiliation with a particular church."[21]

Another difficulty that stood in the way of producing good Catholic history was the widely held conviction that an account should only praise its subject in order to edify its readers. This attitude expected historians to emphasize only positive elements of the past and to ignore embarrassing episodes. "In other words, should the occasion call for it, the historian was not to scruple about indulging generously in the *suppressio veri* in order to avoid giving scandal." Ellis argued against such pious fraudulence and made a conscious effort in his own writings to conceal nothing. He was convinced that many of the inadequacies in Catholic history were due to a misconception of the discipline's proper task. Sanitized, expurgated narratives were tokens of a "frequently self-imposed ghetto mentality" which prevented Catholic investigators from reporting the unvarnished truth for its own sake. In opposition to those one-sided reports, Ellis maintained that "when the . . . exacting labor of true scholarship is intelligently directed and competently expressed it will win its way on its own merits into channels of influence beyond the Catholic pale. Of that one can be certain."[22]

A final predicament facing Catholic historians was identical to the one that vexed other students of the religious past. Ever since scientific history had introduced the procedures of disinterested observation and naturalistic explanation, all church historians had labored under the suspicion that their work did not qualify as acceptable scholarship. So Ellis found that many Catholics feared he might "betray the Catholic cause by candid revelations of misconduct and scandal within what was often termed the household of faith." At the same time, he became "the target of a heavy cross fire from fellow historians of other or no religious faith" who doubted he could portray his church's history objectively enough. To this last charge, he reiterated the answer which other church historians had made: "I can think of no phase of the methodology nor of historical composition that differentiates [the ecclesiastical historian] from his opposite number in the field of profane history." Far from stressing differences between his work and investigations in other topics, he held that a scholar like himself "needs to be on guard that he does not stray too far from that opposite number's milieu." Such a maxim was "patent to every historian of the Church and of religious life," and in embodying it Ellis demonstrated how much Catholic historiography had come of age.[23]

Ellis dissociated himself from confessional bias and any intent to edify those who read his history. In doing so his arguments recapitulated every major change in twentieth-century historiographical development. First he invoked the ideal of objective scrutiny as antidote to ideological preconceptions. Refusing to categorize history as a subsection of theology or as propaganda for ecclesiological reputation, he chose "to allow the documents to speak for themselves so that the reader might have all the evidence before him, and thus in the final analysis make up his own mind." This kind of manifesto did not make Ellis an uncritical advocate of the scientific approach, but it helped put some distance between his work and the parochial attitudes that subverted adequate historical coverage. He sought full disclosure of evidence and relied on data rather than rhetoric "in the conviction that in the long run candor could only serve the cause of truth, and in so doing it would reflect credit upon the Church and upon Catholic historical scholarship."[24]

But Ellis also knew that modern historians had radically modified the old ideals of scientific history, and the rest of his perspective disclosed an acute awareness of contemporary method. He was not "beguiled by the delusion" that he or anyone else could write with complete detachment or let facts speak entirely for themselves. Along with others affected by Becker and Beard, he acknowledged that "no historian worthy of the name has ever written with absolute objectivity." This did not entail reversion to special pleading any more for Catholics than it did for other professional scholars. It meant rather that accurate and candid use of evidence on any topic, accompanied by explicit mention of an interpretive viewpoint, could hold its own with other historical activity based on the same premises. So Ellis was not uncomfortable in admitting "to [a] love of the Catholic priesthood" nor to a desire to serve it by "bringing to light hidden aspects of its American story." Indeed, for Catholic historians to "pretend that this basic sympathy had not informed their narratives would be to speak . . . with less than the candor to which their readers are entitled." Those who studied the past with a concern for accuracy and with a vital interest in their subject "have departed not a whit from the accepted canons of scientific history, for it has been their intent to write history and not to compile a soulless annal."[25] Such a view moved beyond both confessional and naturalistic perspectives to espouse the most sophisticated procedures currently employed in the profession.

Now that we see how Ellis perceived options and placed himself amid historiographical options, what did he hope to accomplish while making Catholic history as good as that in other subjects? His work touched many areas. One early publication provided a selection of more than two hundred documents, the better to encourage study of primary sources. He also urged using those materials "to integrate the story of Catholicism with American history in general."[26] Another, and one of his most widely read volumes, also sought to effect "a better integration of the story of the Catholic Church in this country with the general history of the nation." It could do so because discussion of related topics would "put that story into sharper focus for readers of any or no religious faith."[27]

In a larger work with a narrower focus, Ellis's full-length biography of James Gibbons pursued similarly ambitious objectives by seeking to "recapture the spirit of the man and to recount . . . the great events in which he played so leading a role."[28] Another project found Ellis laboring "to get beneath the surface and to analyze in a balanced and real way the subtle influences that have played upon the souls and minds of candidates for the priesthood" in this country.[29] All these studies of religion in the American context provide instances of the way Ellis used historical information to help transform public opinion about his communion. He employed modern scholarship "so that our fellow citizens may be given an enlightened concept of Catholicism and be thus enabled to dissipate the mistaken notions that may have been their inheritance from childhood."[30]

While combating mistaken notions about the past, Ellis touched upon salient events that occurred over four centuries of Catholic experience. His narratives usually employed an institutional definition of religious factors, stressing ways in which the church contributed positively to national life. He did not focus on intellectual history, lamenting occasionally that his subject contained little innovative religious thought at any point. At times he wrote in a consensus history vein, and when doing so, he emphasized Catholic support for mainstream American values like religious freedom and concern for general social welfare. Considering Ellis's place in the larger framework of modern church history, then, it is clear that he fit at least two major categories. His interpretation of Catholic contributions resembled Sweet and Latourette by emphasizing the cultural significance of religion. He also paralleled the efforts of Mead and Hudson who searched for consensual values in the American past. Ellis did not echo the environmental conditioning point of view which Case represented, the theologically informed agenda backed by Richardson and Nichols, or the intellectual focus found in Smith and Miller.

Catholic experience in the Western Hemisphere began with missionary enterprises, and Ellis depicted the zeal for souls that motivated such work, recounting, too, how the Spanish and French brought certain benefits of material culture to their converts. He provided a wealth of information about local happenings, and he incorporated these data with European components that made colonial Catholicism part of a larger panorama. In discussing English activities, Ellis showed more concern for white Catholic continuance than for Indian beginnings.[31] This tripartite coverage contained one of the ironies in early American history: whereas Spanish missions claimed more converts than the French or English, they had the least permanent influence in American territory. English patterns eventually dominated the land, with French second, while traces of Spanish presence were the least noticeable.

Turning to that later frontier, Ellis reminded other historians that, when English pioneers pushed into the continental heartland after the Revolution, Catholic institutions in French settlements were there to greet them. At places like Vincennes and Bardstown, "a cathedral and a college . . . staffed by bishops and priests" existed amid frontier conditions. Those interested in the whole American experience should note that such institutions were "a significant stabilizing factor in the maturing process of the newborn states," a factor representing "an ancient and fixed tradition to mellow the rough and raw elements of the West."[32]

Concentrating on English and Irish experience as the prototype of what developed into American Catholicism, Ellis traced several recurrent themes through the colonial period. British coreligionists had smarted under a universal anti-Catholic prejudice that had been transplanted to Jamestown and flourished from Maine to Georgia. Despite such hostility, Catholic enclaves clung to their faith during the ensuing 180 years. Wherever they exert political influence, as they had done briefly in Maryland and New York, Catholics introduced the principle of religious toleration. If they lost political standing or never had it in the first place, they suffered discrimination under penal laws. Yet when the Revolution eventuated in religious freedom for all, Catholics fully embraced both the policy and the practice.

Within this scenario Ellis underscored Catholic contributions to, and support for, religious toleration. As early as 1633, George Calvert fostered such a policy along the Chesapeake, admittedly acting with expediency but with high-minded fairness as well. So, for the record, "two years before Roger Williams fled the Puritan wrath of Massachusetts Bay to establish religious toleration in Rhode Island, Baltimore had laid the groundwork for such a policy in Maryland." With that as a precedent, Ellis cited important bishops from John Carroll through James Gibbons to Richard Cushing, and he spoke of "an authentic tradition" of Catholic support for religious freedom from colonial times to the present day. Citations from that tradition not only clarified basic points of historical fact, he hoped they would also allay lingering nativist suspicions in contemporary Protestantism. "The American hierarchy," he proclaimed, "has always held, and still holds, that separation of Church and State in this country is the practical solution of this age-old problem; and nowhere will the student of

American history find that the Holy See has ever rebuked them for their stand."[33]

Other factors important to Catholic development emerged during the early national period. As was usually the case in his work, Ellis described American events against the backdrop of European circumstances, blending socioeconomic, political, and ecclesiastical conditions into a complex yet gracefully readable narrative. Up to the mid-nineteenth century, Catholicism remained a minority faith in this country, and its adherents suffered continually from traditional prejudices which most Americans held. Immigration increased church membership by leaps and bounds, simultaneously giving the organization a distinctly foreign cast. Latent bigotry and overt attacks caused Catholics to turn in upon themselves, establishing separate schools and founding their own newspapers. But at least the federal government was neutral, and this allowed Catholics to expand across the continent without Congressional interference. So Catholics helped push the frontier westward, and here Ellis took the opportunity to supplement the "Turner thesis." If the frontier was crucial in developing American character, it had to include more than farmers and ranchers. Ellis made a telling point by insisting that "if one omits the bishop, the priest, the monk, and the nun, he has missed one of the most important sources out of which the civilization of western America evolved."[34] Though Catholics were feared and scorned by other Christian groups, they had become by midcentury the largest and strongest single denomination in the land.

After the Civil War, which did not rend the Catholic church as it had many Protestant ones, membership continued to grow through natural increase, conversions, and immigration. Ellis thought the decades between 1860 and 1900 were ones plagued by "growing pains" which had almost proved "fatal." At times one might have thought "the immigrant flood, the lack of American Catholic intellectual achievement, and the bigotry of groups like the [American Protective Association] . . . represented differences between Catholic belief and the dominant national mores that would forever stamp the Church as an institution alien to America."[35] But church and people endured, quietly gathered strength, and developed resources for worship and welfare. That steady enlargement was not due to any single individual, but Ellis attributed much of its success to James Gibbons, archbishop of Baltimore from 1877 to

1921. Gibbons lived through difficult times while occupying America's premier see, and he had to deal with many controversies. By the end of his long career, both church leaders and the public at large had come to appreciate his contributions to their general well being. It was perhaps substantially true that "the reason for the deference shown to him was . . . that the public had been won by the gentle and kindly manner, the sound judgment, and the expansive affection with which he seemed to embrace all his fellow citizens."[36]

Ellis dealt with all phases of American Catholic history, early and late, on both sides of the Atlantic, touching lay concerns as well as those of the hierarchy. But he devoted special attention to Cardinal Gibbons and tended to view much of the national experience from that vantage point. The historian judged the prelate a true successor to John Carroll, Baltimore's first archbishop, because his enlightened leadership sustained the genuine Catholic tradition of orthodox faithfulness and patriotism. Over the years Gibbons made many statements that supported separation of church and state in this country. He perpetuated the image of Catholic Americans who would not change constitutional provisions for full religious freedom, if they had the power to do so.[37] He also enlarged on Catholic sympathy for the poor and defended the right of workers to organize against exploitation. In 1887 Gibbons protested incipient papal condemnation of the Knights of Labor and placed the American church solidly on the side of general welfare rather than privilege. In memorably democratic phrasing, he said that "to lose the heart of the people would be a misfortune for which the friendship of the few rich and powerful would be no compensation."[38]

Gibbons epitomized the noblest features of American Catholicism, in Ellis's estimation, especially in his support for the national experiment in religious freedom and in his sensitivity to social justice. Ellis's biography of the prelate incorporated many topics that portrayed Gibbons's Americanism and his empathy with basic human problems. At the same time, Ellis duly acknowledged evidence in the diocesan archives that showed the statesman was pestered with lesser matters, too. Gibbons was nagged by disputes within and among various dioceses, and he did what he could to arbitrate them. He also had to mediate between American sentiment and Rome, a ticklish situation where his patient diplomacy stood him in good stead. Attending to local disputes and parochial matters kept Gibbons from speaking of religion and American civilization as a whole. In this he did not resemble his Protestant counterparts. But Ellis's summary assessment of the churchman's personal impact pointed out how much the average citizen had come to value his efforts to benefit society at large: "High intelligence, exquisite tact, profound wisdom, and interests that were well nigh universal supplemented a noble bearing and a lofty moral tone that bespoke the Christian gentleman and called forth from high and low, from rich and poor, from Catholic, Protestant and Jew a respect seldom accorded to any living man."[39]

Gibbons's death in 1921 coincided with the nation's first laws restricting immigration. Both events marked a new phase in American Catholicism, the end of a struggle for survival and the start of a new maturity. Ellis discerned contradictory signals in twentieth-century phenomena, but he analyzed each in turn with great facility. He noted that American Catholics seemed to be more accepted as citizens, largely due to their patriotism during World War I and to their social progressivism thereafter. Even though immigration virtually ended, the church continued to grow in size and status. But at the same time, the Ku Klux Klan fanned anti-Catholic hostilities into flame again, and a Catholic candidate for president was overwhelmingly repudiated in 1928. Yet while all this was going on, a new emphasis on liturgical renewal began, and a remarkable increase in monastic vocations manifested a greater maturity in American Catholicism. Ellis concluded that his fellow communicants occupied a strong position in mid-twentieth-century culture. They were accepted enough to consider questions about religion and society outside their own narrow interests. But they were distinctive enough to criticize society, too, having retained a theological perspective. Far from identifying uncritically with national life, as mainstream Protestants had done, "Catholicism is non-conformist. . . . that very fact gives it a valuable role to play in American culture, for while it accepts the political premises of the community without question, it can still judge those premises by a standard outside the community's history."[40] That is where matters stood as Ellis brought Catholic history into contact with the living present.

This corpus of writings by the most distinguished modern American Catholic scholar stimulated new research in a number of ways. When Ellis looked at Catholicism in American life, he did so from a mature historiographical perspective. With no interest in apologetics or defensive polemics, he brought a positive attitude to understanding relationships between his church and his country. That view of heritage and that hunger for historical clarity encouraged many others to investigate other parts of the past with the same spirit of open-minded inquiry. His legacy to Catholic history was to move scholars' minds out of the ghetto and into the common world of humanistic learning.

In addition to leading by example, Ellis also encouraged new research by pointing out areas that needed attention. He thought the area of biographical studies had been developed well enough, as had inquiries into anti-Catholic nativism. But he suggested that much more could be done in categories related to colonization, journalism, education, monastic communities, parish histories, and the place of different ethnic groups in each of these areas. Catholic scholarship was also strong in areas related to religious freedom and support for labor. But in the latter category, for instance, why did Catholic concern for the poor take the form of private charity while Protestants were developing the Social Gospel? And why, Catholic scholars needed to know, did the "Bishops' Program" of social legislation succeed after the Social Gospel faded away? To mention just one more theme that called for investigation, Ellis thought scholarship was particularly weak regarding the church and black Americans. This was doubly regrettable because, not only had recruitment of black parishioners been slow, historians seemed reluctant to seek reasons for it. This "peculiar lethargy" was an item that needed relentless probing because it could not be dismissed with a "simple explanation or a facile condemnation."[41]

Ellis urged Catholic historians to move beyond parochial topics and thus participate in the larger questions of religious influences in national history. His own efforts along those lines demonstrated a fundamental shift away from the dated rubrics of denominational history to the general historiographical standards that infuse the best of all modern studies. Ellis articulated the viewpoint which all contemporary historians share, saying "it is our present duty to face up to the far more difficult and exacting task of self-scrutiny," instead of remaining entrenched behind confessional walls. By moving away from preconceptions, he thought Catholic historians could also avoid special pleading and thus conduct new studies with a balanced perspective. Modern Catholic historians could pursue topics with a new sense of freedom because they realized, "the time has passed when an assumed uniformity within our ranks . . . dominates our thinking, a time . . . when we were led to present a united front out of reaction to a hostile society around us. The historical causes that called that attitude into being are no longer with us, and it has in the meantime itself become part of our history."[42]

CHRISTIANITY GRASPED ENTIRE—AGAIN

In 1919 George E. Horr recommended that American church historians expand their horizons enough to include the neglected subject of Eastern Orthodoxy. Few heeded his call. In recent decades, however, Jaroslav Pelikan has contributed significantly to historical theology, and this partially answers Horr's request for a better understanding of Eastern churches. It would be misleading to say that Pelikan concentrates exclusively on Orthodox topics. Since he grew from a Lutheran background and has held professorships at the University of Chicago and Yale, his interests are naturally broader than that. But his works have illuminated Orthodox categories more fully than have the writings of any other modern church historian. So, even though the alignment may be a bit strained, the historians discussed in this chapter cover all three major branches of Christianity: Handy on Protestantism, Ellis on Catholicism, and Pelikan on Orthodoxy. In the last case, Pelikan is determined to grasp all of Christian history. But pointing out his heavy concentration on Orthodox thought underscores the fact that he has explained its content more than anyone else in American scholarship has done.

Pelikan concentrated on questions about the development of doctrine, choosing not to address matters of institutional growth or the impact of religion on culture. He was intrigued by transformations that have occurred in Christian doctrine, and a recurrent theme in his writings is the problem of interpreting continuity and change. Compared to John Tracy Ellis who brought Catholic historiography up to date by adopting contemporary professional standards, Pelikan brought forth a type of church history that bears striking resemblances to nineteenth-century scholarship. He reinvigorated the concept of church history as handmaiden to theology. His productive career demonstrates that this version of the craft has not only survived, it flourishes alongside other options that variegate the field.

Knowing he was part of a venerable tradition in church historiography, Pelikan aligned himself with intellectual giants of earlier centuries. The most important of them was Adolf von Harnack, whose immense learning provided the foundation on which Pelikan sought to build. There were, of course, some flaws that needed correcting. He thought Harnack had erred by overemphasizing philosophy at the expense of liturgy and prayer as historical influences, but his assessment of the erudite German could be one he wished applied to himself. With the magisterial reformers, Harnack had "shared a concern for the 'restoration of the gospel'; with the historians of the Enlightenment he shared a commitment to a 'nonpartisan' reading of the sources . . .; and with his predecessors in the nineteenth century, he shared an interest in going beyond the bare facts of the history of doctrine to an understanding of the processes by which the doctrine had developed." Pelikan also admired John Henry Newman (one of Ellis's favorites, too) because the English cardinal had sought to "define tradition and infuse it in the church of his day." Newman's works, crammed with facts and citations, vindicated tradition "by using history to transcend antitheses and to hold together principles that polemics on all sides had set into opposition." Using a third and simpler reference, Pelikan wanted to employ history as had Peter Abelard: "to make Christians think, not to make [outsiders] accept Christianity."[43]

An essential quality in the tradition which Pelikan wanted Christians to think about was the fact that believers held much of that tradition in common. Shared emphases outweighed institutional and cultural differences. Almost all of Pelikan's scholarship was informed by an ecumenical mind-set, and this transdenominational perspective led him to search for basic affirmations within varying statements. A sensitivity to both continuity and change also sustained his search for what was authentic in doctrinal development. His desire to identify commonly held truths thus pushed investigation "back to the history of how doctrines have developed in patristic theology." Contemporary ecumenics began, then, with understanding ancient initiatives. Citing a classic example, Pelikan noted that "the *homoousion* formula adopted by the Council of Nicea in 325, which most of Protestantism also accepts, legitimates a development of Christian doctrine beyond the language and thought-world of the New Testament." Then he asked, and kept asking through decades of labor, "if such development was legitimate, what finally are the limits of legitimacy?" Historians are not usually concerned with achieving theological accord among communions, but Pelikan thought historical theology could. If historians traced doctrinal change in sufficient detail, he maintained, then theologians could address "questions both of the legitimacy and of the incompleteness of past developments."[44]

In looking at doctrinal development, Pelikan wanted to find out what made doctrine definable, not what made it true. He accepted as given that Christian thought had a history, that parts of it had changed over time. If observers wondered whether some of those changes were legitimate and how far such alterations could go, church history might serve such theological reflection. Indeed, it was prerequisite to normative evaluation because "the fact of development cannot be appreciated nor the issues of legitimacy and limit adjudicated" without historians' having charted "the process by which doctrines have been developed."[45]

Pelikan knew he faced methodological difficulties in attempting to provide such a chart. Without explaining investigative procedures in detail, he nevertheless held that modern historians were warranted in "going beyond the philologically ascertained *ipsissima verba*" of documentary evidence. They could read between the lines of early texts in hope of "finding in them early hints and traces of what, by subsequent development of doctrine, has become the faith of the Church Catholic." But where did historical description give way to theological preference? Where analysis to personal interest? Pelikan acknowledged the difficulty, saying at one place that the historian would "find the theological questions in the history of doctrine ineluctable; and in this sense he, too, will have to speak as a theologian." Elsewhere he tried to separate the two functions more sharply, concluding that "the tough questions in the development of doctrine will not finally be settled by any historical research." The disciplines were always intertwined for him, and the tough questions of normative judgment could "be faced theologically only when [historical] research has done its job."[46]

One of the tasks Pelikan set for himself in charting the processes of change was that of helping secularists "appreciate how it is that otherwise intelligent and critical thinkers of another age could ever have entertained such beliefs as the doctrine of the Trinity and the Incarnation." In addition to that objective, he also wanted to "introduce those who are already believers to dimensions of the tradition that their own denomination has overlooked." This involved wide knowledge of the primary sources on the part of believers and unbelievers alike. Full information was necessary, and "total immersion in the concrete life of the Church's past" could rescue history from selective distortions. Honest inquirers could succeed if they studied "the full range of the life of the Church within its culture." This immersion enabled researchers to analyze texts according to the "various accents of the time" that produced them. Knowing the context allowed historians to render "a responsible judgment about the various processes by which various doctrines have in fact developed in various periods."[47]

Pelikan was not overly precise in defining his task, subject matter, or investigative procedures because the complex materials comprising his evidence defied easy categorization. On one hand he held that "the method of historical theology and the criteria for judging its results are fundamentally historical." But on the other hand, he saw things as overlapping because the "usual locus" of such history "is within the theological enterprise." Secular intellectual history was useful, too, but "it is in the course of the study of theology that scholars usually become acquainted with the history of Christian doctrine, and it is to other theologians that they usually address the results of their work."[48]

At one point Pelikan mused that his work differed from church history proper, since he was interested in the "genetic history of Christian faith and doctrine." But he went on to admit that there is no clear and simple formula for identifying separate concentrations or divisions of labor. To complicate matters further, he also referred to dogma which for him was "a term ordinarily used to designate the orthodox doctrinal affirmations of the Christian Church." Scholars in former generations produced histories of dogma, but more recent ones pursued histories of doctrine. Pelikan used both terms. Modern historians asked how and why doctrines changed; they did not address theological questions as to their truth content. In Pelikan's view even this kind of historical inquiry belonged in the overall category of theological studies.[49]

Previous attempts to deal with the history of Christian doctrine had, in Pelikan's opinion, emphasized either too much change or none at all. Relativists argued that so many alterations had occurred, there was not enough continuity to link ideas of the apostles with those of the present. Absolutists asserted that Christian truth had existed whole at the beginning, and no significant alteration had ever taken place. Pelikan thought the relativists were right to accept change, but he was also taken with the absolutist notion of durable truth. Recognizing the dilemma, he asked,

How, then, may we acknowledge the human, all-too-human nature of the traditions that are our intellectual, moral, political, and spiritual heritage, and nevertheless . . . affirm those traditions as normative and binding, and go so far as to call them, in some meaningful sense, sacred? . . . how may we who affirm as our own . . . these traditions . . . go on calling them a credo without whistling in the dark as we pass by the cemetery where history has buried tradition?

Pelikan hoped to resolve the dilemma with a "confessional" interpretation of doctrinal development. In it Pelikan admitted that successive generations had used different ideas to explain their beliefs, so change was genuine. But he also insisted that those changes in articulation tried to make sense out of a continuing tradition that was kept alive in the churches, so continuity was real, too. Distinguishing his position from both relativists and absolutists, "with the former it shares the recognition that it is not given to any mortal, be he Christian believer or not, to apprehend and to articulate timeless truth in a timeless way; with the latter it shares the conviction that one must affirm the truth of the faith as though his life depended on it, for it does."[50] This confessional perspective accepted relativity in past and present doctrine, still affirming the truth found therein with no conviction lost because of that.

Pelikan included an astonishing amount of sources in his study of developing doctrine. He began naturally enough with ordinary materials like creeds and theological treatises, but these official pronouncements were too limited for him. The living faith which he sought to glimpse existed in more abundant expressions. So

Pelikan aimed at penetrating "the life and worship of the entire Christian community" where doctrine received its continuing vitality. He invoked Newman to substantiate this populist focus, saying that authentic orthodoxy "did not trickle down from theologians, popes, and councils to the people, but filtered up from the faithful (who are the church) to become the subject matter for speculations, controversies, and systems of the dogmatic theologians." Doctrine evolved according to its own "inner logic" in this "communal matrix" where believers sustained ideas within a common experience. For example, it was the sacramental life in early churches which nurtured Cyprian's doctrine of original sin. Similarly, it was Christian devotion, especially those forms developed in monastic settings, that prompted Athanasius to highlight beliefs about the Blessed Virgin Mary.[51] A history of Christian doctrine based on such deep and widespread source materials might, he hoped, move well beyond previous studies because those earlier ones had depended too much on just a handful of official documents.

A broader range of sources also disclosed the fact that Christian doctrine had been expressed in different ways. Formal creeds and juridical rulings yielded important information, and Pelikan studied them as carefully as had earlier historians of dogma. But going beyond those obvious documents, he analysed sermons and scriptural exegesis to find what lay behind the construction of official creeds. He also focused on liturgies and prayer because he thought devotions could illuminate that which religious instruction sought to guide. The matrix for doctrinal evolution comprised all these levels: confession, teaching, and beliefs. By studying the whole context, "it is possible for the historian, after the fact of what was taught and especially of what was confessed, to discern in what was believed how the Church came to teach a doctrine and how it felt obliged eventually to confess it as well."[52] Pelikan remained alert to various combinations within the three areas. By insisting that each of them was an important factor and by allowing them to interact in different ways, he hoped to do their permutations justice and to treat their complex history adequately.

Pelikan made one final suggestion about method which few other historians were willing to hazard. In addition to analyzing and interpreting what the evidence contained, he thought it might be possible to identify basic ideas that were not expressed there at all. People in every age, he declared, presuppose certain axiomatic truths without articulating them. They do not clarify their assumptions because the reality seems so obvious, there is no need to say it. Thus those silences could be a fruitful source of ideas, eloquent with assumptions and implications which the historian might succeed in grasping. One had to begin with explicit statements in tangible documents, of course, but after that Pelikan suggested historians could try "teasing" the "unspoken meaning" out of documentary evidence. Exploring silence in documents, "moving back to an assumption or forward to an implication," might add valuable dimensions to historical understanding.[53] Fortunately Pelikan did not follow this risky procedure in his magnum opus, and it remains to be seen whether future historians can turn it to some advantage.

The Christian Tradition aimed at no less than explaining the rise of every major doctrine which the believing community has produced over two millennia. It was addressed to two sets of readers: "students of theology and church history, who are concerned with the history of Christian doctrine because it is Christian; [and] students of intellectual history, . . . because it contains important and influential ideas." In this sweeping survey that rivals Harnack's *Dogmengeschichte*, Pelikan made his work as comprehensive as possible. With that wide focus, he discussed specific thinkers and issues "only as they belong to the history of the development of doctrine within the Christian tradition as a whole." Individual voices were useful only to show "what the church has believed, taught, and confessed on the basis of the word of God." The author described this tripartite nexus best when he wrote,

Without setting rigid boundaries, we shall identify what is "believed" as the form of Christian doctrine present in the modalities of devotion, spirituality, and worship; what is "taught" as the content of the word of God extracted by exegesis from the witness of the Bible and communicated to the people of the church through proclamation, instruction, and churchly theology; and what is "confessed" as the testimony of the church, both against false teaching from within and against attacks from without, articulated in polemics and in apologetics, in creed and in dogma.

Those were the elements, then, in which one could find the condition and growth of the church's faith and worship, its understanding of the Bible, and its defense of tradition against heresy. In them Pelikan found both a variety of theologies and a unity of the gospel. He accepted genuine change in Christian history and affirmed true development in a tradition that responded to inner dynamics in the Christian message.[54]

Beginning with primitive Christianity and the early church, Pelikan found incipient doctrine already characterized by a unity of life, devoted to Christ as Lord and faithful to revelation in Scripture. Variations soon appeared, especially among gnostic groups, each of which claimed to be continuous with early witness. So one early problem in the church was to find adequate criteria for authenticating continuity. Pelikan thought Irenaeus put it best when he made wholeness a primary consideration. Heretics showed their bias by selecting only one part of the apostolic consensus and elevating an isolated system to a place above other parts of tradition. Heresy began with partial truth and made its incompleteness aberrant; orthodoxy stayed in the mainstream without departing from consensus. So orthodox Christians retained continuity with traditional teachings by keeping believers together. They were as concerned about maintaining consensus as they were about defining beliefs precisely. As Pelikan described the attitude, "Fundamental to the orthodox consensus was an affirmation of the authority of tradition as that which had been believed 'everywhere, always, by all.' The criteria for what constituted the orthodox tradition were 'universality, antiquity, and consensus.'"

By the sixth century, a great deal of doctrine about christology, anthropology, sacraments, and the church had developed. Segments of these beliefs did not always support each other. Definitions of the person of Christ, for instance, did not easily bear the weight of eucharicstic teaching. But those problems laid the foundation for later constructions, and as concepts developed, "the church went on celebrating and believing, teaching and experimenting with metaphors, defending and confessing."[55]

The most important early doctrines clustered around definitions of the Trinity. In dealing with such complex issues, Pelikan confined himself mostly to the internal connections between integrated ideas. He made only passing reference to nontheological factors, though he knew some historians thought church politics and personality clashes had much to do with the final outcome. But Pelikan wanted to study trinitarian doctrine "in its own terms," and he left all secondary matters for others to study if they wished.

What he stressed was that, as controversy about the person of Christ expanded during the first three centuries, various parties used biblical exegesis and philosophical-theological speculation to clarify what they believed. By A.D. 325, ecumenical councils had begun to lay down orthodox premises for such exegesis and to draw boundaries for acceptable speculation. Such authoritative action might seem arbitrary, but Pelikan found it part of the process. Commenting on change and continuity, he observed, "In the sense that these premises and boundaries had not been specified with any real precision before, the formulation of the doctrine of the person of Christ involved genuine novelty. But in the sense that the presuppositions were already present, that formulation could claim to be . . . following the holy fathers."[56] It was, moreover, a culmination of much that preceded it. The Trinity vindicated monotheism and came to terms with Logos terminology. It refuted Marcion again by making creation and redemption inseparable. And by incorporating the Holy Spirit into a single Godhead it helped silence vestiges of montanism. Homoousion doctrine thus served as a bridge from the classical period to later ages.

In medieval times devotional doctrine flourished in Eastern churches, prompting strong debates over icons. Even though cultural factors bore directly on the iconoclastic controversy, Pelikan again expressed no interest in "the exigencies of ecclesiastical and imperial politics." From his perspective the whole matter was "a dispute over the propriety of the use of images in Christian worship and devotion." In Western churches eucharistic doctrine had moved to affirming the real presence and to using the word "transubstantiation" by 1215. Accompanying this development was a greater emphasis on Christ in the Trinity. The Filioque segment of Western creeds was so widely accepted as part of the undisputed orthodox heritage, Pelikan had to explain in some detail why Eastern theologians challenged it. Differences over trinitarian doctrine and liturgical practices exacerbated ecclesiological disputes, all of which eventuated in schism between Roman and Greek churches in 1054. Pelikan viewed all this as contention within a common faith. He thought ecclesiological arguments had bogged down over interpreting one biblical passage, Matthew 16:18–19, and claims about petrine supremacy had stymied further dialogue. So when the inner logic of doctrinal development faltered, the ongoing process stopped. Pelikan's focus remained so fixed on ideas alone, he could say about the rupture that, "if the doctrinal basis of the jurisdictional dispute could have been settled, all these other differences could have been negotiated—or overlooked."[57] From that point of view, it would be easier to reinstate ecumenical discussions in the twentieth century, too.

Until the late 1200s, believers in both East and West took it for granted that the authentic witness of tradition accorded with the authentic biblical message. After that watershed century, there was an increasing number of important differences in philosophical outlook and systematic formulation among Christian thinkers. Finally, by the time of the Protestant Reformation, Christians began to pit Scripture against tradition and eventually to reject much of the content of catholic consensus. In the sixteenth century, Luther and Calvin made the doctrine of justification by faith central to Protestantism. It was for them the chief doctrine of Christianity and the central point of difference separating Reformed and Roman churches. Pelikan interpreted this renewed emphasis on faith as a "vigorous reassertion of Augustinian anthropology" in opposition to pelagianism which Rome had allowed to become "the one perennial heresy of Christian history." In fact, he viewed Luther's theology as a development in "the old dogmatic Christianity" that went back through Anselm and Augustine to the Council of Chalcedon. Luther's doctrine of redemption was a response to unanswered questions about appropriating the benefits of grace. And as such it relied directly on the early leaders. The "emphatic insistence" by magisterial reformers "that the only valid object of justifying faith was the person of Jesus Christ as the incarnate Son of God located this doctrine within the framework of trinitarian theology."[58] In this interpretive context, Protestants and Catholics were not far apart. Indeed, some Catholic responses to unresolved questions about justification, as expressed in the Council of Trent, were no less remarkable than Protestant beliefs.

If the doctrine of justification by faith alone lay at the heart of Reform impulses, the question of authority was its most troubling problem. Protestants gave primacy to Scripture as the word of God, finding in it "the whole substance of the Christian religion." They regarded preaching God's word to be the Church's supreme function; the sacraments depended on God's word and had no significance apart from it. The grace that was offered in sacraments was the same grace offered in the word. It was true that Luther and Calvin also gave some weight to tradition alongside Scripture. They knew that the ancient Church had created the canon by including some books as authentic and excluding others from Scripture. So Pelikan interpreted Protestant and Catholic views on authority as not absolutely opposed to each other. He thought the broad tradition of Christian doctrine had room for both the Reformed position — "Nothing is to be admitted beyond Holy Writ" — and the tridentine affirmation — "Nothing is to be received contrary to Scripture." In Pelikan's assessment, Protestant ideas in the sixteenth century "made a decisive contribution to the development of doctrine of the Catholicity of the church." Protestantism worked as a catalyst, causing heretofore undifferentiated parts of the orthodox catholic tradition to separate into clusters. Christian doctrines that were rooted in the Bible and the apostles "now became the themes of opposing and mutually exclusive systems, only one of which eventually took the name 'Catholic' as its own."[59]

Thereafter, the universal tradition of orthodox Christian doctrine was increasingly filtered through, and identified with, particular doctrinal formularies. Magisterial reformers had been in general agreement with their Catholic counterparts, affirming the Incarnation, Trinity, and Scripture as inspired, and grace as conferring gifts. For all of them, Pelikan pointed out, the mark of authentic doctrine was its continuity with apostolic revelation, whether contained only in Scripture or also available in the Church as a supplementary source. But more radical thinkers rejected infant baptism, trinitarian creeds, the eucharistic presence of the body of Christ, and an ordained priesthood. In subsequent generations it became more than ever clear that "apostolic continuity was a standard around which several different — and opposing — theological armies could rally." Still Pelikan interpreted the several systems of confessional dogmatics as "each a simulacrum of that 'one, holy, catholic, and apostolic' tradition to which in one way or another, they all still pledged allegiance."[60]

This historiographical study ends before Pelikan has completed his monumental coverage of the whole Christian tradition. His plans for treating more recent topics include an analysis of Marian dogmas (Immaculate Conception, 1854; Bodily Assumption, 1950) and the actions of the Vatican Councils (first, 1869–70; second, 1962–65). Those developments alongside the contributions of pietism, Puritanism, and Jansenism will round off his history. And in the end, he hopes this will help contemporary Christians better appreciate their common heritage.

Pelikan's history has done more than supply information about the past. It has afforded insights that could "go beyond polemics to truth and thus, hopefully, a little closer to unity." His version of historical theology began with the facts of doctrinal change, but it led ineluctably to a quest for doctrinal continuity. As Protestants, Catholics, and Orthodox debated over various differences, he showed that they shared an imposing list of common denominators: God as creator and redeemer; Christ as divine and human, whose life and teaching, suffering and death, resurrection and ascension were cosmically significant; humanity as sinful and yet free; grace, issuing in faith, hope, and love, communicated through the holy ones (especially Mary) and sacraments (especially Eucharist); the church as one, holy, catholic, and apostolic. Over the years there have been "continuing points of divergence" regarding this "doctrinal mainstream," but Pelikan thought that the broad consensus was more important than partisan preferences that singled out only a fraction of the heritage.[61]

Historians could not define the nature of truth or identify the locus of authority. Those were "issues of the faith and the teaching of the Church." But they could serve the church by describing previous efforts to determine truth and authority, and thus help current believers understand more adequately what constituted their tradition. All such doctrines have been affected by environmental conditions. Awareness of this contingency in dogmatic formulation could foster toleration of varied doctrinal expressions. Since "one of the chief intellectual forces of modern ecumenism is the dissolution of the claim that one denomination is in possession of the pure and unchanging doctrine, whereas the distinctive teachings of all others have been shaped by history," church historians might nurture reunion by pointing out that all of them had similar roots and acculturating forces.[62]

Historians could aid ecumenism in another way by reminding all coreligionists that change was endemic to human life. Pelikan went even further and held "that the fact of change somehow belongs to the very definition of Christian truth." By that he meant all human experience is partial, and various attempts at describing Christian truth all fall short of perfection. Historical study could thus liberate minds rather than confine them, and "the historical process needs to be seen by Christian theology as a medium of growth, not as a source of embarrassment." Pelikan thought this sort of ecumenicity across time rested on a conception of doctrinal change that embraced both theological variety and dogmatic continuity. Historians could not produce unity in the Church, but they could supply data out of which it might emerge.[63]

Pelikan offered the fruits of his scholarship to intellectual historians, church historians, and ultimately to the Church itself. While professionally aligned with the first two categories, he identified with the last, affirming its doctrines and anticipating its eventual reunion. He represented a distinctive type of church historian in thinking that history can nurture ecumenical consciousness. To enhance that result, he discussed myriad voices that echoed a common Christian heritage that reached back to the early leaders. He thought such a historical compendium could "serve as a means for this generation of Christian believers to repossess the power of their tradition." In the last analysis, he wanted his type of history to encourage "the task of each generation of the church to re-examine the images and metaphors bequeathed to it by the Bible and subsequent Christian tradition, with a view toward finding those which can serve again as bearers of the Word of God."[64]

8
Overview

The differences between church history and secular history were rather sharply etched in the nineteenth century. When scientific ideals dominated the historical profession, one could readily discern that church history based on theological preconceptions contrasted with the new standard. The weight of a naturalistic, nonprovidential perspective slowly crushed the old form of church history. As practitioners from the old school died out, few young historians replaced them. The twentieth century thus provided opportunities for church historians to align their work more closely with the secular rubrics that applied to everyone, regardless of their subject matter.

Since 1906 members of the reconstituted American Society of Church History have utilized every major historiographical trend that has flourished in the general field of historical scholarship. Understandably, differences between church and secular history have not been as sharp as in the previous era. Instead of black-and-white juxtapositions, twentieth-century contrasts have involved various shades of gray, if indeed the differences were noticeable at all. Despite the fact that methods in church history approximate those used in other topics, modern authors have produced a body of work that is worth viewing as a separate genre, distinguished by its choice of topic. After studying how it developed along the lines of various emphases and interpretive patterns, we are now in a better position to understand its relationship to other segments of the overall field.

When innovations first appeared in the larger field, they involved changes in topic, not method. Scientific ideology continued to shape the major contours of American scholarship well into the 1920s, and church historians slowly accommodated themselves to it. But whereas secular history had traditionally focused on political and military themes, new approaches began to emerge. Younger students such as Charles A. Beard inquired into the economic factors that affected government and warefare. Other pioneers such as James Harvey Robinson abandoned those shopworn topics altogether and began studying a wide range of everyday experiences among the common people. Since then, socioeconomic history and general cultural studies have expanded the horizons of historical knowledge on these broad bases. When these new concepts first appeared, church historians did not participate in such attempts to diversify history. Scholars like Robert H. Nichols and Peter Guilday were proof that many of them continued to think of their work as an adjunct to theological curricula. Only in the last few decades have historians started exploring Christianity on the commoner's level and the economic considerations behind ecclesiastical affairs.

In the 1920s another cluster of scholars began stressing the significance of environmental conditions in explaining history, and several church historians found this approach amenable to their use. As a rule they shared with other such historians a progressivist outlook regarding past developments. They ignored questions of origins and genetic development, preferring to focus on how later conditions had produced beneficial change. Practitioners like Peter G. Mode and Henry K. Rowe emphasized important connections between social experimentation and religious freedom in this country, between democracy and voluntary church support. Sometimes allowing for reciprocal influence, sometimes insisting on the larger environment as determinative of religious content, their narratives traced the decline of elitist politics as well as ecclesiastical privilege. In odes to progress, they wrote of American religion and culture as reaching its highest potential when it achieved religious liberty and nurtured democratic participation in church life.

Of all environmentalist church historians, the most vigorous and prolific was Shirley Jackson Case. Focusing on the early church period, Case interpreted Christianity as a protean entity which responded to varying circumstances that determined its beliefs, worship, and behavioral standards. He thought no religion could remain vibrant by relying on tradition, though change in itself did not imply progress. He simply found it axiomatic that religious expressions were fluid, and as the environmental context altered, they adapted to evolving historical conditions. Theological emphases were also human phenomena to him, affirmations that changed in different ages and situations when people were affected by new intellectual and moral outlooks. So the environing nexus was the key whenever some confessing group formed a new organizational structure or expressed a new belief. Case embodied a real change in church historiography, concentrating as he did on social themes drawn from the actual world. He did not base his work on biblical norms, theologically sensitive interpretations, or the genetic unfolding of some authoritative religious standard. Yet he subsumed his environmental history under ideals about the craft that still honored scientific objectivity.

That ideal collapsed in the early 1930s under a barrage of criticism. The decline of scientific ideals did not occur overnight, nor was it due to one individual's influence, but the names of Carl L. Becker and Charles A. Beard stand at the head of the list. Most professional historians had assumed for over half a century that data about the past existed objectively and that historians could eliminate all biases and preconceived judgments in order to read the data without distortion. But Becker pointed out that actual practice belied the ideal. Everyone, he said, brought preconceptions to the evidence they studied, and those biases were shaped by contemporary culture. Historical narratives did not contain permanent or self-evident truth because each account was an imaginative creation based on current perceptions. Historians did not observe events with neutral eyes; patterns were not inherent in the facts themselves; their significance did not manifest itself to a disinterested scholar.

Charles Beard voiced similar reservations about "that noble dream" wherein facts were thought to contain inherent meaning and observers to record dispassionate truth about the past. In addition to the impact Becker had already made, Beard's influence effectively terminated the ideal of scientific objectivity. He argued it was false to assume that the past existed independently, outside human minds; that historians could know this past and reflect it impartially as a mirror does its object; that events possessed inherent meaning; and that historians could divest themselves of all religious, political, social, economic, and moral interests. On the contrary, he argued, when scholars reconstructed the past, their account featured only a portion of what the fragmentary records contained. Every investigator arranged and interpreted material according to ideas absorbed from an acculturated perspective.

The collective professional response to such devastating criticism was to admit that historical investigation did in fact harbor elements of subjectivity, relativity, and indeterminism. Thereafter historians strove to be as honest as possible about their preconceptions and still be as accurate as possible while treating materials in their chosen field. Strangely enough, church historians were only marginally interested in this momentous debate, and except for George E. Horr and William W. Rockwell they hardly participated in it at all. One can only speculate on this silence. It is possible that church historians were already aware that the goal of disinterested observation was unobtainable because they knew preconceived ideas were part of every researcher's intellectual baggage. For whatever reason, though, the decline of ideas about objective truth, absolute reality, and universally valid criteria did not prod religion scholars into much analysis of procedure or a search for better method. It did, however, remove some of the old antagonism between church and secular history. Fewer scholars thought any longer that religious historians followed theological preconceptions while secular researchers investigated things with no presuppositions at all. Differences between subfields stemmed thereafter from subjective insights which everyone admitted. The same procedures applied to all selected evidence, and findings yielded different interpretations according to various priorities and emphases which individual historians preferred.

The end of science as an ideal for history ushered in the modern historiographical period which we still occupy. In this modern period, scholars acknowledge that every investigation contains some subjective elements. This more self-consciously open context makes it possible for church historians to pursue their work without having to justify it, as heretofore, by reference to a single set of arbitrary standards. Since the 1930s they have been free to use differing frames of reference when probing for causal explanations, and they have employed priorities of their own choosing when piecing together an intelligible sequence of events. In these matters they differ not one bit from other historians who comprise many subsections in the historical profession.

In this more flexible era, church historians explored four notable avenues of investigation: (1) reconstructing the ecclesiastical past along lines of cultural influence, (2) stressing the theological significance of the church's place in history, (3) emphasizing its function in retaining a consensus of cultural values, and (4) accentuating its vigor in conveying important ideas. These four approaches did not emerge in any logical order or progressive sequence. They overlapped in time and blended in individual scholars, with fruitful and often unique results. Perhaps most important of all, each viewpoint was one which secular colleagues also embraced and utilized in other fields of historical endeavor.

William Warren Sweet and Kenneth Scott Latourette represented the first of these approaches, using massive accumulations of data to show that churches had made a notable impact on large segments of human society. Sweet held that churches were an important part of American culture because they had been significant agents in shaping the country's values. His work built on foundations laid by Frederick Jackson Turner and Shirley Jackson Case, but Sweet reversed their environmentalism. Instead of cultural conditions imposing characteristics on people, religious guidelines influenced behavior and thus modified the environment in which people lived. In his view American Christianity was a contributing factor to, not a derivation of, cultural change. So the evangelical impulse was vital to American history because it safeguarded moral standards, guaranteed social stability, nurtured civilized manners, guided education, and defended democracy. Latourette wrote in a similar manner to portray religious influences in different cultures, in his case from a global perspective. With impressive sweep he looked at how Christianity had affected art, music, literature, education, and philosophy as well as touching social, economic, and political institutions. Keys to evaluating religious effectiveness for him were these: geographical expansion, the emergence of new movements, and basic improvements in human welfare. Latourette discerned successive pulsations in church history—expansion, recession, resurgence—and he concluded that Christianity had been and still was a beneficial force in human life.

A second option in church history involved emphasizing the subject's spiritual qualities rather than its institutional forms. Cyril C. Richardson represented this approach that valued ecclesiastical experience for its religious importance, not for its cultural function. It is impossible to ascertain what generated this renewed theological appreciation of the Church, but it emerged in the 1940s. Those were the years when church leaders sought a fresh sense of vocation after they decided that religion defined as social utilitarianism was bankrupt and aimless. Church history with a theological rationale apparently wished to recover the self-esteem it had enjoyed before science banished transcendence from causal explanation. Since modern epistemology made room for metaphysics again, these ecumenical, neoorthodox historians used theological sensibilities to stress the distinctively religious quality of the materials they studied. This concern for ultimate meaning did not, however, lead Richardson to distort evidence or recount events in a triumphalist vein. For him the solemn task of church history was to describe events with scrupulous accuracy in order to facilitate seeing the hand of God at work there.

James H. Nichols also plumped for high-church directives, arguing that positivistic views of history gave it no dignity or ultimate significance. He wanted to recapture a "Christian vision of history" by describing various ways in which the Church Catholic had proclaimed its universal message in different settings. This perspective had no interest in assessing the impact of religion on culture. It tried instead to discern direction and meaning in history by showing how the Church contained concrete examples of redemption and new life. For Nichols, the element that made proper church history superior to mundane studies was that it belonged to the story of God's redemption of mankind. If scholars appreciated the Church as a transcendent reality, he thought they could then use tangible evidence to trace the actualization of the Gospel in human history. As with Richardson, Nichols did not allow this theory to lead him into one-sided, celebrationist history, but his ideas about the craft resonated with those of the late nineteenth century. Though few other church historians followed this line of reasoning, such emphases remain for contemporary practitioners to ponder as a possible component in their work.

A third genre emerged in church history at midcentury, corresponding to broader concerns about consensus in cultural priorities. As an alternative to the violence of war and totalitarian regimes around them, students of American and western European culture searched for continuity in a common heritage. Uncertainty about competing ideologies led historians to lay greater stress on institutional stability, social uniformities, and the persistence of basic values across the generations. Two scholars who emphasized fundamental continuities in religious experience were Roland H. Bainton and Sidney E. Mead. Bainton highlighted three perennial themes in Christian history as antidote to what he called "secular paganism." The first concerned pacifism, freedom from the cruelty of war. His second interest placed a premium on open discussion, freedom to seek the truth and to criticize other positions while doing so. The third was tolerance, acceptance of religious differences without resorting to violence in the name of orthodoxy. Through all his surveys and biographical studies, Bainton stressed these fundamental principles, concluding that no institution through the centuries had exhibited such resistance to tyranny or preserved a consensus of important ideas as had the Christian church.

Sidney Mead's essays represented an effort to expound fundamental principles, especially religious ones, that undergirded American life. He thought contemporary times exhibited symptoms of "religious leukemia," a malaise wherein people tried to be good citizens and good church members with "bifurcated minds." For the better part of forty years, he tried to remove this obstacle to consensus, hoping to resolve tension between the values that legitimized religious freedom and the theology which most denominations embraced. Mead noted that on one side of the equation, rationalism had risen above particular creeds to emphasize a cosmopolitan theology where all religions were equal in a pluralistic commonwealth. On the other side, confessional churches had never adjusted their thinking to the new national outlook. So American Christianity, enjoying separation of church and state as a legacy of the Enlightenment, failed to acknowledge its intellectual benefactor and never developed a theoretical justification for its most distinctive practice. The subsequent impasse thwarted what Mead thought Americans could achieve if they had a better grasp of their heritage. So as a historian, he tried to delineate the religion of the Republic, showing how it differed from the religion of the denominations. In that way he hoped to prod contemporary thinkers into seeing the theological issues between the two religions. Historical understanding might also show that these elements were not incompatible and that it was possible to fuse religion and culture into a proper consensus for modern times.

A fourth category in recent historiography stressed the importance of ideas in past experience. A great number of church historians have utilized this perspective, possibly because they have always regarded doctrine to be central in religious affairs. Some scholars, exemplified by H. Shelton Smith and John T. McNeill, inclined to intellectual history which regarded ideas as causes of behavior. Others, such as Perry Miller and Herbert W. Schneider, inclined to the history of ideas which appreciated systems of thought for their own sake without much concern for pragmatic value. But whether treating ideas as motivating agents or as concepts with intrinsic worth, this type of church history made significant contributions to the study of human perceptions, aspirations, and reasons for action. Such work helped achieve one of the most important professional advances at midcentury, and its various forms continue to be quite vigorous today.

By midcentury hundreds of church historians had produced a wealth of monographs in each of these four approaches. Attempts to synthesize those findings into comprehensive narratives began shortly thereafter. Between 1960 and 1972, at least six outstanding texts on American religious experience appeared. Scholars in this country who specialized in ancient, medieval, or modern Europe did not publish eclectic accounts of a similar nature. But correlative studies of American phenomena reached ever higher degrees of sophistication. Clifton E. Olmstead inaugurated the process of tying discrete monographs together. Winthrop S. Hudson, Edwin S. Gaustad, and Martin E. Marty continued that activity, incorporating relevant information about denominational pluralism, intellectual change, and the effect of religion on American society. This kind of enterprise culminated in the magisterial volume by Sydney E. Ahlstrom. His book discussed institutional, intellectual, and social aspects of American religion in such inclusive depth, it is not likely to be surpassed until another accumulation of monographic information requires synthesizing some time in the future. Collections of primary documents—begun by Peter G. Mode, enhanced by H. Shelton Smith, Robert T. Handy, and Lefferts A. Loetscher, and perfected by Edwin S. Gaustad—also demonstrated the current state of excellent scholarship regarding America's religious past.

Many newer church historians pursue studies on the leading edge of contemporary scholarship, and fortunately they are probing a number of neglected topics. Minority experience, especially the religious life of blacks, Hispanics, and American Indians, is a multifaceted area where scholars are recovering vital information from oblivion. Another important field is the study of women in religion, including women's participation at every level of white denominational existence and in minority groups as well. New studies of immigration are now shedding light on religion as related to ethnic consciousness, pluralism, minorities, and women. In addition to exploring these new fields of study, contemporary church historians are also using fresh hypotheses. Different investigative ideas drawn from psychology, anthropology, and other interdisciplinary viewpoints are turning up new information while also yielding beneficial interpretations of familiar evidence. These and many more creative insights give contemporary researchers greater opportunities to combine their hypotheses with new topics in order to enrich the store of historical knowledge.

While general syntheses emerged and new studies discovered material on neglected topics in American religions, several church historians were continuing distinguished careers. Robert T. Handy put fresh questions to the old phenomenon of pluralism in this country. He helped contemporary scholars see that not all the facets of pluralism have been investigated, especially its relation to religious freedom, immigration and ethnic diversity, social action, and association with non-Christian religions. Handy also broke new ground by studying similarities and differences in the religious life of Canada and the United States. Probably his most significant contribution was in tracing the gradual transformation of ideals for Christianizing America into uncritical acceptance of Americanized Christianity. That reversal supplied important information about acculturation, and it explained conditions which lie behind the problems and opportunities which churches face today. Handy's work will stimulate several generations to pursue further research along these lines.

Catholic history came of age in the person of John Tracy Ellis. In an outstanding instance of leadership by example, he published a landmark biography and two surveys of American Catholicism that were the epitome of painstaking accuracy and bold candor. He encouraged a great many other Catholic historians to move out of their intellectual ghetto and to exercise more fully the historiographical options available to them.

Jaroslav Pelikan was a third contemporary scholar whose work pushed beyond the midcentury plateau. In a curious way, he was old and new at the same time. Perhaps no American church historian dared as much as he to encompass the whole spectrum of Christian doctrinal development. For that alone his efforts will have to be reckoned with in succeeding generations. But while exploring history from a new ecumenical perspective, Pelikan also embodies attitudes about the church and its message that was reminiscent of nineteenth-century perspectives. His career proves that, while many historians now investigate aspects of Christianity from secular points of view, others are still capable of writing Christian history in a way that echoes a previous era.

All these trends emerged in the modern historiographical period. That period began around 1935 with the collapse of ideals about history that derived ultimately from Baconian empiricism. Subsequent options emerged after the larger historical profession no longer operated with a single standard regarding perspectives and procedures. This turn of events was a boon in that the tyranny of intellectual uniformity was overthrown, and historians could act according to ideas that made sense to them personally. It was a bane in that nothing replaced the old orthodoxy with another overarching perspective to which practitioners might conform.

The lasting benefit of multiple voices in the guild is richness, a happy diversity that stimulates further inquiry and debate without worry about lockstep conformity to one viewpoint. The troubling element is that historians of all kinds now tacitly accept the fate of being dismissed by those who do not share their perceptions and priorities. This is the mixed blessing of having moved from one canon in the age of science to multiple approaches in a more complex age when historians employ subjective insight and critical judgment as parts of an increasingly sophisticated historical method.

The modern period enjoys freedom of choice, but its options entail feelings of uncertainty. Historians now approach a variety of subjects in different ways. They no longer think there is a single mode of operation for everyone to follow. Relativity allows any history to claim legitimacy, but this raised the question of complete relativism where hopes for general historical validity are sacrificed to special interest groups who sponsor competing studies. The modern period has no canon, and professional historians are no longer certain as to which method or interpretive perspective is the proper one for all of them to follow—or whether there ought to be one at all.

One more aspect of twentiety-century church historiography is worth mentioning, and that concerns the perennial question of how to treat sacred references in a human framework. Historians in previous epochs frequently used earthly means to serve other-worldly ends. They thought of their work as a subsection of theology, enlisting the aid of Clio to discern providential activity in past experience. Most of them pointed to certain events as indicating God's direct intervention or as substantiating support for their favorite part of the Church. All such activities were ones wherein faith affirmations took precedence, influencing both the selection of evidence and the interpretation placed on it. Belief in divine agency was a theoretical prerequisite to proper church history. It was this perspective that contrasted so markedly with scientific history when that methodological ideal denied a place to all presuppositions.

In the modern period, when the decline of scientific rubrics made room for different angles of vision again, some church historians called for a return to theological guidelines in their profession. Most of their colleagues did not respond to their call but remained solidly on the side which defines church history as a branch of humanistic learning. Secular-minded students of ecclesiastical developments have accepted the predominant attitude about documentary restrictions in modern historiography. Instead of seeing a vindication of supernatural agency in human materials, they have confined themselves to interpreting religion as a vital component in people's lives. This collective decision to remain within mundane interpretations is one of the most striking features of the profession's operational ideas at present.

Almost all students of religious developments now acknowledge that interpretations should be based responsibly on the limited materials of research findings, not determined by anterior definitions or higher purposes. They see that retaining supernatural factors in historical interpretation appeals to an agency not found in the records themselves. Most contemporary church historians have stopped trying to locate God in reports about what transpired on the mundane level. Their scholarship is on a par with the restricted but solid work of historians in the general field who also resist ideological distortion.

The old problem of trying to support providentialist interpretations with human evidence has been particularly clear in church history, and scholars in the modern period have gravitated in significant numbers to the humanistic viewpoint. But a few have recently defined some aspect of Christianity as divinely instituted and have invoked a transcendental perspective to support their assertion. They wound up admitting, however, that all they could do was investigate earthly materials and study human expressions in mundane documents. It was impossible, the most astute of them acknowledged, to write the history of the work of God unless one were either a prophet or an apostle. Lacking that status, church historians could not claim higher meaning in the results of their work. The old allegiance to serve theological ends stretched the means of historical data to the breaking point.

Investigative procedures in the modern period bar all responsible historians from discerning God's direct hand in public events. But some scholars still keep a theological interest alive by commenting on the significance of events *after* they write history. Reflections on religious meaning behind historical experience have superseded efforts to describe providential guidance or intervention. Those who now discuss divine agency in history no longer use documentary materials to verify providential action. Their commentaries *follow* research and interpretation rather than determine scholarly inquiry. Comments of this sort rely on historical data that are produced by accepted investigative procedures. They add a metahistorical element to mundane accounts, but they keep the process of research, interpretation, and commentary in proper order. So reflections on the supernatural have not disappeared altogether from modern church history; they have shifted from preconception to afterthought in the list of priorities to which most historians subscribe. Those who speak of religious meaning in history do not manage evidence or impose supernatural causes on it. Their theological reflections rest on the solid ground of humanistic learning, and they add further suggestions about the possible significance of historical knowledge.

Scholars who choose to discuss human records in light of Christian faith supply an additional dimension to historical awareness. For some this is the culmination of all preceding spadework. Different assumptions about providence, doctrine, and moral standards cause such historians to disagree among themselves in their commentaries, not to mention disagreements with those whose naturalistic interests rule out supernatural reflections altogether.

Some church historians argue that historical explanations ought to exclude every idea that lies outside the investigative process. Others point out that subjective insights are part of the researcher's mind-set, and they cannot be excluded by wishing them away. Making a virtue of necessity, they welcome theological reflection because it provides a more comprehensive intelligibility to human existence. Such reflections utilize rigorous methods of historical inquiry and then furnish ideas about intermediate significance in human life while incorporating the whole in thoughts about ultimate destiny.

In summary, then, it is clear that church historians in the modern period have adjusted to the limits placed on interpreting mundane evidence while also accepting subjectivity and relative insights in each researcher's investigative procedures. Their narratives are accepted as worthwhile contributions to modern scholarship, distinguishable from other histories only by choice of subject matter. Some present-day students of religion choose to employ theological reflections on historical change. This optional dimension preserves a place for ideas about the supernatural in history without violating the commonly shared techniques that supply information for comment. Having accommodated to critical investigative procedures, church history has still been able within that rectitude to allow for theological commentary as a supplement to secular intellectual standards. Most church historians do not make such reflective comments, but the inclusive guild is large enough for those with different frames of mind to cooperate with, and to learn from, each other.

NOTES
SELECT BIBLIOGRAPHY
INDEX

Notes

PREFACE

1. Timothy Paul Donovan, *Historical Thought in America: Postwar Patterns* (Norman: University of Oklahoma Press, 1973), 9–10.

2. John Higham, Leonard Krieger, and Felix Gilbert, *History* (Englewood Cliffs, N.J.: Prentice-Hall, 1965), 147.

3. John Higham, *Writing American History: Essays on Modern Scholarship* (Bloomington: Indiana University Press, 1970), 173.

4. Sidney E. Mead, "Church History Explained," *Church History* 32 (March 1963): 21.

5. Bruce Catton, *Prefaces to History* (Garden City, N.Y.: Doubleday, 1970), 93.

CHAPTER 1

1. Williston Walker, *A History of the Congregational Churches in the United States* (New York: Christian Literature Co., 1894); Williston Walker, *Ten New England Leaders* (New York: Silver, Burdett and Co., 1901); Williston Walker, *John Calvin: The Organiser of Reformed Protestantism, 1509–1564* (New York: G. P. Putnam's Sons, 1906); Williston Walker, *The Reformation* (New York: Charles Scribner's Sons, 1915); Williston Walker, *A History of the Christian Church* (New York: Charles Scribner's Sons, 1918).

2. Ephraim Emerton, "The Study of Church History," *Unitarian Review and Religious Magazine* 19 (January 1883): 1–18; Ephraim Emerton, *Medieval Europe* (Boston: Ginn and Co., 1894); Ephraim Emerton, *Desiderius Erasmus of Rotterdam* (New York: G. P. Putnam's Sons, 1899); Ephraim Emerton, *Learning and Living: Academic Essays* (Cambridge: Harvard University Press, 1921).

3. Arthur C. McGiffert, "The Historical Study of Christianity," *Bibliotheca Sacra* 50 (January 1893): 150–71; Arthur C. McGiffert, *The Problem of Christian Creeds as Affected by Modern Thought* (Buffalo: Peter Paul and Co., 1901); Arthur C. McGiffert, *Protestant Thought before Kant* (London: Gerald Duckworth and Co., 1911); Arthur C. McGiffert, *The Rise of Modern Religious Ideas* (New York: Macmillan Co., 1915); Arthur C. McGiffert, *A History of Christian Thought*, 2 vols. (New York: Charles Scribner's Sons, 1932).

4. Philip Schaff, *Principle of Protestantism, As Related to the Present State of the Church* (Chambersburg, Penn.: Publication Office of the German Reformed Church, 1845); Philip Schaff, *What is Church History? A Vindication of the Idea of Historical Development* (Philadelphia: J. B. Lippincott Co., 1846); Philip Schaff, *History of the Christian Church*, 6 vols. (New York: Charles Scribner's Sons, 1882–92).

5. Francis A. Christie, "Report of the Conference on the Teaching of Church History," *Annual Report of the American Historical Association for the Year 1904* (Washington, D.C., 1905): 213.

6. George P. Fisher, "The Function of the Historian as Judge of Historic Persons," *Annual Report of the American Historical Association for the Year 1898* (Washington, D.C., 1899): 26.

7. Henry C. Lea, "Ethical Values in History," *American Historical Review* 9 (1904): 234, 237.

8. Simeon E. Baldwin, "Religion Still the Key to History," *American Historical Review* 12 (1907): 219, 221, 239, 242. This attitude brings to mind Edward Gibbon who abandoned hostility toward Catholicism and substituted a spirit of condescending appreciation of its usefulness; it also echoes James Madison who penned in no. 38 of *The Federalist* a reference to "the authority of superstition" as an element contributive to social stability.

9. J. Franklin Jameson, "The American Acta Sanctorum," *American Historical Review* 13 (1908): 292–93, 295, 298.

10. Ephraim Emerton, "A Definition of Church History," *Papers of the American Society of Church History*, 2d ser., 7 (1923): 56, 59.

11. Samuel M. Jackson, *Bibliographical Sketches of the Principal Christian Writers from the Sixth to the Twelfth Century, with an Analysis of their Writings* (New York: Charles Scribner's Sons, 1892); Samuel M. Jackson, *A Bibliography of American Church History, 1820–1893*, vol. 12, American Church History (New York: Christian Literature Co., 1894), 441–513; Samuel M. Jackson, *Concise Dictionary of Religious Knowledge, Biblical, Doctrinal, Historical, and Practical* (New York: Christian Literature Co., 1889); Samuel M. Jackson, *Huldreich Zwingli, the Reformer of German Switzerland* (New York: G. P. Putnam's Sons, 1901).

12. Edward T. Corwin, *A Manual of the Reformed Church in America, 1628–1902*, 4th ed. (New York: Board of Publication, Reformed Church in America, 1902); Edward T. Corwin, *History of the Reformed Church, Dutch*, vol. 8, American Church History (New York: Christian Literature Co., 1898); Edward T. Corwin, "The Amsterdam Correspondence," *Papers of the American Society of Church History* 8 (1897) and "Letters of the Dutch Ministers to the Classis of Amsterdam, 1655–1664," in *Narratives of New Netherland, 1609–1664*, ed. J. Franklin Jameson, vol. 9, *Original Narratives of Early American History* (New York: Charles Scribner's Sons, 1909), 391–415; Edward T. Corwin, "The Ecclesiastical Condition of New York at the Opening of the Eighteenth Century," *Papers of the American Society of Church History*, 2d ser., 3 (1912): 79–115.

13. Joseph C. Ayer, Jr., "The Development of the Appellate Jurisdiction of the Roman See," *Papers of the American Society of Church History* 8 (1897): 197–227; Joseph C. Ayer, "On the Medieval National Church," *Papers of the American Society of Church History*, 2d ser., 4 (1914): 41–75; Joseph C. Ayer, "Church

Councils of the Anglo-Saxons," *Papers of the American Society of Church History,* 2d ser., 7 (1923): 91–107; Joseph C. Ayer, *A Source Book for Ancient Church History, from the Apostolic Age to the Close of the Conciliar Period* (New York: Charles Scribner's Sons, 1913), viii–ix.

14. Robert H. Nichols, *The Growth of the Christian Church,* 2 vols., (Philadelphia: Westminster Press, 1914); "Courses in the History of the Christian Church," (New York: Columbia University Home Study Service, 1923).

15. Robert H. Nichols, "Aims and Methods of Teaching Church History," *Papers of the American Society of Church History,* 2d ser., 7 (1923): 39, 41, 44, 47.

16. John K. Cartwright, "The American Catholic Historical Association: A Survey of Twenty-Five Years," *Catholic Historical Review* 30 (January, 1945): 384–85.

17. Ibid., 382, 392. See also W. H. Kent, "Catholic Truth and Historical Truth," *Catholic Historical Review* 6 (October 1920): 275–76.

18. Waldo G. Leland, "Concerning Catholic Historical Societies," *Catholic Historical Review* 2 (January 1917): 390–92, 398.

19. Henry J. Ford, "A Change of Climate," *Catholic Historical Review,* n.s. 5 (April 1925): 24–25.

20. John Tracy Ellis, "Peter Guilday, March 25, 1884–July 31, 1947," *Catholic Historical Review* 33 (October 1947): 262–63, 265. See also John Tracy Ellis, "The Catholic University of America, 1927–1979: A Personal Memoir," *Social Thought* 5 (Spring 1979): 40; and John Tracy Ellis, "The Influence of the Catholic University of Louvain on the Church in the United States," *Louvain Studies* 9 (Spring 1983): 280.

21. Peter Guilday, "The American Catholic Historical Association," *Catholic Historical Review* 6 (April 1920): 5.

22. Ford, "Change of Climate," 25–26.

23. Edward P. Lilly, "A Major Problem for Catholic American Historians," *Catholic Historical Review* 24 (January 1939): 434.

24. Guilday, "American Catholic Historical Association," 13–14.

25. Joseph Schrembs, "The Catholic Philosophy of History," in *The Catholic Philosophy of History,* ed. Peter Guilday (New York: P. J. Kenedy and Sons, 1936), 3–4.

26. Peter Guilday, *The English Colleges and Convents in the Catholic Low Countries, 1558–1795,* vol. 1, *The English Catholic Refugees on the Continent, 1558–1795* (London: Longmans, Green and Co., 1914), x.

27. Ibid., xv, xxi, 163.

28. Ibid., xxii–xxiii, 2–3.

29. Peter Guilday, *The Life and Times of John Carroll, Archbishop of Baltimore, 1735–1815* (New York: Encyclopedia Press, 1922), 27, 166, 246, 260–61, 828–29, 830.

30. Peter Guilday, *The Life and Times of John England, First Bishop of Charleston, 1786–1842* (New York: America Press, 1927), 1:3, 35, 359–360; 2:48–67, 71, 117–18.

31. Ibid., vol. 1, viii.

32. Peter Guilday, *A History of the Councils of Baltimore, 1791–1884* (New York: Macmillan Co., 1932), 1–2.

33. James Harvey Robinson, *The New History: Essays Illustrating the Modern Historical Outlook* (New York: Macmillan Co., 1912), 9, 72–73.

34. Edward Eggleston, "The New History," *Annual Report of the American Historical Association for the Year 1900* (Washington, D.C., 1901): 47. As early as 1848, the Regius Professor of History at Oxford University, H. H. Vaughan, called for expansion of historical subject matter in order to cover such areas as popular tastes, pastimes, beliefs, and customs. See Lawrence Stone, "History and the Social Sciences in the Twentieth Century," in *The Future of History: Essays in the Vanderbilt Centennial Symposium,* ed. Charles F. Delzell (Nashville: Vanderbilt University Press, 1977), 4.

35. Frederick Jackson Turner, "The Significance of the Frontier in American History," *Annual Report of the American Historical Association for the Year 1893* (Washington, D.C., 1894), 199–227; Frederick Jackson Turner, *The Rise of the New West, 1818–1829* (New York: Harper and Brothers, 1906); Frederick Jackson Turner, *The Frontier in American History* (New York: Henry Holt and Co., 1920).

36. Charles A. Beard, *An Economic Interpretation of the Constitution of the United States* (New York: Macmillan Co., 1913); Charles A. Beard, *Economic Origins of Jeffersonian Democracy* (New York: Macmillan Co., 1915).

37. John Higham, Leonard Krieger, and Felix Gilbert, *History* (Englewood Cliffs, N.J.: Prentice-Hall, 1965), 112–14, 172–73.

38. Richard Hofstadter, *The Progressive Historians: Turner, Beard, Parrington* (New York: Alfred A. Knopf, 1968), 172, 185, 437–38.

39. Robinson, *New History,* 23–24.

40. Higham, Krieger, and Gilbert, *History,* 111–12, 115–16.

41. George Williams sees Peter G. Mode's concentration on American materials as an aspect of post-World War I isolationism. See George H. Williams, "Church History," *Protestant Thought in the Twentieth Century: Whence and Whither?* ed. Arnold S. Nash (New York: Macmillan Co., 1951), 161. The momentum that led to Mode's work was due to more basic changes in perspective and approach than that. His specialization is a natural development in the general victory of New History categories over nineteenth-century formulas.

42. Peter G. Mode, *Source Book and Bibliographical Guide for American Church History* (Menasha, Wis.: George Banta Publishing Co, 1921), v.

43. Peter G. Mode, *The Frontier Spirit in American Christianity* (New York: Macmillan Co., 1923), ix.

44. Ibid., 1. As will become clear later, it is significant that Mode drew his definition of Christianity from Shirley Jackson Case and his *Evolution of Early Christianity* (Chicago: University of Chicago Press, 1914), 25.

45. Mode, *Frontier Spirit,* 100.

46. Ibid., 13.

47. Ibid., 121–22.

48. Ibid., 41–42, 54.

49. Ibid., 57.

50. Ibid., 57–58.

51. In this instance Williams's "Church History," 165, is closer to the mark in pointing out strong ties between Rowe's interests and those enunciated by James Harvey Robinson.

52. Henry K. Rowe, *History of the Christian Church* (New York: MacMillan Co., 1931), 3–4.

53. Rowe, *History of the Christian Church*, 14; Henry K. Rowe, *The History of Religion in the United States* (New York: Macmillan Co., 1924), vii.

54. Rowe, *Religion in the United States*, vii–viii; and Rowe, *Christian Church*, 10.

55. Rowe, *Religion in the United States*, 55–56, 114–15.

56. Ibid., 405.

57. Ibid., 204–5.

58. Shirley Jackson Case, *Jesus through the Centuries* (Chicago: University of Chicago Press, 1932), 354–55.

59. Shirley Jackson Case, *The Social Origins of Christianity* (Chicago: University of Chicago Press, 1923), 33, 35–37, 252.

60. Shirley Jackson Case, *The Evolution of Early Christianity: A Genetic Study of First-Century Christianity in Relation to Its Religious Environment* (Chicago: University of Chicago Press, 1914), 1–2, 37–38.

61. Shirley Jackson Case, *Christianity in a Changing World* (New York: Harper and Brothers, 1949), 120–21.

62. Shirley Jackson Case, *The Historicity of Jesus: A Criticism of the Contention that Jesus Never Lived, a Statement of the Evidence for His Existence, an Estimate of his Relation to Christianity* (Chicago: University of Chicago Press, 1912), 272–73; Case, *Christianity in a Changing World*, viii; Case, *Evolution of Early Christianity*, 190–91.

63. Case, *Christianity in a Changing World*, 18, 40; Case, *Evolution of Early Christianity*, 47.

64. Case, *Social Origins*, 24, 255; Case, *Evolution of Early Christianity*, 46.

65. Shirley Jackson Case, *The Christian Philosophy of History* (Chicago: University of Chicgao Press, 1943), 47–48, 98.

66. Shirley Jackson Case, *The Historical Method in the Study of Religion* (Lewiston, Maine: N.p., 1907), 10–11; Case, *Evolution of Early Christianity*, 25.

67. Case, *Jesus through the Centuries*, 15–16, 318.

68. Shirley Jackson Case, *Jesus: A New Biography* (Chicago: University of Chicago Press, 1927), 378–79; 384–85; Case, *Christianity in a Changing World*, 46–47.

69. Case, *Evolution of Early Christianity*, 332–33; *Social Origins*, 60–61; *Jesus: A New Biography*, 66, 338–39.

70. Case, *Christianity in a Changing World*, 32.

71. Case, *Jesus through the Centuries*, 4–5; Case, *Evolution of Early Christianity*, 32–34, 368–69; Case, *Social Origins*, 77–78.

72. Shirley Jackson Case, *The Origins of Christian Supernaturalism* (Chicago: University of Chicago Press, 1946), v–vi; Case, *Social Origins*, 75; Case, *Jesus: A New Biography*, 2–5.

73. Shirley Jackson Case, *The Social Triumph of the Ancient Church* (New York: Harper and Brothers, 1933), 35, 37, 115–16.

74. Case, *Evolution of Early Christianity*, 279–80.

75. Case, *Social Triumph*, 91–93, 203, 212.

76. Ibid., 97, 142, 145, 198–99.

77. Case, *Jesus through the Centuries*, 366, 370–75; Case, *Historicity of Jesus*, 328, 336, 344; Case, *Christianity in a Changing World*, 33, 180–81, 184–85.

78. Case, *Social Origins*, 252–53; Case, *Historical Method*, 11, 18–20; Case, *Historicity of Jesus*, 7–8; Case, *Christian Philosophy of History*, vi.

CHAPTER 2

1. Carl L. Becker, "Some Aspects of the Influence of Social Problems and Ideas upon the Study and Writing of History," *American Journal of Sociology* 18 (March 1913): 641; Carl L. Becker, "Everyman His Own Historian," *American Historical Review* 37 (January 1932): 241–43. In another trenchant phrase, he said, "all historical writing, even the most honest, is unconsciously subjective, since every age is bound, in spite of itself, to make the dead perform whatever tricks it finds necessary for its own peace of mind." See also Becker, *The Heavenly City of the Eighteenth Century Philosophers* (New Haven: Yale University Press, 1932), 44.

2. Carl L. Becker, "Detachment and Writing of History," *Atlantic Monthly* 106 (October 1910): 24.

3. Becker, "Everyman His Own Historian," 249–50.

4. Carl L. Becker, "What Are Historical Facts?" *Western Political Quarterly* 8 (September 1955): 47.

5. Becker, "Everyman His Own Historian," 234.

6. Becker, "Some Aspects of the Influence of Social Problems," 664–65; "What Are Historical Facts?" 48, 50–51.

7. Charles A. Beard, "That Noble Dream," *American Historical Review* 41 (October 1935): 84.

8. Ibid., 76.

9. Charles A. Beard, "Written History as an Act of Faith," *American Historical Review* 39 (January 1934): 219–21, 226.

10. John Higham, Leonard Krieger, and Felix Gilbert, *History* (Englewood Cliffs, N.J.: Prentice-Hall, 1965), 126–27; Richard Hofstadter, *The Progressive Historians: Turner, Beard, Parrington* (New York: Alfred A. Knopf, 1968), 305–6, 315–16.

11. Leo Gershoy, "Zagorin's Interpretation of Becker: Some Observations," *American Historical Review* 62 (October 1956): 15; Robert Allen Skotheim, *American Intellectual Histories and Historians* (Princeton: Princeton University Press, 1966), 119.

12. Whitaker T. Deininger, "The Skepticism and Historical Faith of Charles A. Beard," *Journal of the History of Ideas* 15 (October 1954): 573–88; Timothy Paul Donovan, *Historical Thought in America: Postwar Patterns* (Norman: University of Oklahoma Press, 1973), 114; Maurice Mandelbaum, "Causal Analysis in History," *Journal of the History of Ideas* 3 (January 1942): 30–50.

13. Chester McArthur Destler, "Some Observations on Contemporary Historical Theory," *American Historical Review* 55 (April 1950): 519; William B. Munro, "Clio and Her Cousins: Some Reflections upon the Place of History among the Social Sciences," *Pacific Historical Review* 10 (December 1941): 405.

14. Charles W. Cole, "The Relativity of History," *Political Science Quarterly* 48 (June 1933): 162–64.

15. Ibid., 165.

16. Ibid., 170.

17. It may be that church historians have felt less threatened by critiques of scientific history because they were more tentative about its absolute claims. Sophisticated church historians knew that theology played a role in their overall perspective, and this preconception thwarted simple-minded acceptance of naturalistic, empirical explanations. One theologian who wrote at the time of Becker's first essay epitomized this point of view. He noted that the subject matter with which one worked "is not simply a datum to be received" because "the influence of personal subjective presuppositions" played an important part. Church historians attracted to ideals about objectivity also had to ponder the question, "if the conception of Christianity is conditioned by [one's] personal attitude toward it, this personal attitude is conditioned in turn by the age of the world in which one lives, the type of civilization of which one is a member, the stage of culture to which one belongs, and the local and temporal currents or drifts from which one, try hard as one may, cannot hold himself aloof." See George B. Foster, *The Finality of the Christian Belief, Part 1* (Chicago: University of Chicago Press, 1909), 311–12.

18. George H. Williams, "Church History," in *Protestant Thought in the Twentieth Century: Whence and Whither?* ed. Arnold S. Nash (New York: Macmillan Co., 1951), 174, is correct in noting the paucity of debate among church historians, but he is both anachronistic and imprecise in identifying participants and the works which contributed significantly to historiographical advance.

19. George E. Horr, "The Influence of the War Upon the Study of Church History," *Papers of the American Society of Church History*, 2d ser., 7 (1923): 27.

20. Ibid., 28.

21. Ibid., 35.

22. Ibid., 31, 36.

23. William W. Rockwell, "Rival Presuppositions in the Writing of Church History: A Study of Intellectual Bias," *Papers of the American Society of Church History*, 2d ser., 9 (1934): 12. The citation is from Herbert Spencer, *The Principles of Ethics*, vol. 1 (New York: D. Appleton and Co., 1893), 464. In *The Study of Sociology* (New York: D. Appleton and Co., 1873), Spencer outlined five varieties of bias which he categorized as educational, patriotic, class, political, and theological.

24. Rockwell, "Rival Presuppositions," 13. In debate with a recently appointed Roman Catholic professor of history at the University of Strasbourg, Mommsen called for "eine voraussetzungslose Geschichtswissenschaft."

25. Rockwell, "Rival Presuppositions," 14. Albert M. Koeniger answered Mommsen in *Voraussetzungen und Voraussetzungslosigkeit* (München: Kirchenhistorischer Seminar, Veröffentlichungen, 1910), saying that all historians are partial and must be held accountable for their biases. If church historians were allowed to pass over evidence unfavorable to their own beliefs, Koeniger held this would invalidate their contribution: "To allow them to escape the extreme penalty of their misdeeds would be indeed a sad sort of 'benefit of clergy.'"

26. Rockwell, "Rival Presuppositions," 11.

27. Ibid., 25.

28. Ibid., 32–34.

29. Ibid., 34, 46–47. This was the wording contained in the 1907 papal encyclical, *Pascendi Gregis,* that condemned modernism.

30. Rockwell, "Rival Presuppositions," 49, 51.

31. William W. Sweet as cited in James L. Ash, Jr., *Protestantism and the American University: An Intellectual Biography of William Warren Sweet* (Dallas: Southern Methodist University Press, 1982), 107.

32. William W. Sweet, *American Culture and Religion: Six Essays* (Dallas, Southern Methodist University Press, 1951), 75–76; William W. Sweet, "Christianity in the Americas," in *A Bibliographic Guide to the History of Christianity,* ed. Shirley Jackson Case (Chicago: University of Chicago Press, 1931), 173; William W. Sweet, *Men of Zeal: The Romance of American Methodist Beginnings* (New York: Abingdon Press, 1935), 75.

33. Sweet spent a tremendous amount of time, and Chicago's money, visiting local archives to create a depository of primary sources at his university. Some of the results of this effort came to light in doctoral dissertations, while four major assemblages appeared as denominational source books. Those extensive compilations, edited by Sweet, are listed chronologically from *Religion on the American Frontier:* Vol. 1, *The Baptists, 1783–1830* (New York: Henry Holt and Co., 1931); vol. 2, *The Presbyterians, 1783–1840* (New York: Harper and Brothers, 1936); vol. 3, *The Congregationalists, 1783–1850* (Chicago: University of Chicago Press, 1939); vol. 4, *The Methodists, 1783–1840* (Chicago: University of Chicago Press, 1946).

34. William W. Sweet, "The Frontier Spirit in American Christianity," in *Environmental Factors in Christian History,* ed. J. T. McNeill, M. Spinka, and H. R. Willoughby (Chicago: University of Chicago Press, 1939), 380, 397.

35. Sweet, *The Baptists,* 3.

36. William W. Sweet, ed., *Circuit-Rider Days along the Ohio: Being the Journals of the Ohio Conference from its Organization in 1812 to 1826* (New York: Methodist Book Concern, 1923), 11.

37. Sweet, "The Frontier Spirit in American Christianity," 381.

38. The best summary discussion of this important theme can be found in Ray A. Billington, *America's Frontier Heritage* (New York: Holt, Rinehart and Winston, 1966), 3, 25.

39. William W. Sweet, *Methodism in American History* (New York: Methodist Book Concern, 1933), 143; William W. Sweet, *The Story of Religions in America,* 6th ed. (New York: Harper and Brothers, 1950), 4–5; *The Baptists,* 18.

40. William W. Sweet, "Religion and the Westward March," *Ohio State Archaeological and Historical Quarterly* 50 (January–March, 1941), 72–73; William W. Sweet, "The Protestant Churches," *Annals of the American Academy of Political and Social Science* 256 (March 1948), 46; Sweet, *Men of Zeal,* 199; Sweet, "The Frontier Spirit in American Christianity," 390; Sweet, *The Baptists,* 18.

41. For the best analysis on this point see Ash, *Protestantism and the American University,* 45.

42. William W. Sweet, *The American Churches: An Interpretation* (New York: Abingdon-Cokesbury Press, 1948), 7–8.

43. Sweet, "The Frontier Spirit in American Christianity," 395–96; Sweet, *Men of Zeal*, 201.

44. Sweet, *The American Churches*, 49; William W. Sweet, ed., *The Rise of Methodism in the West: Being the Journal of the Western Conference, 1800–1811* (New York: Methodist Book Concern, 1920), 62.

45. Sweet, "The Frontier Spirit in American Christianity," 396.

46. Sweet, *The Story of Religions in America*, 6.

47. Ibid., 5.

48. Sweet, *The American Churches*, 51–52; Sweet, *American Culture and Religion*, 108.

49. Sweet, *American Culture and Religion*, 38: Sweet, *The Story of Religions in America*, 8.

50. Sweet, *The American Churches*, 7, 14–15.

51. Sweet, *American Culture and Religion*, 107; Sweet, *The Rise of Methodism in the West*, 67; Sweet, *The American Churches*, 75–76; Sweet, "The Frontier Spirit in American Christianity," 396.

52. Sweet claimed, for example, that the midwestern frontier had become the seat of Methodist predominance in the early national period. But his supporting data show instead that eastern urban centers were more significant. See William W. Sweet, *The Methodist Episcopal Church and the Civil War* (Cincinnati: Methodist Book Concern, 1912), 63, 80.

53. Sweet, *Men of Zeal*, 17; William W. Sweet, *Makers of Christianity: From John Cotton to Lyman Abbott* (New York: Henry Holt and Co., 1937), 235.

54. Sweet, *American Culture and Religion*, 28–29; Sweet, *Men of Zeal*, 15–16.

55. At no other point did Sweet depart from other interpretations of Turner's frontier thesis than here. Once he dissociated the frontier concept from land as a determining factor, Sweet moved to categories bearing little relation to its historiographical roots, save as an evocative symbol that could be manipulated. See Sweet, *The American Churches*, 50, 57–58, 99–100.

56. Sweet, *American Culture and Religion*, 63.

57. Kenneth S. Latourette, *A History of the Expansion of Christianity*, 7 vols. (New York: Harper and Brothers, 1937–1945), 1:xvii.

58. Ibid., xvii–xviii.

59. Kenneth S. Latourette, *A History of Christianity* (New York: Harper, 1953), xx; Kenneth S. Latourette, *Christianity in a Revolutionary Age: A History of Christianity in the Nineteenth and Twentieth Centuries*, 5 vols. (New York: Harper, 1958–1962), 1:xiii.

60. Latourette, *History of Christianity*, xxi.

61. Latourette, *Christianity in a Revolutionary Age*, 1:531.

62. Latourette, *History of Christianity*, xxi; Latourette, "The Christian Understanding of History," *American Historical Review* 54 (January 1949): 270.

63. Latourette, *Christianity in a Revolutionary Age* 5:515.

64. Latourette, "Christian Understanding of History," 267–68.

65. Ibid., 271.

66. Latourette, *History of Christianity*, 8.

67. Kenneth S. Latourette, "New Perspectives in Church History," *Journal of Religion* 21 (October 1941): 432.

68. Latourette, "New Perspectives," 433.

69. Kenneth S. Latourette, *Anno Domini: Jesus, History, and God* (New York: Harper and Brothers, 1940), 206; *Expansion of Christianity* 1:x–xv.

70. For the shortest statement of this ubiquitous pattern, see his essay, "The Church and Christian Society Today in the Perspective of History," in *The Gospel, the Church and the World*, ed. Kenneth S. Latourette (New York: Books for the Library Press, 1946), 86ff.

71. Latourette, "Church and Christian Society," 86; *History of Christianity*, xvi–xvii; Latourette, "Christian Understanding of History," 263.

72. Latourette, *History of Christianity*, xvii–xviii.

73. Latourette, *Anno Domini*, 227; Latourette, *Christianity in a Revolutionary Age* 5: 534; Latourette, "Christian Understanding of History," 272, 275.

74. Latourette, *History of Christianity*, 5.

75. Ibid., 1474.

76. Ibid., 1474–76; *Anno Domini*, 230–31, 235.

77. Latourette, *Christianity in a Revolutionary Age*, 5: 534.

CHAPTER 3

1. Charles M. Destler, "Some Observations on Contemporary Historical Theory," *American Historical Review* 55 (April 1950): 507. Another important observer pointed out that, if one said skepticism made history unreliable, "one has no good grounds for doing so. Not because history is not relative to such basic decisions, but because every human cognitive enterprise is. One could not be sceptical about history without being sceptical about everything else, and this, finally, destroys whatever specific force relativism might be thought to have with regard to history. . . . History is no more and no less subject to the relativistic factors than science is." See Arthur C. Danto, *Analytical Philosophy of History* (Cambridge: Cambridge University Press, 1965), 110. See also Ralph H. Gabriel, "History and the American Past," in *American Perspectives: The National Self-Image in the Twentieth Century*, eds. Robert E. Spiller and Eric Larrabee (Cambridge: Harvard University Press, 1961), 16; and Robert F. Berkhofer, Jr., *A Behavioral Approach to Historical Analysis* (New York: Free Press, 1969), 26.

2. Timothy Paul Donovan, *Historical Thought in America: Postwar Patterns* (Norman: University of Oklahoma Press, 1973), 116–17; see also John Higham, Leonard Krieger, and Felix Gilbert, *History* (Englewood Cliffs, N.J.: Prentice-Hall, 1965), 130.

3. David M. Potter, "Explicit Data and Implicit Assumptions in Historical Study," in *Generalization in the Writing of History*, ed. Louis Gottschalk (Chicago: University of Chicago Press, 1963), 186–87, 190.

4. Winthrop S. Hudson, "Shifting Trends in Church History," *Journal of Bible and Religion* 28 (April 1960): 237; see also George H. Williams, "Church History," in *Protestant Thought in the Twentieth Century: Whence and Whither?* ed. Arnold S. Nash (New York: Macmillan, 1951), 148.

5. Williams, "Church History," 173; see also Henry F. May, "The Recovery of American Religious History," *American Historical Review* 70 (October 1964): 89.

6. W. H. Kent, "Catholic Truth and Historical Truth," *Catholic Historical Review* 6 (October 1920); 292–93.

7. Henry J. Browne, "American Catholic History: A Progress Report on Research and Study," *Church History* 26 (December 1957): 375.

8. John Lukacs, "The Historiographical Problem of Belief and Believers: Religious History in the Democratic Age," *Catholic Historical Review* 64 (April 1978): 164–65.

9. Cyril C. Richardson, "Church History Past and Present," *Union Seminary Quarterly Review* 5 (November 1949): 12–13.

10. Ibid., 13–14.

11. Cyril C. Richardson, *The Sacrament of Reunion: A Study in Ecumenical Christianity with Particular Reference to the Proposed Concordat between the Presbyterians and Protestant Episcopal Churches* (New York: Charles Scribner's Sons, 1940), 4–5.

12. Cyril C. Richardson, *The Doctrine of the Trinity* (Nashville: Abingdon, 1958), 13, 16, 148.

13. Richardson, *Sacrament of Reunion*, ix, 5–6, 29–30.

14. Cyril C. Richardson, *The Church through the Centuries* (New York: Charles Scribner's Sons, 1938), 2, 79, 144.

15. Ibid., 225–26.

16. Ibid., 245–46.

17. Williams, "Church History," 172.

18. James H. Nichols, "Church History and Secular History," *Church History* 13 (June 1944): 98–99.

19. James H. Nichols, "The Art of Church History," *Church History* 20 (March 1951): 5–6; James H. Nichols, "History in the Theological Curriculum," *Journal of Religion* 26 (July 1946): 183–84.

20. Nichols, "Art of Church History," 3, 6.

21. Ibid., 5; James H. Nichols, *Romanticism in American Theology: Nevin and Schaff at Mercersburg* (Chicago: University of Chicago Press, 1961), 4.

22. James H. Nichols, "The History of Christianity," in *Religion*, ed. Paul Ramsey (Englewood Cliffs, N.J.: Prentice-Hall, 1965), 175.

23. Ibid., 201.

24. Nichols, "Art of Church History," 6, 9. The borrowed words are those of Walter Nigg who used them in reference to the work of Karl Mueller.

25. Nichols, "History of Christianity," 170.

26. Ibid.

27. Nichols, "Art of Church History," 8; Nichols, "History of Christianity," 157.

28. Nichols, "History of Christianity," 171–72.

29. Nichols, "Art of Church History," 8–9.

30. Nichols, "History in the Theological Curriculum," 184.

31. Ibid., 186–89.

32. James H. Nichols, *Primer for Protestants* (New York: Association Press, 1947), 11, 134.

33. Ibid., 50, 148.

34. Ibid., 51–52; see also 7–8, 34.

35. James H. Nichols, *History of Christianity, 1650–1950: Secularization of the West* (New York: Ronald Press, 1956), iii; James H. Nichols, ed., *The Mercersburg Theology* (New York: Oxford University Press, 1966), 17–18.

36. Nichols, *Romanticism in American Theology*, 44, 130, 139.

37. Nichols, *Primer for Protestants*, 7–8.

38. James H. Nichols, *Democracy and the Churches* (Philadelphia: Westminster Press, 1951), 267–68.

39. Ibid., 268, 270–71.

40. Ibid., 274.

41. Ibid., 273; Nichols, *Primer for Protestants*, 147; Nichols, *History of Christianity, 1650–1950*, 212–15, 231, 367–71, 374.

42. Nichols, *Democracy and the Churches*, 276–77.

43. Nichols, *History of Christianity, 1650–1950*, 10–12.

44. Ibid., 10–11.

45. Ibid., 11–12.

46. Leonard J. Trinterud, "The Task of the American Church Historian," *Church History* 25 (March 1956): 5, 7.

47. Leonard J. Trinterud, "Some Notes on Recent Periodical Literature on Colonial American Church History," *Church History* 20 (December 1951): 73.

48. Trinterud, "Task of the American Church Historian," 6–8.

49. Ibid., 3–4, 14.

50. Ibid., 11–12.

51. Ibid., 10–11.

52. Ibid., 9.

53. Ibid., 12.

54. Ibid., 13.

55. See for example Leonard J. Trinterud, "A.D. 1689: The End of the Clerical World," in *Theology in Sixteenth- and Seventeenth-Century England*, eds. Winthrop S. Hudson and Leonard J. Trinterud (Los Angeles: William Andrews Clark Library, 1971), 35, 50.

56. Leonard J. Trinterud, ed., *Elizabethan Puritanism* (New York: Oxford University Press, 1971), 15–16.

57. Leonard J. Trinterud, *The Forming of an American Tradition: A Reexamination of Colonial Presbyterianism* (Philadelphia: Westminster Press, 1949), 15, 45–46, 61, 119, 148, 199, 255, 294–95, 307–8.

CHAPTER 4

1. Timothy Paul Donovan, *Historical Thought in America: Postwar Patterns* (Norman: University of Oklahoma Press, 1973), 35.

2. John Higham, "Beyond Consensus: The Historian as Moral Critic," *American Historical Review* 67 (April 1962): 613.

3. Richard Hofstadter, *The Progressive Historians: Turner, Beard, Parrington* (New York: Alfred A. Knopf, 1968), 438–39.

4. John Higham, Leonard Krieger, and Felix Gilbert, *History* (Englewood Cliffs, N.J.: Prentice-Hall, 1965), 136; see also John Higham, *Writing American History: Essays on Modern Scholarship* (Bloomington: Indiana University Press, 1970), 165.

5. Roland H. Bainton, *The Travail of Religious Liberty: Nine Biographical Studies* (Philadelphia: Westminster Press, 1951), 14, 253; Roland H. Bainton, *Christendom: A Short History of Christianity and Its Impact on Western Civilization*, vol. 2 (New York: Harper and Row, 1966), 197.

6. Roland H. Bainton, *Yesterday, Today, and What Next?* (Minneapolis: Augsburg Publishing House, 1978), 100–101, 118.

7. Roland H. Bainton, *Christian Unity and Religion in New England* (Boston: Beacon Press, 1964), 23.

8. Roland H. Bainton, *Christian Attitudes Toward War and Peace: A Historical Survey and Critical Re-evaluation* (New York: Abingdon Press, 1960), 53, 85, 103, 112; Roland H. Bainton, *Studies on the Reformation* (Boston: Beacon Press, 1963), 248.

9. Bainton, *Christian Attutudes*, 64, 66, 81.

10. Ibid., 230, 243.

11. Ibid., 244–46; Roland H. Bainton, *Erasmus of Christendom* (New York: Charles Scribner's Sons, 1969), 120, 124.

12. Bainton, *Christian Attitudes*, 248, 250–51.

13. Bainton, *Erasmus*, vii–viii, 167, 185, 192, 262.

14. Bainton, *Travail*, 260.

15. Bainton, *Christian Attitudes*, 235–36, 238–39.

16. Roland H. Bainton, *The Reformation of the Sixteenth Century* (Boston: Beacon Press, 1952), 212–13.

17. Bainton, *Travail*, 30.

18. Bainton, *Christian Unity*, vii–viii, 52, 62.

19. Bainton, *Travail*, 259–60; Roland H. Bainton, *Hunted Heretic: The Life and Death of Michael Servetus, 1511–1553* (Boston: Beacon Press, 1953), 210.

20. Bainton, *Travail*, 17.

21. Ibid., 22–25, 29.

22. Ibid., 25; Bainton, *Christian Unity*, 79–81, 247–48.

23. Roland H. Bainton, *Here I Stand: A Life of Martin Luther* (Nashville: Abingdon-Cokesbury Press, 1950), 376–79.

24. Bainton, *Hunted Heretic*, 214–15; Bainton, *Travail*, 94.

25. Bainton, *Reformation of the Sixteenth Century*, 226–27.

26. Winthrop S. Hudson, *The Great Tradition of the American Churches* (New York: Harper and Brothers, 1953), 9, 17–19.

27. Ibid., 10, 25–26; Winthrop S. Hudson, ed., *Nationalism and Religion in America: Concepts of American Identity and Mission* (New York: Harper and Row, 1970), xi.

28. Winthrop S. Hudson, *John Ponet (1516?–1556): Advocate of Limited Monarchy* (Chicago: University of Chicago Press, 1942), v, 161–62, 180.

29. Hudson, *Great Tradition*, 43–44, 46–47, 49–50.

30. Ibid., 9, 18, 42, 62.

31. Ibid., 45–46, 60–62. In later writings Hudson modified these ideas to

acknowledge more influence on the part of rationalists, but the overall interpretation remained essentially the same. See Winthrop S. Hudson, *Religion in America: An Historical Account of the Development of American Religious Life*, 3d ed. (New York: Charles Scribner's Sons, 1981), 92–94, 99–105.

32. Hudson, *Great Tradition*, 47–48, 54–55; Hudson, *Nationalism and Religion*, 34–35.

33. Hudson, *Great Tradition*, 19–20; Hudson, *Nationalism and Religion*, 55–56, 93–94, 109–10.

34. Winthrop S. Hudson, *Understanding Roman Catholicism: A Guide to Papal Teachings for Protestants* (Philadelphia: Westminster Press, 1959), 31, 154.

35. Ibid., 32–34.

36. Ibid., 63, 156.

37. Ibid., 106, 108–9.

38. Ibid., 160. In later writings Hudson modified several of these judgments, and in this particular area, his revised views became notably more appreciative. See Hudson, *Religion in America*, 402–3, 408–9.

39. Hudson, *Understanding Roman Catholicism*, 150, 152.

40. Hudson, *Great Tradition*, 109, 198–99.

41. Ibid., 201–2, 217–20. See Hudson, *Religion in America*, 415–17, for an example of interpretive patterns which did not change during subsequent decades of research and writing. For additional corroboration, see Winthrop S. Hudson, *American Protestantism* (Chicago: University of Chicago Press, 1961), 131–34, 168; Winthrop S. Hudson, *Baptist Concepts of the Church: A Survey of the Historical and Theological Issues Which Have Produced Changes in Church Order* (Philadelphia: Judson Press, 1959), 213–16.

42. Hudson, *American Protestantism*, 41–42, 46–47.

43. Hudson, *Great Tradition*, 10–11, 252, 262.

44. Hudson, *Great Tradition*, 244–45, 262; Hudson, *Baptist Concepts*, 218.

45. Sidney E. Mead, *The Nation with the Soul of a Church* (New York: Harper and Row, 1975), vi–vii; Sidney E. Mead, *The Old Religion in the Brave New World: Reflections on the Relation Between Christendom and the Republic* (Berkeley: University of California Press, 1977), 1–3, 18–19, 108–9.

46. Sidney E. Mead, *The Lively Experiment: The Shaping of Christianity in America* (New York: Harper and Row, 1963), 15; Sidney E. Mead, *History and Identity* (Missoula, Mont.: Scholars Press, 1979), 25, 29, 47.

47. Mead, *Nation*, 4–5, 117–18. Setting himself apart from those who tried to write church history with an exalted conception of the Church, Mead lodged a telling point by observing that a "proliferation of religious groups in the modern world, and especially in America under religious freedom, has made absurd any one group's claim to be the only institutionalized incarnation of the 'body of Christ.'" Then he quipped, "So today the doleful saint of many church historians is Mary Magdalene, and with her they lament, 'they have taken away my Lord's body and I know not where to find it.'" See Mead, *History and Identity*, 28.

48. Mead, *Old Religion*, 7–9; 42–43; Mead, *Nation*, 103–5.

49. Mead, *Old Religion*, 16–17; Mead, *Nation*, 30–31, 93.

50. Mead, *Old Religion*, 83–84.

51. Ibid., 84–85.

52. Mead, *Nation*, 21–22, 59–61. In language reminiscent of Bainton's concern for free speech and continuous search for truth, Mead held that religious pluralism "does not necessarily undermine belief in the efficacy of sectarian forms to express the universal. Indeed it encourages the free, open, and uncurbed proclamation of all sectarian specific notions" regarding duties to the Creator and the manner of discharging them. Echoing Madison, Mead held that it "encourages even vehement conflict of opinion between them on the premises . . . that truth is great and will prevail if left to herself." See Mead, *Nation*, 60–61.

53. Mead, *Lively Experiment*, 35–36.

54. Ibid., 40–41, 43.

55. Mead, *Nation*, 73–74; Mead, *Lively Experiment*, 36, 43.

56. Mead, *Lively Experiment*, 38.

57. Ibid.

58. Ibid., 52–53, 55–56.

59. Mead, *Old Religion*, 77–78; Mead, *Nation*, 124.

60. Mead, *Old Religion*, 36–37, 41, 127.

61. Mead, *History and Identity*, 14.

62. Mead, *Nation*, 22–24; Mead, *Lively Experiment*, 66, 139–40.

63. Mead, *Lively Experiment*, 127–28, 138, 141–42, 156–57.

64. Mead, *Nation*, 24–26, 76.

65. Ibid., ix; Mead, *Lively Experiment*, 135.

66. Mead, *Nation*, 27, 38, 42–43, 47, 49.

67. Ibid., 9–10, 63–65, 67, 76–77.

68. Mead, *Lively Experiment*, 187; Mead, *Old Religion*, 132; Mead, *Nation*, 19.

CHAPTER 5

1. Robert Allen Skotheim, *American Intellectual Histories and Historians* (Princeton: Princeton University Press, 1966), 71, 86.

2. Winthrop S. Hudson, "Shifting Trends in Church History," *Journal of Bible and Religion* 28 (April 1960): 237; Rush Welter, "The History of Ideas in America: An Essay in Definition," *Journal of American History* 51 (March 1965): 607–10.

3. John Higham, "The Rise of American Intellectual History," *American Historical Review* 56 (April 1951): 453, 462–64; John Higham, *Writing American History: Essays on Modern Scholarship* (Bloomington: Indiana University Press, 1970), 164; John Higham, "American Intellectual History: A Critical Appraisal," *American Quarterly* 13 (Summer Supplement, 1961): 221.

4. Welter, "History of Ideas," 600, 620; Richard Hofstadter, *The Progressive Historians: Turner, Beard, Parrington* (New York: Alfred A. Knopf, 1968), 442–43.

5. Welter, "History of Ideas," 600, 604–5; Higham, "Critical Appraisal," 229–30.

6. The exponent is Perry Miller, as cited in Skotheim, *American Intellectual Histories*, 190–91.

7. John Higham, Leonard Krieger, and Felix Gilbert, *History* (Englewood Cliffs, N.J.: Prentice-Hall, 1965), 226–27; Skotheim, *American Intellectual Histories*, 250–52.

8. Henry F. May, "The Recovery of American Religious History," *American Historical Review* 70 (October 1964): 79; Skotheim, *American Intellectual Histories*, 249–50.

9. James H. Nichols, "The Art of Church History," *Church History* 20 (March 1951): 7; May, "Recovery," 82–83.

10. Ralph H. Gabriel, *The Course of American Democratic Thought* (New York: Roland Press, 1940), 214, 282–85, 382–86; Merle Curti, *The Growth of American Thought* (New York: Harper and Brothers, 1943), 531–35, 558–62.

11. H. Shelton Smith, *Faith and Nurture* (New York: Charles Scribner's Sons, 1941), 5–17, 93–99, 157–60.

12. H. Shelton Smith, *Changing Conceptions of Original Sin: A Study in American Theology since 1750* (New York: Charles Scribner's Sons, 1955), ix, 3, 5–7.

13. Ibid., 35, 63, 68.

14. Ibid., 26, 38, 55.

15. Ibid., 78, 119.

16. Ibid., 69–71, 96, 110, 125, 127–33, 140, 178, 199.

17. Ibid., 164–68, 170–71, 174, 176–77, 183, 187, 191–92.

18. Lyman Abbott as cited in ibid., 180; see also 179, 196–97.

19. Ibid., 202–3, 207–8.

20. H. Shelton Smith, ed., *Horace Bushnell* (New York: Oxford University Press, 1965), 17, 38–39, 153–58; Smith, *Changing Conceptions*, 141, 159–61.

21. H. Shelton Smith, *In His Image, But . . . Racism in Southern Religion, 1780–1910* (Durham, N.C.: Duke University Press, 1972), vii–viii.

22. Ibid., 4, 7, 9.

23. Ibid., 18, 24, 35–36, 46–48, 69, 73.

24. Ibid., 74–76. Smith's treatment of denominational controversies are located as follows: Presbyterians (1837), 77–90; Methodists (1844), 96–112; and Baptists (1845), 114–26.

25. Ibid., 129, 132, 134, 137, 143–48, 152.

26. Ibid., 168, 171, 177, 188–90, 205.

27. Ibid., 228, 230, 242, 251, 254, 260–62.

28. Ibid., 265, 287–88, 291, 293, 296, 299, 302, 304–5.

29. After completing a doctoral dissertation on the subject in 1920, McNeill produced several helpful studies: *The Celtic Penitentials* (Paris: E. Champion, 1923); *Medieval Handbooks of Penance* (New York: Columbia University Press, 1935); and *The Celtic Churches: A History* A.D. *200 to 1200* (Chicago: University of Chicago Press, 1974). His main contention is that Irish monks evangelized and tutored Germanic Europe through exemplary piety, zeal, and learning.

30. John T. McNeill, ed., *Calvin: Institutes of the Christian Religion,* vol. 1 (Philadelphia: Westminster, 1960), xxix, li; John T. McNeill, *The History and Character of Calvinism* (New York: Oxford University Press, 1954), 93.

31. McNeill, *History and Character of Calvinism*, 209, 211–25, 299.

32. John T. McNeill, *Unitive Protestantism: A Study in Our Religious Resources* (Cincinnati: Abingdon Press, 1930), 39–40, 43–45, 65; McNeill, *History and Character of Calvinism*, 138–39, 160, 196.

33. McNeill, *Unitive Protestantism*, 38–39; see also 15–16, 337, and chapters 4, 5, 7, and 8 passim.

34. McNeill, *History and Character of Calvinism*, 353–89 passim.

35. John T. McNeill, *Christian Hope for World Society* (New York: Willet, Clark and Co., 1937), 3, 8, 29–30.

36. Ibid., 46–48, 54, 89–91.

37. Ibid., 101, 121, 133–36, 154–56.

38. John T. McNeill, *Modern Christian Movements* (Philadelphia: Westminster, 1954), 14; McNeill *Christian Hope*, 181–89, 193–95, 207.

39. McNeill, *Christian Hope*, 240–42, 390–410.

40. Ibid., 436–37. For his treatment of the various issues mentioned, see 237–350.

41. Two good examples of studies in the interstices between religious history and literature are Kenneth B. Murdock, whose works include *Increase Mather: The Foremost Puritan* (Cambridge: Harvard University Press, 1925) and *Literature and Theology in Colonial New England* (Cambridge: Harvard University Press, 1949); and William Haller, whose works include *The Rise of Puritanism* (New York: Columbia University Press, 1938) and an edited collection *Tracts on Liberty in the Puritan Revolution, 1638–1647*, 3 vols. (New York: Columbia University Press, 1934).

42. There is a surfeit of secondary material on Miller. The best single source, notable for inclusive references and judicious use of them, is Francis T. Butts, "The Myth of Perry Miller," *American Historical Review* 87 (June 1982): 665–94.

43. Perry Miller, *Orthodoxy in Massachusetts, 1630–1650* (Cambridge: Harvard University Press, 1933; New York: Harper and Row, 1970), xxv–xxvi of latter edition.

44. Perry Miller, *The New England Mind: The Seventeenth Century* (New York: Macmillan, 1939; Cambridge: Harvard University Press, 1954; Boston: Beacon Press, 1961), vii of Beacon Press edition. Hereafter cited as *NEM:SC*. See also Skotheim, *American Intellectual Histories*, 192, 210–11.

45. Perry Miller, *Errand Into the Wilderness* (Cambridge: Harvard University Press, 1956; New York: Harper and Row, 1964), ix of latter edition; Perry Miller and Thomas H. Johnson, eds., *The Puritans: A Sourcebook of their Writings*, 2 vols. (New York: American Book Co., 1938; New York: Harper and Row, 1963) 1:2–3, 5 of latter edition.

46. Miller, *Errand*, 185; Miller, *NEM:SC*, 4, 6; Miller and Johnson, *The Puritans* 1:58–59, 281.

47. Miller, *NEM:SC*, 67–69; see also 76, 85, 90, 102–8; Skotheim, *American Intellectual Histories*, 195–96.

48. Miller, *Errand*, 50–53.

49. Miller, *NEM:SC*, 25, 264. It is difficult to determine just what Miller thought the Puritan doctrine of human depravity really emphasized. In *Errand*, 80–81, for instance, he said: "This line of argument indicates a

predisposition in the minds of early New England theologians to minimize the power of original sin. . . . Adam in his disobedience had broken a bond. . . . The punishment which he received as a consequence was not deterioration so much as it was the infliction of a judicious sentence; . . . not inherent pollution."

50. Miller, *NEM:SC*, 26–27, 280–81; Miller, *Errand*, 74.

51. Miller, *NEM:SC*, 239, 397; Miller, *Errand*, 60.

52. Miller, *Errand*, 61–66, 70–72, 92–93.

53. Ibid.

54. Miller, *NEM:SC*, 375, 380–81, 384–85, 388, 394. For a critical response to Miller's analysis, especially as it pertains to covenantal thinking, see George M. Marsden, "Perry Miller's Rehabilitation of the Puritans: A Critique," *Church History* 39 (March 1970): 91–105.

55. Miller dwelled at length on the influence of Peter Ramus on Puritan ideas throughout the entire system. This explained how they reasoned from universals to single entities and then arranged these objectively real phenomena into useful classifications. See Miller, *NEM:SC*, 116, 140, 149.

56. Ibid., 489–90.

57. Miller, *Orthodoxy*, 119–20, 127–28, 146, 157; Miller, *NEM:SC*, 433, 435, 461–62.

58. Miller, *Orthodoxy*, 281–83; Miller, *Errand*, 5, 89.

59. Miller, *Errand*, 150–51; Miller, *NEM:SC*, 429–30.

60. Miller, *Orthodoxy*, 171–72; Miller, *NEM:SC*, 439, 454–55; Miller, *Errand*, 147–49.

61. Perry Miller, *The New England Mind: From Colony to Province* (Cambridge: Harvard University Press, 1953; Boston: Beacon Press, 1961), 14 of latter edition.

62. Ibid., 9, 49, 76, 80, 95–98, 371, 380–81, 460.

63. Ibid., 172, 213–14, 463.

64. Ibid., 484–85.

65. Perry Miller, *Jonathan Edwards* (New York: William Morrow, 1949; New York: Meridian Books, 1959), foreword; Miller, *Errand*, 98.

66. For a complete bibliography on Schneider, see Craig Walton and John P. Anton, eds., *Philosophy and the Civilizing Arts: Essays Presented to Herbert W. Schneider* (Athens: Ohio University Press, 1974), 495–504. Some of his best books on freedom and morals include *Making the Fascist State* (New York: Oxford University Press, 1928); *Adam Smith's Moral and Political Philosophy* (New York: Hafner, 1948); and *Three Dimensions in Public Morality* (Bloomington: Indiana University Press, 1956). Volumes edited with others include *Religion in Various Cultures* (New York: Henry Holt and Co., 1932); and *Fountainheads of Freedom: The Growth of the Democratic Idea* (New York: Reynal and Hitchcock, 1941).

67. Herbert W. Schneider, *The Puritan Mind* (New York: Henry Holt, 1930), 3–4.

68. Ibid., 5.

69. Ibid., 208.

70. Ibid., 264. In several of his publications, Schneider acknowledged the help of a graduate student researchers, Joseph Haroutunian. This young

scholar took Schneider's thesis further in a notable book of his own, *Piety versus Moralism: The Passing of the New England Theology* (New York: Henry Holt and Co., 1932).

71. Schneider, *The Puritan Mind*, 6–7, 208–9. Another arresting metaphor put Schneider's position this way: "To understand both the origin and the fruit of an idea, one must examine the teeming world by which it was generated and into which it falls. One can, of course, follow an idea into its undying dialectical implications without examining the social landscape in which it lived, just as a botanist might study the glass flowers in the Harvard museum. Such an alignment of ideas, according to their appointed niches in the mind's eternal architecture, must not be mistaken for an understanding of their temporal and earthly meanings to those human beings who from time to time held them and in whose lives they played a living part."

72. For a paradigm of his ability to provide a concise synthesis of ideas from Ramus to Edwards, see Herbert W. Schneider, *A History of American Philosophy* (New York: Columbia University Press, 1946; 1963), 3–26.

73. Schneider, *The Puritan Mind*, 51–52.

74. Ibid., 73, 77–78, 94.

75. Ibid., 106–7, 125–26.

76. Ibid., 98, 201–2, 254–56.

CHAPTER 6

1. Clifton E. Olmstead, *History of Religion in the United States* (Englewood Cliffs, N.J.: Prentice-Hall, 1960), v–vi.

2. Ibid., 16, 71–72, 82, 84.

3. Ibid., 178–79, 242, 256, 352–53, 590.

4. Ibid., 446–47.

5. Ibid., 447.

6. Ibid., 562–63, 589, 592–93.

7. H. Shelton Smith, Robert T. Handy, and Lefferts A. Loetscher, eds., *American Christianity: An Historical Interpretation with Representative Documents*, 2 vols. (New York: Scribner, 1960, 1963), 1:vii–viii.

8. Ibid., 1:433–35.

9. Ibid., 1:314–15, 519–25, 561–64; 2:10–12.

10. Ibid., 2:222, 255, 359, 422.

11. Winthrop S. Hudson, *Religion in America: An Historical Account of the Development of American Religious Life* (New York: Scribner, 1965; rev. eds., 1973, 1981, 1987), vii, viii of the 1965 edition.

12. Hudson, *Religion in America* (1981), vii.

13. Ibid., viii.

14. Ibid., ix, 3–4.

15. Ibid., 59–60, 82; see also 149–58.

16. Ibid., 292, 317–18.

17. Ibid., 329, 360, 411.

18. Edwin S. Gaustad, *A Religious History of America* (New York: Harper and Row, 1966), xxv. For a later and more elaborate display of primary source

materials, see Gaustad's two-volume treasure trove, *A Documentary History of Religion in America,* 2 vols. (Grand Rapids, Mich.: Eerdmans, 1982, 1983). This work surpasses the Smith, Handy, Loetscher book in capturing the rich diversity in America's religious past.

19. Edwin S. Gaustad, *American Religious History* (Washington, D.C.: American Historical Association, 1966), 1, 15.

20. Edwin S. Gaustad, *Religion in America: History and Historiography* (Washington, D.C.: American Historical Association, 1973), 58–59.

21. For approaches that were innovative in their day, see Henry K. Carroll, *The Religious Forces of the United States Enumerated, Classified, and Described* (New York: Christian Literature Co., 1893; rev. ed., 1912) and Leonard Woolsey Bacon, *A History of American Christianity* (New York: Christian Literature Co., 1897).

22. Gaustad, *A Religious History of America,* 54–55, 150–52, 208, 214.

23. For this particular quote, see Edwin S. Gaustad, *Historical Atlas of Religion in America* (New York: Harper and Row, 1962; rev. ed., 1976), xii of the second edition.

24. Martin E. Marty, *Righteous Empire: The Protestant Experience in America* (New York: Dial, 1970); second edition issued as *Protestantism in the United States: Righteous Empire* (New York: Scribner, 1986). All references are to the first edition, in this case to two unnumbered pages of the foreword.

25. Marty, *Righteous Empire,* 76–77, 90–91.

26. Ibid., 138, 177–79, 265.

27. Ibid., 258–59, 263–64.

28. Sydney E. Ahlstrom, *A Religious History of the American People* (New Haven: Yale University Press, 1972), xiii.

29. Ibid., xiv. See also Sydney E. Ahlstrom, "The Problem of the History of Religion in America," *Church History* 39 (1970): 233–34.

30. Ahlstrom, "Problem," 234.

31. Ibid., 231–35.

32. Ahlstrom, *Religious History,* xvi, 1079, 1081.

33. Peter W. Williams, *Popular Religion in America: Symbolic Change and the Modernization Process in Historical Perspective* (Englewood Cliffs, N.J.: Prentice-Hall, 1980); Catherine L. Albanese, *America: Religions and Religion* (Belmont, Calif.: Wadsworth, 1981); Mary F. Bednarowski, *American Religion: A Cultural Perspective* (Englewood Cliffs, N.J.: Prentice-Hall, 1984).

34. Gayraud S. Wilmore, *Black Religion and Black Radicalism: An Examination of the Black Religious Experience* (Garden City, N.Y.: Doubleday, 1972); Carol V. R. George, *Segregated Sabbaths: Richard Allen and the Emergence of Independent Black Churches, 1760–1840* (New York: Oxford University Press, 1973); C. Eric Lincoln, ed., *The Black Experience in Religion* (Garden City, N.Y.: Doubleday, 1974); Harry V. Richardson, *Dark Salvation: The Story of Methodism As It Developed Among Blacks in America* (Garden City, N.Y.: Doubleday, 1976); Albert J. Raboteau, *Slave Religion: The "Invisible Institution" in the Antebellum South* (New York: Oxford University Press, 1978); Randall K. Burkett, *Garveyism as a Religious Movement: The Institutionalization of a Black Civil Religion* (Metuchen, N.J.: Scarecrow Press, 1978); Randall K. Burkett and Richard

Newman, eds., *Black Apostles: Afro-American Clergy Confront the Twentieth Century* (Boston: G. K. Hall, 1978); Gayraud S. Wilmore and James H. Cone, eds., *Black Theology: A Documentary History* (Marynoll, N.Y.: Orbis Books, 1979); Walter L. Williams, *Black Americans and the Evangelization of Africa, 1877–1900* (Madison: University of Wisconsin Press, 1982); Arthur E. Paris, *Black Pentecostalism: Southern Religion in an Urban World* (Amherst: University of Massachusetts Press, 1982); Robert Weisbrot, *Father Divine and the Struggle for Racial Equality* (Urbana: University of Illinois Press, 1983); Mark D. Morrison-Reed, *Black Pioneers in a White Denomination* (Boston: Beacon Press, 1984); Milton C. Sernett, ed., *Afro-American Religious History: A Documentary Witness* (Durham, N.C.: Duke University Press, 1985); Leroy Fitts, *A History of Black Baptists* (Nashville: Broadman Press, 1985); James M. Washington, *Frustrated Fellowship: The Black Baptist Quest for Social Power* (Macon, Ga.: Mercer University Press, 1986).

35. Eleanor Hull, *Women Who Carried the Good News* (Valley Forge, Pa.: Judson Press, 1975); Mary Ewens, *The Role of the Nun in Nineteenth Century America* (New York: Arno Press, 1978); Linda K. Kerber, *Women of the Republic: Intellect and Ideology in Revolutionary America* (Chapel Hill: University of North Carolina Press, 1980); Janet W. James, ed., *Women in American Religion* (Philadelphia: University of Pennsylvania Press, 1980); Amanda Porterfield, *Feminine Spirituality in America: From Sarah Edwards to Martha Graham* (Philadelphia: Temple University Press, 1980); Judith L. Weidman, ed., *Women Ministers: How Women Are Redefining Traditional Roles* (San Francisco: Harper and Row, 1981); Barbara L. Epstein, *The Politics of Domesticity: Women, Evangelism, and Temperance in Nineteenth-Century America* (Middletown, Conn.: Wesleyan University Press, 1981); Hilah Thomas and Rosemary Skinner Keller, eds., *Women in New Worlds: Historical Perspectives on the Wesleyan Tradition*, 2 vols. (Nashville: Abingdon Press, 1981, 1982); Rosemary R. Ruether and Rosemary S. Keller, eds., *Women and Religion in America: A Documentary History*, 3 vols. (San Francisco: Harper and Row, 1981–1983); John Patrick McDowell, *The Social Gospel in the South: The Woman's Home Mission Movement in the Methodist Episcopal Church South, 1886–1939* (Baton Rouge: Louisiana State University Press, 1982); Lois Boyd and R. Douglas Brackenridge, *Presbyterian Women in America: Two Centuries of a Quest for Status* (Westport, Conn.: Greenwood Press, 1983); Leonard I. Sweet, *The Minister's Wife: Her Role in Nineteenth-Century American Evangelicalism* (Philadelphia: Temple University Press, 1983); Nancy Hardesty, *Women Called to Witness: Evangelical Feminism in the Nineteenth Century* (Nashville: Abingdon Press, 1984); Edward C. Lehman, Jr., *Women Clergy: Breaking Through Gender Barriers* (New Brunswick, N.J.: Transaction Books, 1985).

36. David D. Hall, *The Faithful Shepherd: A History of the New England Ministry in the Seventeenth Century* (Chapel Hill: University of North Carolina Press, 1972); Sacvan Bercovitch, *The Puritan Origins of the American Self* (New Haven: Yale University Press, 1975); Paul Lucas, *Valley of Discord: Church and Society Along the Connecticut River, 1636–1725* (Hanover, N.H.: University Press of New England, 1976); Philip Greven, *The Protestant Temperament: Patterns of Childrearing, Religious Experience, and the Self in Early America* (New York:

256 NOTES TO PAGE 184

Alfred A. Knopf, 1977); Winton U. Solberg, *Redeem the Time: The Puritan Sabbath in Early America* (Cambridge: Harvard University Press, 1977); William K. B. Stoever, *"A Faire and Easie Way to Heaven": Covenant Theology and Antinomianism in Early Massachusetts* (Middletown, Conn.: Wesleyan University Press, 1978); Sacvan Bercovitch, *The American Jeremiad* (Madison: University of Wisconsin Press, 1978); Norman Fiering, *Moral Philosophy at Seventeenth-Century Harvard: A Discipline in Transition* (Chapel Hill: University of North Carolina Press, 1981); Charles Hambrick-Stowe, *The Practice of Piety: Puritan Devotional Disciplines in Seventeenth-Century New England* (Chapel Hill: University of North Carolina Press, 1982); John Demos, *Entertaining Satan: Witchcraft and the Culture of Early New England* (New York: Oxford University Press, 1982); Kenneth Silverman, *The Life and Times of Cotton Mather* (New York: Harper and Row, 1984); Harry S. Stout, *The New England Soul: Preaching and Religious Culture in Colonial New England* (New York: Oxford University Press, 1986).

37. Donald M. Scott, *From Office to Profession: The New England Ministry, 1750–1850* (Philadelphia: University of Pennsylvania Press, 1978); Norman Fiering, *Jonathan Edwards's Moral Thought and Its British Context* (Chapel Hill: University of North Carolina Press, 1981); Stephen A. Marini, *Radical Sects in Revolutionary New England* (Cambridge: Harvard University Press, 1982).

38. Norris Magnuson, *Salvation in the Slums: Evangelical Social Work, 1865–1920* (Metuchen, N.J.: Scarecrow Press, 1977); Paul Boyer, *Urban Masses and Moral Order in America* (Cambridge: Harvard University Press, 1978); Marie Caskey, *Chariot of Fire: Religion and the Beecher Family* (New Haven: Yale University Press, 1978); James H. Moorhead, *American Apocalypse: Yankee Protestants and the Civil War, 1860–1869* (New Haven: Yale University Press, 1978); Joan Jacobs Brumberg, *Mission for Life: The Story of the Family of Adoniram Judson . . . and the Course of Evangelical Religion in the Nineteenth Century* (New York: Free Press, 1980); Janet Forsythe Fishburn, *The Fatherhood of God and the Victorian Family: The Social Gospel in America* (Philadelphia: Fortress Press, 1981).

39. Donald G. Mathews, *Religion in the Old South* (Chicago: University of Chicago Press, 1977); E. Brooks Holifield, *The Gentleman Theologians: American Theology in Southern Culture, 1795–1860* (Durham, N.C.: Duke University Press, 1978); Anne C. Loveland, *Southern Evangelicals and the Social Order, 1800–1860* (Baton Rouge: Louisiana State University Press, 1980); Charles Reagan Wilson, *Baptized in Blood: The Religion of the Lost Cause, 1865–1920* (Athens: University of Georgia Press, 1980); John W. Kuykendall, *Southern Enterprise: The Work of National Evangelical Societies in the Antebellum South* (Westport, Conn.: Greenwood Press, 1982); S. Charles Bolton, *Southern Anglicanism* (Westport, Conn.: Greenwood Press, 1982).

40. Donna Merwick, *Boston Priests, 1848–1910: A Study of Social and Intellectual Change* (Cambridge: Harvard University Press, 1973); Richard M. Linkh, *American Catholicism and European Immigrants, 1900–1924* (Staten Island: Center for Migration Studies, 1975); Donald F. Crosby, *God, Church, and Flag: Senator Joseph R. McCarthy and the Catholic Church, 1950–1957* (Chapel Hill, N.C.: University of North Carolina Press, 1978); Jay P. Dolan, *Catholic Revivalism: The American Experience, 1830–1900* (Notre Dame: University of Notre Dame Press,

1978); William M. Halsey, *The Survival of American Innocence: Catholicism in an Era of Disillusionment, 1920–1940* (Notre Dame: University of Notre Dame Press, 1980); Patrick Carey, *An Immigrant Bishop: John England's Adaptation of Irish Catholicism to American Republicanism* (Yonkers, N.Y.: U.S. Catholic Historical Society, 1982); Mel Piehl, *Breaking Bread: The Catholic Worker and the Origin of Catholic Radicalism in America,* (Philadelphia: Temple University Press, 1982).

41. Alan Graebner, *Uncertain Saints: The Laity in the Lutheran Church–Missouri Synod, 1900–1970* (Westport, Conn.: Greenwood Press, 1975); Jay P. Dolan, *The Immigrant Church: New York's Irish and German Catholics, 1815–1865* (Baltimore: Johns Hopkins University Press, 1975); Randall M. Miller and Thomas D. Marzik, eds., *Immigrants and Religion in Urban America* (Philadelphia: Temple University Press, 1977); James D. Bratt, *Dutch Calvinism in Modern America: A History of a Conservative Sub-Culture* (Grand Rapids, Mich.: Eerdmans, 1984).

42. Dickson D. Bruce, Jr., *And They All Sang Hallelujah: Plainfolk Camp-Meeting Religion, 1800–1845* (Knoxville: University of Tennessee Press, 1974); Sandra S. Sizer, *Gospel Hymns and Social Religion: The Rhetoric of Nineteenth-Century Revivalism* (Philadelphia: Temple University Press, 1978); William G. McLoughlin, *Revivals, Awakenings, and Reform: An Essay on Religion and Social Change in America* (Chicago: University of Chicago Press, 1978); Carol Flake, *Redemptorama: Culture, Politics, and the New Evangelicalism* (Garden City, N.Y.: Anchor Press, 1984); Jerry D. Cardwell, *Mass Media Christianity: Televangelism and the Great Commission* (Lanham, Md.: University Press of America).

43. Cushing Strout, *The New Heavens and New Earth: Political Religion in America* (New York: Harper and Row, 1974); Samuel S. Hill and Dennis E. Owen, *The New Religious-Political Right in America* (Nashville: Abingdon Press, 1982).

44. William R. Hutchison, *The Modernist Impulse in American Protestantism* (Cambridge: Harvard University Press, 1976); Catherine L. Albanese, *Corresponding Motion: Transcendental Religion and the New America* (Philadelphia: Temple University Press, 1977); James R. Moore, *The Post-Darwinian Controversies* (New York: Cambridge University Press, 1979); George M. Marsden, *Fundamentalism and American Culture: The Shaping of Twentieth-Century Evangelicalism, 1870–1925* (New York: Oxford University Press, 1980); Philip F. Gura, *The Wisdom of Words: Language, Theology, and Literature in the New England Renaissance* (Middletown, Conn.: Wesleyan University Press, 1981); Ferenc Morton Szasz, *The Divided Mind of Protestant America, 1880–1930* (University, Ala.: University of Alabama Press, 1982); Bruce Kuklick, *Churchmen and Philosophers: From Jonathan Edwards to John Dewey* (New Haven: Yale University Press, 1985); David F. Wells, ed., *Reformed Theology in America: A History of Its Modern Development* (Grand Rapids, Mich.: Eerdmans, 1985).

45. Melvin B. Endy, Jr., *William Penn and Early Quakerism* (Princeton: Princeton University Press, 1973); Jack D. Marietta, *The Reformation of American Quakerism, 1748–1783* (Philadelphia: University of Pennsylvania Press, 1984).

46. Stephen Gottschalk, *The Emergence of Christian Science in American Religious Life* (Berkeley: University of California Press, 1973); John M. Whitworth, *God's Blueprints: A Sociological Study of Three Utopian Sects* (London:

Routledge and K. Paul, 1975); James A. Beckford, *The Trumpet of Prophecy: A Sociological Study of Jehovah's Witnesses* (New York: Wiley, 1975); Lawrence Foster, *Religion and Sexuality: Three American Communal Experiments of the Nineteenth Century* (New York: Oxford University Press, 1981); Klaus J. Hansen, *Mormonism and the American Experience* (Chicago: University of Chicago Press, 1981); Jan Shipps, *Mormonism: The Story of a New Religious Tradition* (Urbana: University of Illinois Press, 1985); Thomas G. Alexander, *Mormonism in Transition: A History of the Latter-day Saints, 1890–1930* (Urbana: University of Illinois Press, 1986).

47. Jacob Needleman, *The New Religions* (Garden City, N.Y.: Doubleday, 1970); Robert S. Ellwood, Jr., *Alternative Altars: Unconventional and Eastern Spirituality in America* (Chicago: University of Chicago Press, 1979).

48. David Edwin Harrell, Jr., *All Things Are Possible: The Healing and Charismatic Revivals in Modern America* (Bloomington: Indiana University Press, 1976); Robert Mapes Anderson, *Vision of the Disinherited: The Making of American Pentecostalism* (New York: Oxford University Press, 1979); Timothy P. Weber, *Living in the Shadow of the Second Coming: American Premillennialism, 1875–1982* (New York: Oxford University Press, 1979); Meredith B. McGuire, *Pentecostal Catholics: Power, Charisma, and Order in a Religious Movement* (Philadelphia: Temple University Press, 1982).

CHAPTER 7

1. Robert T. Handy, *The American Tradition of Religious Freedom: An Historical Analysis* (New York: The National Conference of Christians and Jews, 1973), 3–13.

2. Robert T. Handy, ed., *Religion in American Experience: The Pluralistic Style* (Columbia: University of South Carolina Press, 1972), vii–xiii.

3. Ibid., xiv–xvi, xxi.

4. Robert T. Handy, ed., *The Social Gospel in America, 1870–1920: Gladden, Ely, Rauschenbusch* (New York: Oxford University Press, 1966), 6, 15. See also 7–9 for a good example of the way Handy treated ideas as instruments to action.

5. Robert T. Handy, *A History of the Churches in the United States and Canada* (New York: Oxford University Press, 1977), 75; Robert T. Handy, "The 'Lively Experiment' in Canada," in *The Lively Experiment Continued*, ed. Jerald C. Brauer (Macon: Mercer University Press, 1987), 204–6.

6. Handy, *History*, 113–14, 161.

7. Handy, *History*, 228–29; Handy, "Lively Experiment," 208.

8. Handy, "Lively Experiment," 207, 210–13.

9. Handy, *History*, 371; Handy, "Lively Experiment," 214.

10. Handy, *History*, 308–9; 344–45, 375–76, 392–411.

11. Robert T. Handy, *A Christian America: Protestant Hopes and Historical Realities* (New York: Oxford University Press, 1971; enl. ed., 1984), vii, ix. All references are to the first edition.

12. Ibid., 3, 20, 26.

13. Ibid., viii, 31, 35, 42, 58, 63, 174–75.

14. Ibid., 110, 210–11.

15. Ibid., 112–13, 141. The Santayana quote can also be found in Handy, *History,* 310. Its original source is George Santayana, *Character and Opinion in the United States* (New York, 1920), 14–15.

16. Handy, *Christian America,* 65, 143–44, 155.

17. Ibid., 195–97, 207–10.

18. Ibid., 213–15, 225.

19. John Tracy Ellis, "Fragments from My Autobiography, 1905–1942," *Review of Politics* 36 (October 1974): 568, 570, 577.

20. Indicative of his early interest and expertise in European topics are these works: John Tracy Ellis, *Anti-Papal Legislation in Medieval England, 1066–1377* (Washington, D.C.: Catholic University of America Press, 1930); and John Tracy Ellis, *Cardinal Consalvi and Anglo-Papal Relations, 1814–1824* (Washington, D.C.: Catholic University of America Press, 1942). The only historian whose excellent work resembled the quality of that produced by Ellis was Thomas T. McAvoy. For comparative purposes, see McAvoy's titles: *The Catholic Church in Indiana, 1789–1834* (New York: Columbia University Press, 1940); *The Great Crisis in American Catholic History, 1895–1900* (Chicago: Regnery, 1957); *The Americanist Heresy in Roman Catholicism, 1895–1900* (Notre Dame: University of Notre Dame Press, 1963); *The Formation of the American Catholic Minority, 1820–1860* (Philadelphia: Fortress, 1967); and *A History of the Catholic Church in the United States* (Notre Dame: University of Notre Dame Press, 1969).

21. John Tracy Ellis, "The Ecclesiastical Historian in the Service of Clio," *Church History* 38 (March 1969): 114–16; John Tracy Ellis, ed., *The Catholic Priest in the United States: Historical Investigations* (Collegeville, Minn.: St. John's University Press, 1971), xv.

22. Ellis, "Service of Clio," 110; John Tracy Ellis, "American Catholics and the Intellectual Life," *Thought* 30 (September 1955): 355, 386. As an example of how tenacious the "edifying history" mind-set was, Ellis related that, as a result of a candid disclosure, "one of the ranking Catholic churchmen . . . had been so disturbed . . . that he ordered the destruction of the papers of his predecessors in the archdiocesan archives lest the biography of any of them should be marred at the hands of an indiscreet historian who would cause them to suffer a fate similar to the one that had befallen Cardinal Gibbons." See Ellis, "Service of Clio," 112.

23. Ellis, "Fragments," 571; "Service of Clio," 109.

24. John Tracy Ellis, *The Life of James Cardinal Gibbons, Archbishop of Baltimore, 1834–1921,* 2 vols. (Milwaukee: Bruce, 1952) 1:x.

25. Ellis, *Catholic Priest,* xvi.

26. John Tracy Ellis, ed., *Documents of American Catholic History* (Milwaukee: Bruce, 1956), vii.

27. John Tracy Ellis, *American Catholicism* (Chicago: University of Chicago Press, 1956), xii.

28. Ellis, *Gibbons* 1:vii.

29. John Tracy Ellis, "The Formation of the American Priest: An Historical Perspective," in *Catholic Priest,* 11.

30. John Tracy Ellis, *Perspectives in American Catholicism* (Baltimore: Helicon, 1963), 73.

31. John Tracy Ellis, *Catholics in Colonial America* (Baltimore: Helicon, 1965), 120–21, 315–18. Despite their apparent length, chapters 12 to 15 actually contain quite a compact summary of events along the Atlantic seaboard between 1630 and 1790.

32. Ellis, *American Catholicism*, 17–18.

33. Ibid., 19, 23–24; *Perspectives*, 2–3, 8.

34. Ellis, *American Catholicism*, 80–81; *Perspectives*, 275.

35. Ellis, *American Catholicism*, 120.

36. Ellis, *Gibbons*, 2:236.

37. Ellis, *Gibbons*, 1:101, 178, 180, 193, 221, 302–3, 308–9, 319, 376; 2:4–7, 16, 35–37, 108–9, 233, 258–59, and especially 500–563.

38. Ellis, *Gibbons*, 1:165–66, 215, 305, 346–47, 486–546. The quotation is cited in *Perspectives*, 123.

39. Ellis, *Perspectives*, 121.

40. Ellis, *Perspectives*, 57, 64; *American Catholicism*, 153–54.

41. John Tracy Ellis, *A Guide to American Catholic History* (Milwaukee: Bruce, 1959), v–vi; John Tracy Ellis, "Contemporary American Catholicism in the Light of History," *The Critic* 24 (June–July, 1966), 10, 12–13, 15; *American Catholicism*, 103.

42. Ellis, *Perspectives*, 65.

43. Jaroslav Pelikan, *Historical Theology: Continuity and Change in Christian Doctrine* (Philadelphia: Westminster Press, 1971), 67; Jaroslav Pelikan, *The Vindication of Tradition* (New Haven: Yale University Press, 1984), 25–26. The last quotation is from vol. 1, 16, of Pelikan's most sustained effort, *The Christian Tradition: A History of the Development of Doctrine*, 4 vols. (Chicago: University of Chicago Press, 1971–). Each of the four extant volumes has a separate subtitle, but all references hereafter shall cite only *Christian Tradition* with appropriate volume and page numbers.

44. Jaroslav Pelikan, *Development of Christian Doctrine* (New Haven: Yale University Press, 1969), 69; Jaroslav Pelikan, "Mary—Exemplar of the Development of Christian Doctrine," in *Mary: Images of the Mother of Jesus in Jewish and Christian Perspective* (Philadelphia: Fortress, 1986), 79–80.

45. Jaroslav Pelikan, "An Essay on the Development of Christian Doctrine," *Church History* 35 (March 1966): 4–5, 11; *Development*, 40–42, 53.

46. Ibid.

47. Pelikan, *Historical Theology*, 83; "Christian Doctrine," 8; *Development*, 48.

48. Pelikan, *Historical Theology*, xv–xvi.

49. Ibid., 130, 141.

50. Ibid., 159; *Vindication*, 48–49, 51–52.

51. Pelikan, *Historical Theology*, xviii; *Vindication*, 30; *Development*, 144.

52. Pelikan, *Historical Theology*, 96–97, 109–10; *Christian Tradition*, 1:1.

53. Pelikan, *Vindication*, 75–76.

54. Pelikan, *Christian Tradition*, 1:x–xi, 3–4, 7, 9–11, 262; 3:vii–viii, 2, 12, 23.

55. Ibid. 1:70, 109, 112, 120, 167, 170–71, 332–33.

56. Ibid. 1:172–73, 242–43, 3:21.

57. Ibid. 2:91–92, 172–73; 3:21.

58. Ibid. 3:269–70, 4:128, 138–39, 148, 156–57, 252–53. See also Jaroslav Pelikan, *Obedient Rebels: Catholic Substance and Protestant Principle in Luther's Reformation* (New York: Harper and Row, 1964), 14–17, 98–100.

59. Pelikan, *Christian Tradition*, 4:187–89, 245, 262–64.

60. Ibid. 4:323–35.

61. Pelikan, *Development*, 24, 54–55.

62. Pelikan, *Historical Theology*, 76, 156.

63. Ibid., 156–58, 160–61.

64. Jaroslav Pelikan, *The Light of the World: A Basic Image in Early Christian Thought* (New York: Harper and Row, 1962), 14, 16.

Select Bibliography

WORKS OF GENERAL INTEREST

Books

Berkhofer, Robert F., Jr. *A Behavioral Approach to Historical Analysis.* New York: Free Press, 1969.

Curti, Merle, ed. *American Scholarship in the Twentieth Century.* Cambridge: Harvard University Press, 1953.

Curtis, L. P., Jr., ed. *The Historian's Workshop: Original Essays by Sixteen Historians.* New York: Alfred A. Knopf, 1970.

Danto, Arthur C. *Analytical Philosophy of History.* Cambridge: Cambridge University Press, 1965.

Donovan, Timothy Paul. *Historical Thought in America: Postwar Patterns.* Norman: University of Oklahoma Press, 1973.

Higham, John. *Writing American History: Essays on Modern Scholarship.* Bloomington: Indiana University Press, 1970.

Higham, John, Leonard Krieger, and Felix Gilbert. *History.* Englewood Cliffs, N.J.: Prentice-Hall, 1965.

Holt, W. Stull. *Historical Scholarship in the United States, and Other Essays.* Seattle: University of Washington Press, 1967.

Kammen, Michael, ed. *The Past Before Us: Contemporary Historical Writing in the United States.* Ithaca: Cornell University Press, 1980.

Murphey, Murray G. *Our Knowledge of the Historical Past.* Indianapolis: The Bobbs-Merrill Co., 1973.

Smith, Page. *The Historian and History.* New York: Alfred A. Knopf, 1964.

Tillinghast, Pardon E. *The Specious Past: Historians and Others.* Reading, Mass.: Addison-Wesley Publishing Co., 1972.

Articles

Ahlstrom, Sydney E. "The Problem of the History of Religion in America." *Church History* 39 (June 1970): 224–35.

Browne, Henry J. "American Catholic History: A Progress Report on Research and Study." *Church History* 26 (December 1957): 372–80.

Carter, Paul A. "Recent Historiography of the Protestant Churches in America." *Church History* 37 (March 1968): 95–107.

Clebsch, William A. "A New Historiography of American Religion." *Historical*

Magazine of the Protestant Episcopal Church 32 (September 1963): 225–57.

Cochrane, Eric. "What is Catholic Historiography?" *The Catholic Historical Review* 61 (April 1975): 169–90.

Hudson, Winthrop S. "Shifting Trends in Church History." *Journal of Bible and Religion* 28 (April 1960): 235–38.

Lukacs, John. "The Historiographical Problem of Belief and Believers: Religious History in the Democratic Age." *The Catholic Historical Review* 64 (April 1978): 153–67.

May, Henry F. "The Recovery of American Religious History." *American Historical Review* 70 (October 1964): 79–92.

O'Brien, David J. "American Catholic Historiography: A Post-Conciliar Evaluation." *Church History* 37 (March 1968): 80–94.

O'Connor, Thomas F. "Trends and Portends in American Catholic Historiography." *The Catholic Historical Review* 33 (April 1947): 3–11.

Sorenson, Lloyd R. "Historical Currents in America." *American Quarterly* (Fall 1955): 234–46.

Stephenson, Wendell H. "A Quarter Century of American Historiography." *Mississippi Valley Historical Review* 45 (June 1958): 3–22.

Williams, George H. "Church History." In *Protestant Thought in the Twentieth Century: Whence and Whither?* edited by Arnold S. Nash. New York: Macmillan Co., 1951.

CHAPTER 1

Books

Case, Shirley Jackson. *Christianity in a Changing World*. New York: Harper and Brothers, 1941.

———. *The Christian Philosophy of History*. Chicago: University of Chicago Press, 1943.

———. *The Evolution of Early Christianity: A Genetic Study of First-Century Christianity in Relation to its Religious Environment*. Chicago: University of Chicago Press, 1914.

———. *The Historical Method in the Study of Religion*. Lewiston, Maine: N.p., 1907.

———. *The Historicity of Jesus: A Criticism of the Contention That Jesus Never Lived, a Statement of the Evidence for His Existence, an Estimate of his Relation to Christianity*. Chicago: University of Chicago Press, 1912.

———. *Jesus: A New Biography*. Chicago: University of Chicago Press, 1927.

———. *Jesus Through the Centuries*. Chicago: University of Chicago Press, 1932.

———. *The Origins of Christian Supernaturalism*. Chicago: University of Chicago Press, 1946.

———. *The Social Origins of Christianity*. Chicago: University of Chicago Press, 1923.

———. *The Social Triumph of the Ancient Church*. New York: Harper and Brothers, 1933.

Donnan, Elizabeth, and Leo F. Stock, eds. *An Historian's World: Selections from the Correspondence of John Franklin Jameson*. Philadelphia: American Philosophical Society, 1956.

Guilday, Peter, ed. *The Catholic Philosophy of History*. P. J. Kenedy and Sons, 1936.

———. *The English Catholic Refugees on the Continent, 1558–1795*. Vol. 1, *The English Colleges and Convents in the Catholic Low Countries, 1558–1795*. London, 1914.

———. *A History of the Councils of Baltimore, 1791–1884*. New York: Macmillan Co., 1932.

———. *The Life and Times of John Carroll, Archbishop of Baltimore, 1735–1815*. New York: The Encyclopedia Press, 1922.

———. *The Life and Times of John England, First Bishop of Charleston, 1786–1842*. New York: America Press, 1927.

Jackson, Samuel M. *Bibliographical Sketches of the Principal Christian Writers from the Sixth to the Twelfth Century, With an Analysis of their Writings*. New York: Charles Scribner's Sons, 1892.

———. *Concise Dictionary of Religious Knowledge, Biblical, Doctrinal, Historical, and Practical*. New York: Christian Literature Co., 1889.

———. *Huldreich Zwingli: The Reformer of German Switzerland*. New York: G. P. Putnam's Sons, 1901.

Jennings, Louis B. *The Bibliography and Biography of Shirley Jackson Case*. Chicago: University of Chicago Press, 1949.

McNeill, John T., Matthew Spinka, and Harold R. Willoughby, eds. *Environmental Factors in Christian History*. Chicago: University of Chicago Press, 1939.

Mode, Peter G. *The Frontier Spirit in American Christianity*. New York: Macmillan Co., 1923.

———. *The Influence of the Black Death on the English Monasteries*. Menasha, Wis.: George Banta Publishing Co., 1916.

———. *Source Book and Bibliographical Guide for American Church History*. Menasha, Wis.: George Banta Publishing Co., 1921.

Nichols, Robert H. *The Growth of the Christian Church*. 2 vols. Philadelphia: Westminster Press, 1914.

Robinson, James Harvey. *The New History: Essays Illustrating the Modern Historical Outlook*. New York: Macmillan Co., 1912.

Rowe, Henry K. *The History of Religion in the United States*. New York: Macmillan Co., 1924.

———. *History of the Christian People*. New York: Macmillan Co., 1931.

———. *Modern Pathfinders of Christianity: The Lives and Deeds of Seven Centuries of Christian Leaders*. New York: Fleming H. Revell Co., 1928.

Walker, Williston. *A History of the Christian Church*. New York: Charles Scribner's Sons, 1918.

———. *A History of the Congregational Churches in the United States*. New York: Christian Literature Co., 1894.

———. *John Calvin: The Organiser of Reformed Protestantism, 1509–1564*. New York: G. P. Putnam's Sons, 1906.

———. *The Reformation*. New York: Charles Scribner's Sons, 1915.

———. *Ten New England Leaders*. New York: Silver, Burdett and Co., 1901.

Articles

Aubert, Roger. "The Freedom of the Catholic Historian." In *Truth and Freedom*, edited by Louis de Raeymaeker. Pittsburgh: Duquesne University Press, 1954.

Baldwin, Simeon E. "Religion Still the Key to History." *American Historical Review* 12 (January 1907): 219–43.

Brinton, Crane. "The New History: Twenty-five Years Later." *Journal of Social Philosophy* 1 (January 1936): 134–47.

Cartwright, John K. "The American Catholic Historical Association: A Survey of Twenty-five Years." *The Catholic Historical Review* 30 (January 1945): 382–93.

Ellis, John Tracy. "Jameson and American Religious History." In *J. Franklin Jameson: A Tribute,* edited by Ruth A. Fisher and William L. Fox. Washington: Catholic University of America Press, 1965.

———. "Peter Guilday, March 25, 1884–July 31, 1947." *The Catholic Historical Review* 33 (October 1947): 257–68.

English, Adrian T. "The Historiography of American Catholic History, 1785–1884." *The Catholic Historical Review* 5 (January 1926): 561–98.

Ford, Henry J. "A Change of Climate." *The Catholic Historical Review* n.s. 5 (April 1925): 8–28.

Guilday, Peter. "The American Catholic Historical Association." *The Catholic Historical Review* 6 (April 1920): 3–14.

Hoffman, Ross J. S. "Catholicism and Historismus." *The Catholic Historical Review* 24 (January 1939): 401–12.

Jameson, J. Franklin. "The American Acta Sanctorum." *American Historical Review* 13 (January 1908): 286–302.

Kent, W. H. "'Catholic Truth and Historical Truth.'" *The Catholic Historical Review* 6 (October 1920): 275–93.

Leland, Waldo G. "Concerning Catholic Historical Societies." *The Catholic Historical Review* 2 (January 1917): 386–99.

Lilly, Edward P. "A Major Problem for Catholic American Historians." *The Catholic Historical Review* 24 (January 1939): 427–48.

Nichols, Robert H. "Aims and Methods of Teaching Church History." *Papers of the American Society of Church History* 2d ser., 7 (1923): 39–51.

CHAPTER 2

Books

Ash, James L., Jr. *Protestantism and the American University: An Intellectual Biography of William Warren Sweet.* Dallas: Southern Methodist University Press, 1982.

Becker, Carl L. *The Heavenly City of the Eighteenth Century Philosophers.* New Haven: Yale University Press, 1932.

Benson, Lee. *Turner and Beard: American Historical Writing Reconsidered.* Glencoe, Ill.: Free Press, 1960.

Hofstadter, Richard. *The Progressive Historians: Turner, Beard, Parrington.* New York: Alfred A. Knopf, 1968.

Latourette, Kenneth S. *Anno Domini: Jesus, History, and God*. New York: Harper and Brothers, 1940.

———. *Christianity in a Revolutionary Age: A History of Christianity in the Nineteenth and Twentieth Centuries*. 5 vols. New York: Harper and Row, 1958–1962.

———, ed. *The Gospel, the Church and the World*. New York: Books for the Library Press, 1946.

———. *A History of Christianity*. New York: Harper and Row, 1953.

———. *A History of the Expansion of Christianity*. 7 vols. New York: Harper and Brothers, 1937–1945.

Popper, Karl R. *The Poverty of Historicism*. London: Routledge and Kegan Paul, 1957.

The Social Sciences in Historical Study: A Report of the Committee on Historiography. New York: Social Science Research Council, 1954.

Sweet, William W. *The American Churches: An Interpretation*. New York: Abingdon-Cokesbury Press, 1948.

———. *American Culture and Religion: Six Essays*. Dallas: Southern Methodist University Press, 1951.

———, ed. *Circuit-Rider Days along the Ohio: Being the Journals of the Ohio Conference from its Organization in 1812 to 1826*. New York: Methodist Book Concern, 1923.

———. *Makers of Christianity: From John Cotton to Lyman Abbott*. New York: H. Holt and Co., 1937.

———. *Men of Zeal: The Romance of American Methodist Beginnings*. New York: Abingdon Press, 1935.

———. *Methodism in Modern History*. New York: Methodist Book Concern, 1933.

———. *The Methodist Episcopal Church and the Civil War*. Cincinnati: Methodist Book Concern, 1912.

———, ed. *Religion on the American Frontier*. Vol. 1, *The Baptists, 1783–1830*. New York: Henry Holt and Co., 1931. Vol. 2, *The Presbyterians, 1783–1840*. New York: Harper and Brothers, 1936. Vol. 3, *The Congregationalists, 1783–1850*. Chicago: University of Chicago Press, 1939. Vol. 4, *The Methodists, 1783–1840*. Chicago: University of Chicago Press, 1946.

———. *The Story of Religions in America*. New York: Harper and Brothers, 1930.

Theory and Practice in Historical Study: A Report of the Committee on Historiography. New York: Social Science Research Council, 1946.

Wilkins, Burleigh Taylor. *Carl Becker: A Biographical Study in American Intellectual History*. Cambridge: MIT Press and Harvard University Press, 1961.

Articles

Ash, James L., Jr. "American Religion and the Academy in the Early Twentieth Century: The Chicago Years of William Warren Sweet." *Church History* 50 (December 1981): 450–64.

Aydelotte, William O. "Notes on the Problem of Historical Generalization." In *Generalization in the Writing of History*, edited by Louis Gottschalk. Chicago: University of Chicago Press, 1963.

Beard, Charles A. "That Noble Dream." *American Historical Review* 41 (October 1935): 74–87.

――――. "Written History as an Act of Faith." *American Historical Review* 39 (January 1934): 219–29.

Becker, Carl L. "Detachment and the Writing of History." *The Atlantic Monthly* 106 (October 1910): 525–36.

――――. "Everyman His Own Historian." *American Historical Review* 37 (January 1932): 221–36.

――――. "Some Aspects of the Influence of Social Problems and Ideas upon the Study and Writing of History." *American Journal of Sociology* 18 (March 1913): 641–75.

――――. "What Are Historical Facts?" *Western Political Quarterly* 8 (September 1955): 327–40.

――――. "What is Historiography?" *American Historical Review* 44 (October 1938): 20–28.

Beer, Samuel H. "Causal Explanation and Imaginative Re-enactment." *History and Theory* 3 (1963): 6–29.

Cole, Charles W. "The Relativity of History." *Political Science Quarterly* 48 (June 1933): 161–71.

Deininger, Whitaker T. "The Skepticism and Historical Faith of Charles A. Beard." *Journal of the History of Ideas* 15 (October 1954): 573–88.

Destler, Chester McArthur. "Some Observations on Contemporary Historical Theory." *American Historical Review* 55 (April 1950): 503–29.

Gabriel, Ralph H. "History and the American Past." In *American Perspectives: The National Self-Image in the Twentieth Century,* edited by Robert E. Spiller and Eric Larrabee, Cambridge: Harvard University Press, 1961.

Gershoy, Leo. "Zagorin's Interpretation of Becker: Some Observations." *American Historical Review* 62 (October 1956): 12–17.

Gottschalk, Louis. "A Professor of History in a Quandry." *American Historical Review* 59 (January 1954): 273–86.

Horr, George Edwin. "The Influence of the War Upon the Study of Church History." *Papers of the American Society of Church History* 2d ser., 7 (1923): 27–36.

Mandelbaum, Maurice. "Causal Analysis in History." *Journal of the History of Ideas* 3 (January 1942): 30–50.

Munro, William B. "Clio and Her Cousins: Some Reflections upon the Place of History among the Social Sciences." *Pacific Historical Review* 10 (December 1941): 403–10.

Potter, David M. "Explicit Data and Implicit Assumptions in Historical Study." In *Generalization in the Writing of History,* edited by Louis Gottschalk. Chicago: University of Chicago Press, 1963.

Rockwell, William Walker. "Rival Presuppositions in the Writing of Church History: A Study of Intellectual Bias." *Papers of the American Society of Church History* 2d ser., 9 (1934): 3–52.

Smith, Theodore C. "The Writing of American History in America." *American Historical Review* 40 (April 1935): 439–49.

Stone, Lawrence. "History and the Social Sciences in the Twentieth Century."

In *The Future of History: Essays in the Vanderbilt Centennial Symposium*, edited by Charles F. Delzell. Nashville: Vanderbilt University Press, 1977.

CHAPTER 3

Books

Hudson, Winthrop S., and Leonard J. Trinterud. *Theology in Sixteenth- and Seventeenth-Century England*. Los Angeles: William Andrews Clark Memorial Library, 1971.

Marsden, George, and Frank Roberts, eds. *A Christian View of History?* Grand Rapids: William B. Eerdmans Publishing Co., 1975.

Nichols, James Hastings. *Democracy and the Churches*. Philadelphia: Westminster Press, 1951.

──────. *History of Christianity, 1650–1950: Secularization of the West*. New York: Ronald Press Co., 1956.

──────, ed. *The Mercersburg Theology*. New York: Oxford University Press, 1966.

──────. *Primer for Protestants*. New York: Association Press, 1947.

──────. *Romanticism in American Theology: Nevin and Schaff at Mercersburg*. Chicago: University of Chicago Press, 1961.

Richardson, Cyril C. *The Church through the Centuries*. New York: Charles Scribner's Sons, 1938.

──────. *The Doctrine of the Trinity*. Nashville: Abingdon, 1958.

──────. *The Sacrament of Reunion: A Study in Ecumenical Christianity with Particular Reference to the Proposed Concordat between the Presbyterian and Protestant Episcopal Churches*. New York: Charles Scribner's Sons, 1940.

Trinterud, Leonard J., ed. *Elizabethan Puritanism*. New York: Oxford University Press, 1971.

──────. *The Forming of an American Tradition: A Re-examination of Colonial Presbyterianism*. Philadelphia: Westminster Press, 1949.

Articles

Brauer, Jerald C. "Changing Perspectives on Religion in America." In *Reinterpretation in American Church History*, edited by Jerald C. Brauer. Chicago: University of Chicago Press, 1968.

Clebsch, William A. "History and Salvation: An Essay in Distinctions." In *The Study of Religion in Colleges and Universities*, edited by Paul Ramsey and John F. Wilson. Princeton: Princeton University Press, 1970.

──────. "Toward a History of Christianity." *Church History* 43 (March 1974): 5–16.

Harbison, E. Harris. "The 'Meaning of History' and the Writing of History." *Church History* 21 (June 1952): 97–107.

──────. "The Problem of the Christian Historian: A Critique of Arnold Toynbee." *Theology Today* 5 (October 1948): 388–405.

Nichols, James Hastings. "The Art of Church History." *Church History* 20 (March 1951): 3–9.

──────. "Church History and Secular History." *Church History* 13 (June 1944): 87–99.

———. "History in the Theological Curriculum." *The Journal of Religion* 26 (July 1946): 183–89.

———. "The History of Christianity." In *Religion*, edited by Paul Ramsey. Englewood Cliffs, N.J.: Prentice-Hall, 1965.

Outler, Albert C. "Theodosius' Horse: Reflections on the Predicament of the Church Historian." *Church History* 34 (September 1965): 251–61.

Pauck, Wilhelm. "The Idea of the Church in Christian History." *Church History* 21 (September 1952): 191–214.

Richardson, Cyril C. "Church History Past and Present." *Union Seminary Quarterly Review* 5 (November 1949): 5–15.

Spitz, Lewis W. "History: Sacred and Secular." *Church History* 47 (March 1978): 5–22.

Trinterud, Leonard J. "The Task of the American Church Historian." *Church History* 25 (March 1956): 3–15.

CHAPTER 4

Books

Bainton, Roland H. *Christendom: A Short History of Christianity and Its Impact on Western Civilization.* 2 vols. New York: Harper and Row, 1966.

———. *Christian Attitudes Toward War and Peace: A Historical Survey and Critical Re-evaluation.* New York: Abingdon Press, 1960.

———. *Christian Unity and Religion in New England.* Boston: Beacon Press, 1964.

———. *Erasmus of Christendom.* New York: Charles Scribner's Sons, 1969.

———. *Here I Stand: A Life of Martin Luther.* Nashville: Abingdon-Cokesbury Press, 1950.

———. *Hunted Heretic: The Life and Death of Michael Servetus, 1511–1553.* Boston: Beacon Press, 1953.

———. *The Reformation of the Sixteenth Century.* Boston: Beacon Press, 1952.

———. *Studies on the Reformation.* Boston: Beacon Press, 1963.

———. *The Travail of Religious Liberty: Nine Biographical Studies.* Philadelphia: Westminster Press, 1951.

———. *Women of the Reformation: In France and England.* Minneapolis: Augsburg Publishing House, 1973.

———. *Yesterday, Today, and What Next?* Minneapolis: Augsburg Publishing House, 1978.

Hudson, Winthrop S. *American Protestantism.* Chicago: University of Chicago Press, 1961.

———, ed. *Baptist Concepts of the Church: A Survey of the Historical and Theological Issues Which Have Produced Changes in Church Order.* Philadelphia: Judson Press, 1959.

———. *The Great Tradition of the American Churches.* New York: Harper and Brothers, 1953.

———. *John Ponet (1516?–1556): Advocate of Limited Monarchy.* Chicago: University of Chicago Press, 1942.

———, ed. *Nationalism and Religion in America: Concepts of American Identity and Mission.* New York: Harper and Row, 1970.

_____. *Religion in America: An Historical Account of the Development of American Religious Life.* New York: Charles Scribner's Sons, 1965; rev. eds., 1973, 1981, 1987.

_____. *Understanding Roman Catholicism: A Guide to Papal Teaching for Protestants.* Philadelphia: Westminster Press, 1959.

Mead, Sidney E. *History and Identity.* Missoula, Mont.: Scholars Press, 1979.

_____. *The Lively Experiment: The Shaping of Christianity in America.* New York: Harper and Row, 1963.

_____. *The Nation with the Soul of a Church.* New York: Harper and Row, 1975.

_____. *The Old Religion in the Brave New World: Reflections on the Relation Between Christendom and the Republic.* Berkeley: University of California Press, 1977.

Articles

Higham, John. "Beyond Consensus: The Historian as Moral Critic." *American Historical Review* 67 (April 1962): 609–25.

Mead, Sidney E. "Church History Explained." *Church History* 32 (March 1963): 17–31.

_____. "The Task of the Church Historian." *The Chronicle: A Baptist Historical Quarterly* 12 (July 1949): 127–43.

CHAPTER 5

Books

Ekirch, Arthur A. Jr. *American Intellectual History.* Washington, D.C.: American Historical Association, 1963.

McNeill, John T. *Books of Faith and Power.* New York: Harper and Brothers, 1947.

_____, ed. *Calvin: Institutes of the Christian Religion.* 2 vols. Philadelphia: Westminster Press, 1960.

_____. *The Celtic Churches: A History A.D. 200 to 1200.* Chicago: University of Chicago Press, 1974.

_____. *The Celtic Penitentials.* Paris: E. Champion, 1923.

_____. *Christian Hope for World Society.* New York: Willet, Clark and Co., 1937.

_____. *The History and Character of Calvinism.* New York: Oxford University Press, 1954.

_____. *Makers of Christianity: From Alfred the Great to Schleiermacher.* New York: Henry Holt and Co., 1935.

_____. *Medieval Handbooks of Penance.* New York: Columbia University Press, 1935.

_____. *Modern Christian Movements.* Philadelphia: Westminster Press, 1954.

_____. *Unitive Protestantism: A Study in Our Religious Resources.* Cincinnati: Abingdon Press, 1930.

Miller, Perry. *Errand into the Wilderness.* Cambridge: Belknap Press of Harvard University Press, 1956.

_____. *Jonathan Edwards.* New York: William Morrow, 1949.

_____. *The New England Mind: From Colony to Province.* Cambridge: Harvard University Press, 1953.

————. *The New England Mind: The Seventeenth Century.* New York: Macmillan Co., 1939.

————. *Orthodoxy in Massachusetts, 1630–1650.* Cambridge: Harvard University Press, 1933.

Miller, Perry, and Thomas H. Johnson, eds. *The Puritans: A Sourcebook of Their Writings.* New York: American Book Co., 1938.

Schneider, Herbert W. *Adam Smith's Moral and Political Philosophy.* New York: Hafner, 1948.

————. *A History of American Philosophy.* New York: Columbia University Press, 1946.

————. *Making the Fascist State.* New York: Oxford University Press, 1928.

————. *The Puritan Mind.* New York: Henry Holt and Co., 1930.

————. *Three Dimensions of Public Morality.* Bloomington: Indiana University Press, 1956.

Skotheim, Robert Allen. *American Intellectual Histories and Historians.* Princeton: Princeton University Press, 1966.

Smith, H. Shelton. *Changing Conceptions of Original Sin: A Study in American Theology since 1750.* New York: Charles Scribner's Sons, 1955.

————. *Faith and Nurture.* New York: Charles Scribner's Sons, 1941.

————, ed. *Horace Bushnell.* New York: Oxford University Press, 1965.

————. *In His Image, But . . . Racism in Southern Religion, 1780–1910.* Durham: Duke University Press, 1972.

Articles

Butts, Francis T. "The Myth of Perry Miller." *American Historical Review* 87 (June 1982): 665–94.

Gilbert, Felix. "Intellectual History: Its Aims and Methods." In *Historical Studies Today,* edited by Felix Gilbert and Stephen R. Graubard. New York: W. W. Norton and Co., 1971.

Greene, John C. "Objectives and Methods in Intellectual History." *Mississippi Valley Historical Review* 44 (June 1957): 58–74.

Higham, John. "American Intellectual History: A Critical Appraisal." *American Quarterly* 13 (Summer 1961): 219–33.

————. "Intellectual History and Its Neighbors." *Journal of the History of Ideas* 15 (June 1954): 339–47.

————. "The Rise of American Intellectual History." *American Historical Review* 56 (April 1951): 453–71.

Marsden, George M. "Perry Miller's Rehabilitation of the Puritans: A Critique." *Church History* 39 (March 1970): 91–105.

May, Henry F. "Intellectual History and Religious History." In *New Directions in American Intellectual History,* edited by John Higham and Paul Conkin. Baltimore: Johns Hopkins University Press, 1979.

Skotheim, Robert Allen. "The Writing of American Histories of Ideas: Two Traditions in the XXth Century." *Journal of the History of Ideas* 25 (April–June 1964): 257–78.

Swint, Henry L. "Trends in the Teaching of Social and Intellectual History." *Social Studies* 46 (November 1955): 243–51.

Welter, Rush. "The History of Ideas in America: An Essay in Redefinition." *The*

Journal of American History 51 (March 1965): 599–614.

CHAPTER 6

Books

Ahlstrom, Sydney E. *A Religious History of the American People.* New Haven: Yale University Press, 1972.

Albanese, Catherine L. *America: Religions and Religion.* Belmont, Calif.: Wadsworth, 1981.

Bednarowski, Mary F. *American Religion: A Cultural Perspective.* Englewood Cliffs, N.J.: Prentice-Hall, 1984.

Gaustad, Edwin S. *Historical Atlas of Religion in America.* Rev. ed. New York: Harper and Row, 1976.

_____. *Religion in America: History and Historiography.* Washington, D.C.: American Historical Association, 1973.

_____. *A Religious History of America.* New York: Harper and Row, 1966.

Hudson, Winthrop S. *Religion in America: An Historical Account of the Development of American Religious Life.* New York: Charles Scribner's Sons, 1965; rev. eds., 1973, 1981, 1987.

Marty, Martin E. *Righteous Empire: The Protestant Experience in America.* New York: Dial, 1970.

Olmstead, Clifton E. *History of Religion in the United States.* Englewood Cliffs, N.J.: Prentice-Hall, 1960.

Smith, H. Shelton, Robert T. Handy, and Lefferts A. Loetscher, eds. *American Christianity: An Historical Interpretation with Representative Documents.* 2 vols. New York: Charles Scribner's Sons, 1960–1963.

Williams, Peter W. *Popular Religion in America: Symbolic Change and the Modernization Process in Historical Perspective.* Englewood Cliffs, N.J.: Prentice-Hall, 1980.

CHAPTER 7

Books

Ellis, John Tracy. *American Catholicism.* Chicago: University of Chicago Press, 1956.

_____. *Anti-Papal Legislation in Medieval England, 1066–1377.* Washington, D.C.: Catholic University of America Press, 1930.

_____. *Cardinal Consalvi and Anglo-Papal Relations, 1814–1824.* Washington, D.C.: Catholic University of America Press, 1942.

_____, ed. *The Catholic Priest in the United States: Historical Investigations.* Collegeville, Minn.: St. John's University Press, 1971.

_____. *Catholics in Colonial America.* Baltimore: Helicon, 1965.

_____, ed., *Documents of American Catholic History.* Milwaukee: Bruce, 1956.

_____. *A Guide to American Catholic History.* Milwaukee: Bruce, 1959.

_____. *The Life of James Cardinal Gibbons, Archbishop of Baltimore, 1834–1921.* Milwaukee: Bruce, 1952.

_____. *Perspectives in American Catholicism.* Baltimore: Helicon, 1963.

_____, ed. *A Select Bibliography of the History of the Catholic Church in the United*

States. New York: McMullen, 1947.

Handy, Robert T. *The American Tradition of Religious Freedom: An Historical Analysis.* New York: The National Conference of Christians and Jews, 1973.

————. *A Christian America: Protestant Hopes and Historical Realities.* New York: Oxford University Press, 1971.

————. *A History of the Churches in the United States and Canada.* New York: Oxford University Press, 1977.

————, ed. *Religion in the American Experience: The Pluralistic Style.* Columbia: University of South Carolina Press, 1972.

————, ed. *The Social Gospel in America, 1870–1920: Gladden, Ely, Rauschenbusch.* New York: Oxford University Press, 1966.

Pelikan, Jaroslav. *The Christian Tradition: A History of the Development of Doctrine.* Vol. 1, *The Emergence of the Catholic Tradition (100–600).* Vol. 2, *The Spirit of Eastern Christendom (600–1700).* Vol. 3, *The Growth of Medieval Theology (600–1300).* Vol. 4, *Reformation of Church and Dogma (1300–1700).* Vol. 5, *Christian Doctrine and Modern Culture (since 1700).* Chicago: University of Chicago Press, 1971–1984.

————. *Development of Christian Doctrine: Some Historical Prolegomena.* New Haven: Yale University Press, 1969.

————. *Historical Theology: Continuity and Change in Christian Doctrine.* Philadelphia: Westminster Press, 1971.

————. *The Light of the World: A Basic Image in Early Christian Thought.* New York: Harper and Brothers, 1962.

————. *Obedient Rebels: Catholic Substance and Protestant Principle in Luther's Reformation.* New York: Harper and Row, 1964.

————. *The Vindication of Tradition.* New Haven: Yale University Press, 1984.

Articles

Ellis, John Tracy. "American Catholics and the Intellectual Life." *Thought* 30 (September 1955): 351–88.

————. "The Catholic University of America: 1927–1979: A Personal Memoir." *Social Thought* 5 (Spring 1979): 35–62.

————. "Contemporary American Catholicism in the Light of History." *The Critic* 24 (June–July 1966): 8–19.

————. "The Ecclesiastical Historian in the Service of Clio." *Church History* 38 (March 1969): 106–120.

————. "Fragments from My Autobiography, 1905–1942." *The Review of Politics* 36 (October 1974): 565–91.

————. "The Influence of the Catholic University of Louvain on the Church in the United States." *Louvain Studies* 9 (Spring 1983): 265–83.

————. "John Henry Newman, A Bridge for Men of Good Will." *The Catholic Historical Review* 56 (April 1970): 1–14.

Handy, Robert T. "The 'Lively Experiment' in Canada." In *The Lively Experiment Continued,* edited by Jerald C. Brauer. Macon, Ga.: Mercer University Press, 1987.

Pelikan, Jaroslav. "An Essay on the Development of Christian Doctrine." *Church History* 35 (March 1966): 3–12.

Index

22, 27–28, 34–35, 149, 198, 219, 221
Secularization, 81–82, 110, 145–46, 167–68, 175
Secular paganism, 92
Separation, of church and state, 104, 113, 116–17, 121, 190, 201–2, 225
Servetus, Michael, 96, 98, 100
Shea, John G., 10, 197
Sidney, Algernon, 104
Slavery, 93, 109, 137–39, 145, 166, 193
Smith, H. Shelton, 131–41, 147, 158, 162, 168, 171, 186, 200, 226
Social Gospel, 53, 130, 136, 188, 205
Social reform efforts, 53–57, 105, 109, 144–45, 165, 167, 169–70, 173, 175–76, 178, 180, 188–89, 194, 200, 203–4, 227
Spanish colonization, 169, 200
Spencer, Herbert, 46
Spengler, Oswald, 146
Stoddard, Solomon, 157
Studies in American Church History series, 10
Suarez, Francisco de, 145
Subjectivity, in history, 42, 59, 66, 75, 90, 113, 148–49, 199, 222, 231
Suppressio veri, 197
Sweet, William W., 50–57, 66, 75, 84, 164–65, 200, 223
Synthetic narratives, 164–83, 226

Taylor, John, 133
Taylor, Nathaniel W., 133–34
Temperance, 105, 109, 194
Theodosius I, 144

Third Reich, 146
Trent, Council of, 215–16
Trinterud, Leonard J., 82–89
"Truce of God," 144
Turner, Frederick J., xi, 15–16, 18–19, 34, 51–52, 55, 165, 202, 223
"Two-party system," 177–79

Ultramontanism, 191
Union Theological Seminary, 68, 141, 186
United Church of Canada, 190
United States Catholic Historical Society, 9
University of Chicago, 18, 24, 50–51, 73, 112, 141, 206
University of Iowa, 112
University of Louvain, 12
Urbanization, 21, 57, 173, 177, 194

Vatican Council, First, 106
Vatican Council, Second, 106, 174

Walker, Williston, 1, 34
Ware, Henry, 133
Westminster Confession, 132
Willard, Samuel, 157
Williams, Roger, 201
Women's studies, 183–84
Women's suffrage, 173
World War I, 43–44, 46, 55, 135, 165, 195, 204
World War II, 90, 101, 176

Yale University, 3, 57, 92, 206

Zwingli, Huldreich, 5

Henry Warner Bowden is Professor of Religion and Departmental Chair at Rutgers, the State University of New Jersey. During his twenty-five years of undergraduate teaching there he has pursued questions about historiographical change, publishing his findings in two volumes. In 1984 he served as president of the American Society of Church History and edited its bicentennial volume, *A Century of Church History: The Legacy of Philip Schaff.* His current research interests range from historiographical topics to contemporary ecclesiastical issues and the vitality of ethnic minorities, especially American Indians.

Albanese ?